# LEIGH
# STOWELL
# & COMPANY
INCORPORATED

With Best Wishes
From
Leigh Stowell & Company

Market Place Tower, 2025 First Avenue, Suite 310 ▪ Seattle, Washington 98121

# BEYOND
## THE MARKETING POWER
# MIND
## OF PSYCHOGRAPHICS
# GAMES

Rebecca Piirto

AMERICAN
DEMOGRAPHICSBOOKS.

# AMERICAN
## DEMOGRAPHICSBOOKS.

A Division of American Demographics, Inc.
127 West State Street, Ithaca, NY 14850
Telephone: 607-273-6343

This publication is designed to provide accurate and authoritative information in regard to the subject matter covered. It is sold with the understanding that the publisher is not engaged in rendering legal, accounting, or other professional services. If legal advice or other expert assistance is required, the services of a competent professional should be sought.

*From a Declaration of Principles Jointly Adopted by a Committee of the American Bar Association and a Committee of Publishers and Associations.*

ISBN 0-936889-08-X
Library of Congress Catalog Number 91-058121


## CATALOGING IN PUBLICATION DATA

Piirto, Rebecca, 1958–
Beyond mind games




ISBN 0-936889-08-X

Printed in the United States of America


Designed and composed by Stephen Masiclat
Cover design by Rebecca Wilson

# BEYOND

## THE MARKETING POWER

# MIND

## OF PSYCHOGRAPHICS

# GAMES

Rebecca Piirto

# Table of Contents

Acknowledgments ........................................................... vi

Preface ......................................................................... 1

## Part I: The Evolution of Psychographic Research

Chapter 1   Measures of the Mind: The Beginnings ......................... 6

Chapter 2   The Birth of Psychographics: Focus on the Person ...... 18

## Part II: Psychographics Realized

Chapter 3   Portraits of America: The Original VALS .................... 32

Chapter 4   The American Pulse: Yankelovich's Monitor .............. 50

Chapter 5   Disillusionment and the New VALS 2 ........................ 68

## Part III: Applying Psychographics

Chapter 6   Psychographics in Advertising ................................... 96

Chapter 7   Motivational Revival: From Mining Emotions
            to Bonding with Brands ............................................. 124

Chapter 8     Going Global: International Psychographics ............ 142

Chapter 9     Going Local: Broadcast Markets ................................ 168

Chapter 10    Getting Specific: Attitudes and Behavior of
              Users and Doers ......................................................... 188

Chapter 11    Retailing in an Era of Diversity ................................ 202

Chapter 12    Packaged Goods: Attitudes of the Core Consumer .... 220

Chapter 13    Geodemographics: You Are Where You Live ............. 232

Chapter 14    Advice from the Experts: Avoiding the Pitfalls
              of Psychographic Research ........................................ 238


*Appendix*    A Listing of Advertising Agencies & Market
              Research Firms ......................................................... 247

*Bibliography*  ............................................................................. 252

*Index*  ....................................................................................... 256

# Acknowledgments

**M**any people were instrumental in the making of this book. I must first express my thanks to the numerous marketing and advertising research professionals who offered their thoughts during hundreds of hours of conversation while developing this book. I am particularly grateful to Ernest Dichter, Russell Haley, Joseph Smith, Valentine Appel, Florence Skelly, Bud Roper, Harrison Gough, Susan Hayward, Francois Christen, Anthony Schlee, Barbara Feigin, Fred Elkind, Joseph Plummer, Judy Langer, Sharon Livingston, Deborah Moroney, Eckart Guthe, Jacqueline Silver, Bruce McEvoy, Susie Wong, Melody Douglas Tate, Margaret Mark, Paula Drillman, Henry Bernstein, Martin Horn, Max Blackston, Jay Faberman, Peter Kim, John O'Toole, Fred Posner, Patty Comini, Tony Adams, Josh McQueen, Tom Snyder, and Karen Olshan. Special thanks go to William Wells and Daniel Yankelovich for their insight and thoughtful comments on early drafts of this book.

At American Demographics Books, Dick Wright, Jim Madden, and Diane Crispell were tireless in their administrative, creative, and editorial support coming into the home stretch. Kathy Brandenburg, along with Nancy Ten Kate, Mary Colella, and Patricia Driscoll, executed the editorial changes with patience and competency. Thanks go to designers Rebecca Wilson and Stephen Masiclat for the final appearance of the book, and to Meg Ambry who offered valuable editorial guidance early in the process. And spurring the project on was Peter Francese, who has steadfastly offered me his confidence and support even when I interrupted work to have my first child.

Most essential to my perseverance, despite the trials of pregnancy and new parenthood, have been the love, support, and counsel of my husband, Douglas Heather, and the refreshing moments of pure joy provided by our son, Jackson. In this, as in everything, they are my ultimate inspiration. I dedicate this book to them.

# *Preface*

A business trying to sell a product in America today is faced with an increasingly difficult task. It's a strategic mistake to try to sell widgets with the same appeal in Tuscaloosa as in Boston, or to try to win buyers in San Francisco with the appeal that works in Fort Worth. Beyond location and income, the age, sex, and education of consumers may also determine whether they buy your widgets. But what happens when demographics no longer work to determine demand? All other factors being equal, why would an expensive imported sedan sell like gangbusters in Beverly Hills, but have little appeal in Bal Harbor, two areas with similar average demographics? It all has to do with what goes on in consumers' minds.

In the last 70 years, business researchers have variously embraced and discarded theories from every discipline in the social sciences, trying to find the magic yardstick that provides the ultimate insight into consumers' minds. Along the way, market researchers have borrowed liberally from the academics, adopting a technique here and a methodology there.

In the beginning, there was survey sampling. Then came demographic segmentation and motivational research. At first, there was a deep rift between those advocating the qualitative approach and proponents of quantitative methods of market research. Since then, the process has evolved further, the rift has faded, and eventually something called psychographics evolved that synthesized the quantifiable measurements of the statisticians with the human insights gained by the motivationists.

The first problem one encounters when trying to untangle the origins and evolution of psychographic research is the lack of consensus about something as basic as the definition of the term. "Psychographics" in its broadest sense encompasses not only demographics (sex, age, income, education, etc.), but all aspects of an individual's way of living. The most widely accepted definition of psychographics and lifestyle includes: the activities that occupy leisure time; interests such as family, home, job, and community; and people's opinions—about themselves, social and cultural issues, the future, and products. In its broadest sense, "psychographics" also includes the underlying emotions that drive brand choice.

Psychographics is a tool researchers use to understand the more intangible psychological aspects of consumers, so it's not surprising that psychographics as a field of inquiry has been somewhat shrouded by ambiguity. The American marketplace is a churning sea of human beings with infinitely varied wants, needs, beliefs, opinions, interests, and motivations. Their personalities, life paths, and circumstances are as individual and distinct from one another as are their fingerprints. Psychographic research is what businesses use to make sense of the complex series of external stimuli and internal responses that make a person buy one product rather than another.

One research director at a top advertising agency likens the consumer to an onion. You peel away one layer (the demographics), only to find another layer (the attitudes), and another (the motivations), and still more layers beneath. For each individual, the layers are vastly different in content and order. What motivates one person to buy may well drive another away. To complicate matters further, there is no single reason why people buy. Demand is determined by an intricate combination of human, product, and economic variables, and the equation is different for each consumer and for every product category.

Given this tangled web, the most effective way to market would be to appeal to each consumer directly. Imagine the effect of a television ad that featured a burly man in a plaid shirt speaking directly to Ralph Johnson and telling him to get right down to his local Sears store to buy the power screwdriver that was going on sale. Ralph would probably do it because the man looked like his neighbor, he had been wanting a power screwdriver for all his home fix-ups, and he liked to buy things on sale.

That, at least for the present, is science fiction. Because it is impossible to speak directly to the 250 million-plus consumers in the American market, segmentation was invented. In segmenting the market, researchers search for common attributes that allow them to sort consumers into larger homogeneous groups. But any attempt to sort and categorize the swirling mass of consumers that is the American market is inherently flawed from the start. No such simplification can truly capture the richness of the market in all its diversity. No set of eight or ten abstract consumer profiles can recreate the disparate reality of the American population.

Yet it is these general psychographic typologies that most people think of when they think of psychographic research. This use of the term is unfortunate because serious problems inherent in these broad-based typologies have served to discredit the entire idea of psychographic research for a whole contingent of marketers. These general psychographic segmentations create consumer archetypes such as Succeeders, Climbers, Achievers, and Strugglers, and provide colorful descriptions of fictional consumer groups. But they are of dubious use in predicting consumer behavior. For this reason, it is important to distinguish between this single type of psychographic research and the idea of psychographic inquiry itself.

Broad-based segmentations (the original Values and Lifestyles Program of SRI is the best example) that define groups solely by personality attributes or values have been largely discredited as reliable predictors of consumer behavior. The personality or value constructs on which they are based often have little to do with the reasons people buy toothpaste, breakfast cereal, or even a new car. Such systems have fallen out of favor in the past decade, and most experienced market researchers have learned, often by trial and error, that the best predictor of consumer behavior today is either past behavior or specific consumer attitudes about a product or category. Recognizing the limits of psychological factors alone has led the most sophisticated (and successful) psychographic researchers to include specific behaviors or product attitudes in the equation.

Like any dynamic organism, psychographics is continuously evolving, and its definition must change as applications change. Psychographic research today includes much more than general lifestyles or attitude segmentations; it is multidimensional. It might start with general demographics and broad psychographic segmentations, then narrow down to a product category, and finally, zero in on specific brands. At each level, psychographics—an examination of the relevant psychological aspects—is critical. Advertisers today use many different methods to find out what mind-set distinguishes liquid detergent users from nonusers or to explore the attitudes, images, and emotions that make a group of consumers consistently choose Coke over Pepsi or reach for Heineken instead of Pabst.

For the purposes of this book, "psychographics" will be defined in this broadest sense. Most psychographic studies today include product-related attitudes and behaviors, and this book will examine both the general segmentation schemes as well as recent industry- and product-specific psychographic research. Wherever possible, it will also analyze how well psychographics works with illustrative case studies.

One aspect of this broader perspective on psychographics is something called "nondemographic segmentation," a term social scientist Daniel Yankelovich coined as early as 1964, long before he published his landmark book, *New Rules*. In a *Harvard Business Review* article, Yankelovich described how to segment markets by "values, purposes, needs, and attitudes relevant to the product being studied." It is misleading, he said, to classify a person according to psychological or personality factors and to make assumptions about buying behavior based on those traits, because people behave differently depending upon what product they're buying. A person who always buys the cheapest watch may buy expensive Italian shoes or drive a BMW. When looking for insight into specific buying behavior, Yankelovich says, it is better to draw from the broadest spectrum of nondemographic variables to identify the key determinants of demand for the product or category.

Ironically, this is the approach many advertising agencies and corporate research departments are taking today. They may not call it psychographic research, but it is. It has taken 30 years of false starts and blind alleys for the market research community to arrive at a general consensus that product-related attitudes are more relevant to demand than are personality, values, or social character. This book will examine these changing perspectives and the consequences for psychographic research.

The goal of this book—tracing the origins, evolution, and subsequent business applications of psychographic research—may be an impossible mission. It's rather like trying to untangle the complex etymological roots of the English language. Sociology, psychology, social psychology, anthropology, and psychometrics have all contributed at one time or another to the theoretical foundation of psychographic research. The academic literature is so rich and varied, it is beyond the scope of this book to discuss all pertinent research. The discussion focuses instead on highlighting the important milestones that facilitated the development and subsequent progression of psychographic research.

This book is not intended to be a how-to manual on the various statistical methodologies at the heart of psychographic segmentation. Rather, the text is consciously non-technical, written in a way that precludes statistical expertise. It was my intention to demystify psychographics so as to make both the successes and failures of this form of research more accessible for managers, executives, creatives, and other nonstatisticians. The emphasis of this book is not so much on form as it is on content and application. It is assumed that those who need or want to know the technical intricacies of psychographic survey design, implementation, and analysis already know. Those who desire more technical information should turn to the original sources listed in the bibliography. Almost all of the published academic research includes detailed methodological information.

While researching this book, I interviewed more than 100 market research professionals and academics and pored over hundreds of books and articles. One curious point emerged: old theories and techniques, given new names, keep resurfacing in market research. Some are still being used despite the fact that their effectiveness has been seriously questioned. Some observers, myself included, explain this phenomenon as a lack of historic memory. Without scholarly attention to previous work, market researchers, like Sisyphus, are forced to roll the psychographic rock up that steep slope again and again for eternity.

This shortness of collective recall among many practitioners is one reason why psychographic research is so poorly understood. Because it is inadequately understood, it is sometimes not done well, which is one reason many researchers have become disillusioned with it. That's where this book intends to help.

As George Santayana said, "Those who cannot remember the past are condemned to repeat it." This book is offered in hopes that market researchers of the 1990s and beyond will learn from the past and continue to build and expand on what has gone before. The ability to synthesize the best aspects of established theories with the groundbreaking dynamism of new ideas is the essential catalyst for advancement in any area of knowledge.

Rebecca Piirto
Ithaca, New York
June 1991

# Part I

## The Evolution of Psychographic Research

# 1 Measures of the Mind: The Beginnings

*What is it about this distraction with personality differences that generations of market researchers keep coming back to? Part of it might be a lack of historic memory. If you don't approach this thing in a scholarly way, you reinvent the wheel every year. But more than that, it's so terribly seductive...*

*I think you can confidently predict that someone else writing the same book 20 years from now is going to cover almost exactly the same material. The words will change, but the seduction is a permanent one. The desire to match personalities with brands is irresistible. It's independent of history. It's independent of validity. It just keeps rolling along, like old man river.*
*— Daniel Yankelovich*

**M**ANY VETERAN researchers still point to something that happened in the late 1950s as the finest hour of marketing research. General Mills had developed Betty Crocker brand cake mixes that required consumers to add only water. Executives considered the easy, foolproof product a sure-fire success, so they were quite surprised when it bombed. General Mills called in Ernest Dichter, a Vienna-born psychologist specializing in consumer motivations, to find out what was going on.

One of the first things Dichter's in-depth interviewing revealed was that the housewives who were the main consumers for the product felt left out because the product gave them nothing to do. Frequently, just to participate, they would add some milk, which would overload the cake mix with calcium and ruin the final product. Further research into the symbolism of cakes suggested that baking a cake was an unconscious metaphor for giving birth. At the very least, a cake was a gift from a woman to her family. Dichter suggested that General Mills change the formula to allow the consumer to add an egg so she could re-establish ownership of the cake. The reformulated mix was a hit, and the rest, as they say, is marketing history.

This classic case owes its success to motivational research, which could be viewed as the flip side of Post-War optimism and prosperity as reflected in popular television shows of the time like "Father Knows Best." Back in the 1950s, approaches borrowed from Freud looked for unconscious motivations rooted in forbidden desires (such as a boy's Oedipal wish to have Mom all to himself) as the real reason people bought things like soup or cars. There was a squeaky-clean facade on mainstream American life, and motivation research may have been an attempt to uncover the base human motivations behind this insufferably wholesome, one-dimensional view of the average American. In an era where Ozzie and Harriet represented the perfect family and Senator Joe McCarthy was actually taken seriously, is it any wonder some market researchers thought housewives used food as a weapon and gum chewers were really frustrated breast feeders?

Despite its infamous follies, facades, and persecutions, the 1950s was a decade wracked by unprecedented controversy over something as seemingly trivial as market research methods. Out of the controversy, as often happens, came the knowledge that paved the way for the research advances that spawned psychographics.

## The Great Debate

In the mid-1950s, Madison Avenue was rocked by a classic debate between the traditional statistical researchers, led by Alfred Politz, and the motivationists, led by Ernest Dichter. In a series of articles and public statements, each lambasted the other's theories and techniques. Politz called motivational research "pseudo science" and "pure unadulterated balderdash," while Dichter called Politz's approach "nose-counting."

The dispute had its origins in a powerful ideological line of differentiation that started in academia, was carried over to the commercial world, and became personified in the forms of Politz and Dichter. University departments became divided over the quantitative-versus-qualitative issue, and the market research community became firmly divided between Politz's quantitative "only-numbers-tell-the-truth" stance and Dichter's qualitative "truth-is-in-the-subconscious" approach. This division also laid the groundwork for the synthesis of quantitative methods and qualitative ideas that led to the development of psychographics.

Both Politz and Dichter were well-known researchers who headed their own firms, and both had a flamboyant love of controversy, but that's where the similarity ends. Politz was widely considered a leader in the use of statistical survey sampling and quantitative marketing research techniques. He helped further the development of probability sampling and based his reputation on statistical accuracy. His company, Alfred Politz Research Inc., specialized in major audience measurement studies for publications such as *Time* and *Life* magazines and other national media.

Dichter, on the other hand, was a student of the grayer area of the human psyche. His image was that of the quintessential Freudian psychoanalyst; he spoke with an Austrian accent and sported a goatee. He relished the limelight and had a flair for getting attention. As one example of his modus operandi, Dichter recalls the time he was asked to analyze soap operas when he worked for CBS in the 1940s. To the surprise of his boss, CBS president Frank Stanton, Dichter called a press conference to announce that his research revealed soap operas promoted fascist ideology. The programs, he said, always featured one strong personality who solved the problems of all the others, who were weak and indecisive, much the way people looked to fascist dictators to do their thinking for them. Frank Stanton, Dichter says, was not amused. Soon afterwards, Dichter started his Institute for Motivational Research, which championed the idea of using in-depth interviewing and projective tests to uncover the hidden motivations of consumers.

Politz represented the longer-held view, first postulated by the opinion pollers and survey samplers of the early part of the century—that the only accurate picture of a market or a population is a quantifiable one in which questions are asked, responses are tallied, and results are verified by replication. He dismissed Dichter's studies, which equated housewives' bread-baking with the process of birth and young girls' use of soap with ritual virginal cleansing, as subjective nonsense. Dichter, on the other hand, viewed the purely statistical approach as lacking in true human insights.

One famous debate occurred in 1955 in Madison, Wisconsin, with Dichter arguing for motivational research and Elmo Roper, founder of what is now The Roper Organization Inc., arguing against. Before a meeting of the American Association for Public Opinion Research, Roper presented a spoof of a motivational study to prove the point that motivational research was unscientific. He donned a white coat and had an associate reclining on a couch. He proceeded to ask the "subject" what she ate when she woke up in the morning. She replied, "A roll in bed with honey." He then asked her if she were an egg whether she would be scrambled or fried. She replied, "coddled." From this, Roper announced that he would advise the cereal manufacturer client to get out of the cereal business and go into the egg business. What's more, he said, he also advised that they put their money into developing a square egg, because they would stack better in the refrigerator and wouldn't roll off counters. The stunt had the audience of opinion pollers rolling in the aisles.

"It was devastating," recalls Roper's son, Bud Roper, now chairman of The Roper Organization. "Needless to say, Dichter clearly lost that debate." Bud Roper says that on the train home from Chicago, Dichter and Elmo Roper had a frank confrontation during which Dichter asked Roper why he had it in for him. "My father said he resented that Dichter would do three interviews, come up with an idea, and then say it was based on research," says Bud Roper. "That's what he couldn't forgive Dichter for."

Though the debate sounds academic now, it created a deep fissure among researchers that can be detected in psychology departments today, albeit in a milder form. In the early 1950s, the controversy was so intense that the Advertising Research Foundation set up a special Committee on Motivation Research. "Psychology departments split up over this issue," says renowned social scientist Daniel Yankelovich, co-founder of the Yankelovich Monitor. Yankelovich studied at Harvard during the 1940s, then attended the Sorbonne in Paris. He was research director at a New York design firm during the height of the debate. "The qualitative people were looked at as soft and unscientific, and they in turn looked down their noses at the number crunchers as being trivial," he says. "It was an era where a lot of passion was stirred up over this."

## Sampling Was the Name of the Game

Up until the end of the 1800s, government census takers were the only researchers getting information from average Americans. The first documented research for commercial purposes in the U.S. was done in 1879 by N.W. Ayer & Son for the Nichols-Shepard Company, a threshing-machine manufacturer. Ayer wired state officials across the country to get information on expected grain production and used the data to construct a rudimentary, but serviceable, market survey by counties.

Market research quickly gained practitioners after 1900. Some pre-1915 efforts were done for the E.I. DuPont and De Mours Co., the Kellogg Co., *The Chicago Tribune*, the Curtis Publishing Co., and the newly established Bureau of Business Research at Harvard University. Most of these studies provided only volumetric measurements of trading in various markets. But Kellogg's 1911 study was remarkable in that it was the first documented example of a mail survey that attempted to determine which magazines were read by different classifications of people. In 1923 the newly formed Young & Rubicam advertising agency hired George Gallup to conduct consumer research. The Research Group of the Advertising Group of New York was formed in 1924.

Opinion polling was also an important precursor to the later development of psychographic research, because the early pollers proved that a small representative sample of people could accurately indicate the views or behavior of the larger population. They also showed businesses and governments the value of knowing what consumers or voters were thinking.

Elmo Roper ran a jewelry store in a small Iowa town in the late 1920s, which failed because he "was trying to run a Tiffany-style store in a non-Tiffany-style town." This lesson was one Roper would take with him to his next position as a salesman for one of the jewelry distributors he used to buy from. He eventually worked his way up to a position that involved making decisions about what lines of jewelry to produce. Unlike the other sales managers, Roper based his decisions on what the jewelry-store owners, his old customers, said they would be willing to buy. Though his "research" was strictly unquantified, his lines consistently outsold those of his colleagues. Armed with this knowledge about the power of asking questions, Roper decided to start his own polling company. With the help of an account supervisor at the J. Walter Thompson agency, Roper met Paul Cherington and Richards on Wood. Together, they started Cherington, Roper and Wood in October 1933.

Although Daniel Starch and Archibald Crosley had already started firms specializing in advertising readership and radio audience measurement, Roper's partnership was the first general-opinion polling company in the country. The partnership's first clients were utility companies that wanted to find out why electrical usage was so low. Roper and his associates went door-to door and asked people directly about their electrical usage and their opinions. They reported back to their clients that the problem was pricing—both electricity and appliances were way out of reach of the average consumer. The utility industry recovered from the Depression and went on to become the ubiquitous service it is today.

Roper soon had competition in the form of George Gallup, who started his polling company in 1935. One of Gallup's early efforts involved polling Iowa voters on their opinions about candidates for state office, one of whom happened to be Gallup's mother-in-law. To many observers, her victory, despite her underdog standing, was one more proof of the value of identifying people's perceptions early in the process. The sooner the public's opinions were known, the sooner the product, whether it be a bar of soap or a candidate, could be repositioned for optimal appeal.

Opinion pollsters Gallup and Roper really proved the value of survey sampling by correctly predicting the outcome of the 1936 presidential election. "One of the reasons they got in (to the election) was to deal with the skepticism they constantly faced about the whole methodology," Bud Roper says. "Skeptics didn't believe that you could determine what a nation thought from a small sample." Never mind that the polling firms' results proved to be consistent with government surveys, cynics charged that they manipulated the results purposely to come out within a few percentage points of the government.

Predicting an election that no one could predetermine seemed the perfect way to prove the validity of survey sampling methods. All three of the major polling firms, with their samples of 4,000 to 5,000 voters, predicted Franklin D. Roosevelt's win against Alfred Landon. The *Literary Digest*, with a survey of more than 2 million readers, incorrectly chose Landon, most likely because its readers were more affluent and more educated than the rest of the voting public. "This focused public attention for the first time on the polling operation," Roper said. "It showed that 4,000 people could determine what a nation of 40 million would do."

The opinion polling firms enjoyed a steady string of successes during the war years that effectively silenced the skeptics. Pollers aided the war effort by effectively monitoring everything from troop morale to the opinions of Europeans about American soldiers' conduct. These successes won avid proponents for survey sampling, first in the commercial realm, and later in public policy areas.

As the number of attitude research firms and research practitioners increased, the methodology and data sources became more sophisticated, and market research became an accepted field of study. On the urging of business researchers, the Department of Commerce undertook the first Census of Distribution in 1929 and began improving its scope and accuracy during the 1930s. This annual survey now covers retailing, wholesaling, and service industries. By the late 1930s, at least six college textbooks on market research techniques had been published, indicating that the field had gained credibility in academia.

Before World War II, market research was involved mainly in volumetric measurement, using techniques derived from survey research and economic analysis. Market researchers paid strict attention to sampling methodology. Accuracy of the sampling was paramount, and little importance was attached to psychological considerations.

The earliest mention of psychology in commercial terms was in 1895 by Professor Harlow Gale at the University of Minnesota. Gale sent out a mail questionnaire to 200 advertising professionals around the St. Paul area trying to gain insight into the psychological impact of advertising. Despite a survey response rate of 10 percent, Gale was optimistic about the future of psychology in advertising. "It is an entirely new field for psychological work and one of great and increasing importance. It is our aim to find the mental processes which go on in the minds of the customers from the time they see an advertisement until they have purchased the article advertised," Gale wrote in *On the Psychology of Advertising*, published in 1900.

Gale's impact on other researchers, however, was slight. Between 1900 and 1930, there were fewer than half a dozen practicing commercial psychologists, though they included respected names like E. K. Strong and famed behavioral psychologist John B. Watson, who worked for J. Walter Thompson as a consultant.

One early commercial study that involved psychological probing was done by Professor Dale Houghton of New York University in the 1930s. He studied 18 common irritants of humans, such as constipation, dirty teeth, coughs, and headaches, and how readily images of products to relieve them flashed in people's minds at the mention of the irritants. Another notable study of the early 1930s was done by social scientist Paul Lazarsfeld of Columbia University's Bureau of Applied Social Research. He suggested that any research designed to understand consumer behavior should look at three sets of variables; predisposition, influences, and product attributes. Here was the cornerstone for a more humanized approach to quantitative research.

Most market research, however, continued to be dominated by statistical and demographic criteria. It wasn't until after World War II that broader interest turned to the use of psychoanalytical techniques. One of the reasons for this was the wealth of empirical data on attitudes, sentiments, and behavior that came out of research done on American soldiers during the war. *The American Soldier* was a compendium of this research and went a long way to make the careers of the sociologists and psychologists involved.

One of the most widely used paper-and-pencil inventories for personality assessment also had its origins in World War II research. Dr. Erwin Wexberg, a leader in personality assessment, headed the clinical psychology section at Camp Beale, California, during the war. Harrison G. Gough worked under Wexberg at Camp Beale and later went on to author the California Psychological Inventory (CPI). This paper-and-pencil personality inventory, written in 1951, has become a standard for measuring personality attributes for a wide range of uses today. Subjects respond to a series of self-rating scales that are then scored to produce a personality profile. As shall be seen, market researchers later borrowed this measurement technique, sometimes without any modifications whatsoever, in designing psychographic tools to measure consumer behavior.

Interest in the human psyche and personality peaked among business researchers in the 1950s. By the end of the decade, the business world saw an explosion in research aimed at finding correlations between personality and consumer behavior. The development of personality assessment techniques (such as the CPI and the Myers-Briggs Type Indicator™) was significant because they categorized people into types defined by personality traits, a concept that would later provide the basis for certain types of psychographic research.

At the same time, business researchers were becoming fascinated with exploring consumers' unconscious motivations. Projective techniques, such as Rorschach Ink Blots, Thematic Apperception Tests, and in-depth interviews, were employed to get at motivations that consumers themselves didn't even know they had. A major influence in the rise of motivational research came from the work of Ernest Dichter.

## Cult of Personality

Dichter was a product of pre-Nazi Vienna. Today, at 83, Dichter still does research consulting work for corporate clients. In recalling his early days in Austria, Dichter says it was impossible to live in Vienna in the 1920s and 1930s without becoming interested in psychology. "There were lectures, " he remembers. "It was on every evening on the radio. There was Alfred Adler. In Switzerland, there was Carl Jung. It was like Viennese music. It was part of the climate of the times."

Dichter studied psychology at the Psycho-Economics Institute (Wirtschafts Psychologices Institute) of the University of Vienna. Though an admirer of Freud, he had to study him surreptitiously because Freud wasn't officially recognized by the school's classical psychology professors. Coincidentally, one of his teachers was statistician and social scientist Paul Lazarsfeld, who later emigrated to the U.S. under a grant and eventually headed the Bureau of Applied Social Research at Columbia University.

Dichter fled from Austria in 1938, fearing the rise of Hitler and his brownshirts in neighboring Germany. He went to Paris and worked for a while as a journalist for the Paris bureau of a Viennese paper. With war imminent, he and his wife decided to emigrate to the U.S. After several attempts, he convinced the vice consul he was a good risk and secured American visas. He didn't have the $10,000 price of transportation for his wife and himself, but the vice consul arranged for the International Organization for Displaced Scientists to pay his way.

In reflecting on his early days in America, Dichter says it was not easy at first to get people to listen to his idea of applying psychoanalysis to consumer behavior. Shortly after his arrival, Dichter called Lazarsfeld and asked him if he knew of any companies that would pay him to study the psychological impact of their products. "I was laughed at," Dichter says. "He told me my idea would never work, that Americans didn't understand psychology. It was too sophisticated for them." Nevertheless, Lazarsfeld put him in touch with someone at Compton, the agency that then handled the Procter & Gamble account. They wanted him to analyze the appeal of Ivory soap. Dichter describes that first study:

"Instead of just asking people, 'Why are you using Ivory soap?' I asked them when they took their baths and which of their baths were particularly important. I also interviewed some young girls who said (they used it) before they went out on a date. I sort of smiled and asked why that was important. They answered, 'Well, you never know.' What they meant by it was quite obvious. Out of that came the idea that when you're taking a bath, you're not just getting clean, you're also washing all your sins away, like in baptism. They used the slogan for several years: 'Be smart, get a fresh start, with Ivory soap.' "

In 1939, *Time* magazine ran a feature on Dichter detailing his escape from Europe and his triumph with Ivory soap. The article sparked new interest. His next study was commissioned by Chrysler, which wanted to find out how to improve sales of the beleaguered Plymouth line. He was asked to determine who made the car-buying decision. The company had surveyed 1,000 American men on the topic, and the majority claimed they had decided what car the family would buy. The company was suspicious about that result, so they asked Dichter to get the facts.

He interviewed male car-buyers and asked them to describe the circumstances surrounding their last car purchase—what they did before and after and who they were with. The study found that the majority were accompanied by wives or girlfriends. Dichter concluded that women had significant input into the car-buying decision. As a result, Chrysler altered its selling approach to appeal both directly and indirectly to women. Further exploration showed that women couldn't wait to ride in a new car, while the men couldn't wait to start polishing and tinkering with it. One period ad featured a young couple looking over a Plymouth admiringly and the line, "Imagine us in a car like that." Another showed a stylish young woman next to a Plymouth with the legend, "My Car Fits Me Like a Glove." Plymouth sales picked up and so did Dichter's new career. Shortly after, at the age of 30, he was hired by J. Stirling Getchell advertising agency as director of psychological research.

With those successes under his belt, Dichter became a celebrity in the U.S. business world. A highly recognizable figure who made the most of his German accent and "long-hair" appeal, Dichter took on the lecture circuit, preaching the advantages of "interpretive" over "descriptive" research. "With that, I was really made," says Dichter. "All of a sudden I was the wonder kid from Vienna. I had many discussions over the radio. I was sort of the ugly duckling, trying to challenge the established market research people."

Dichter strongly argued that you couldn't ask people directly why they did what they did, because most of the time they didn't know. People's real motivations were hidden. This was reminiscent of what Lazarsfeld had written 20 years earlier in his article "The Art of Asking Why." Dichter, however, advocated that the way to uncover motivations was through the use of psychoanalytic techniques. When researchers asked people directly why they did something, they were bound to get inaccurate results, he says, because most people try to rationalize their behavior in an intelligent way, when in reality there is no rational explanation. "It's about as intelligent as a physician asking his patient who complained about a stomachache why he had a stomachache and then putting the answer down as a diagnosis," Dichter says. The way to find out why people buy, he said, was to ask about the circumstances surrounding their actions. "It raised a lot of controversy among the established market researchers because it was contrary to everything they had been doing."

Dichter formed the Institute for Motivational Research in Peekskill, New York, and went on to consult for nearly every major agency and the biggest U.S. advertisers. He found ice cream to be representative of mother's milk, childhood, and oral voluptuousness. Dichter says his methods also helped equate convertibles with mistresses, told Heinz to show its ketchup just as it started seeping out of a bottle, and put the tiger in Exxon's tank.

Not all of Dichter's recommendations, however, were so useful. Dichter once advised an oil company that women could be induced to purchase more gasoline if gas pumps were shaped more like female breasts than phallic symbols. In another instance, he counseled American Airlines on how to reduce consumers' fear of flying. He said putting fake oak beams on the cabin ceiling would lend a feel of solidity, and that if the pilot (a father figure) made frequent strolls through the cabin, passengers would be reassured. American Airlines decided it was safer to have the pilot stay in the cockpit. During an early consulting job for the tea industry, Dichter suggested that more males might drink tea if it was their favorite color—blue. Needless to say, the tea industry was not too keen on that idea.

Dichter, though one of the most written about, was certainly not the only consumer motivationist. Louis Cheskin, who founded the Chicago research firm Color Research Institute of America, published a 1948 paper, "Indirect Approach to Market Reactions," in the *Harvard Business Review*. It was one of the first published pieces seeking to legitimize motivational research techniques. Cheskin was also responsible for rounding and feminizing the corners on the Fleischmann's Gin label to appeal more to women.

At about the same time, articles detailing the depth psychoanalytic approach to marketing research appeared regularly in the *Journal of Marketing* and *Printers' Ink*. The number of researchers examining consumer motivations increased. One early study was done in 1950 by Mason Haire. He used a projective technique to discover why housewives didn't use instant coffee, and he found they thought it would brand them as lazy, unorganized housekeepers. Franklin B. Evans did a landmark study in 1958 on the personality characteristics of Ford versus Chevrolet buyers. He found no significant differences, but that has since been attributed to the fact that he didn't alter his questions to fit the product.

Other names associated with research involving psychological attributes at the time were G.H. Smith, who wrote *Motivation Research in Advertising and Marketing* in 1955; Burleigh Gardner and Herta Herzog, who studied media; and Joseph Smith, who started Oxtoby-Smith in 1954, and was responsible for NBC choosing the peacock as the network's symbol.

## Rumors of Big Brother

Motivationism became so popular among U.S. market researchers that by 1954, half of the 64 members of the Jury of Marketing Opinion of the trade journal *Printers' Ink* said they had successfully used motivation research. The techniques were so popular among advertising agencies in the 1950s, Joseph Smith said, that agencies would grab anybody with a German accent and a cigarette holder to head their psychological research departments. Dichter was undoubtedly the model for that stereotype.

The motivationist movement relied on projective techniques borrowed from clinical psychology that were designed to get subjects to talk about and reveal their unconscious motivations. One popular technique was the in-depth interview in which the subject responds at length to a series of general questions designed to make "yes" or "no" responses impossible. Designed to keep respondents under the surface of their awareness, these techniques are projective because they allow respondents to project their own feelings on neutral stimuli. The Thematic Apperception Test, for example, consists of 30 cards printed with pictures from paintings and drawings. The respondent must make up a story about each picture. Another technique is the Rorschach Test, consisting of ten inkblots designed to measure personality. The subject is asked to look at the inkblot and describe what he sees. Other projective techniques include word association and sentence completion exercises.

As with any practice that can be perceived as exploiting innocence for commercial gain, motivation research was bound to become controversial. One of the fanners of the flame was Vance Packard's book *The Hidden Persuaders*, published in 1957. Written in a popular style designed to capture the attention of the general public, the book criticized motivational research on moral grounds and warned consumers that they were being subconsciously manipulated by advertising.

Ad men were seen as malevolent exploiters preying on the unconscious desires of the public. Soup ads were designed to appeal to the subconscious memory of the nourishing environment of the womb. Cigarettes and chewing gum were used by people who didn't get enough suckling as infants and were advertised accordingly. Cigars were phallic symbols or adult equivalents of thumb sucking. A Maidenform ad campaign of the time showed a women undressed except for her underwear in the middle of traffic with the legend, "I Dreamed I Stopped Traffic in My Maidenform Bra." It was designed, Packard implied, to appeal to the exhibitionism present in the female subconscious.

Children, Packard suggested, were especially vulnerable to the seductions of advertisers, and television was rapidly conditioning them to become loyal followers of brands. Manufacturers put the snap-crackle-pop into breakfast cereals because motivational researchers found it had irresistible appeal—the crunchiness allowed children to appease their hostility toward their parents. The country, in short, was in danger of becoming a nation of zombies, subconsciously programmed to consume.

The book was intentionally sensational and succeeded in directing a lot of positive publicity at the author and a lot of negative publicity at Dichter, who was frequently mentioned by name. But as frightening as this tale of subliminal persuasion was to the general public, it was perhaps more damaging to Dichter than it was to motivational research in general. In fact, at least one observer of the time says that Packard's book made motivational research more popular. "It was the best thing that ever happened to motivation research," says William Wells, then a professor of psychology and marketing at the University of Chicago's Graduate School of Business. "It convinced marketers that motivation research was necessary. Without it, motivation research would have remained a curiosity."

By the early 1960s, however, the Freudian aspect of motivational research and Dichter's overpowering personality had received too much adverse publicity. Many found the

Freudian emphasis not only morally unsavory, but too esoteric. Finding out that a woman hated her father wasn't too helpful to a researcher trying to learn why she didn't buy Tide detergent. Most marketers were realizing that unconscious motivations were too deep to have much bearing on a superficial action like buying a product.

Another problem was Dichter himself. He became so well-known personally and his research methods so notorious that, according to some observers, people stopped using motivational research in reaction. Whatever the reasons, many researchers lost interest in consumers' deepest unconscious motivations by the early 1960s, just as computers were becoming more available, a technological advance that paved the way for the next hot new research method—psychographic segmentation.

Perhaps the most persistent problem with motivational research was that Politz and the others were right. Motivational research was unreliable. It failed one of the cardinal rules of scientific methods—replicability. Two researchers might draw two totally different conclusions from the same interviews, because motivational research was so dependent upon individual interpretation.

It's ironic that in the final analysis of current research methods, both the motivationists and the quantitative factions have come out approximately even. Politz's survey sampling methods are an integral part of marketing research, as are in-depth interviewing and focus groups. Despite the flaws inherent in qualitative research, by most accounts its use is increasing as companies slash marketing costs and look for less costly ways to gain consumer insights. The debate about quantitative versus qualitative research is still raging, albeit in much more subdued tones *(see Chapter 14)*.

What's more, interest in consumer motivations has remained high. Many of the projective techniques described earlier are still being used today, although adapted or customized in some way by individual research firms *(see Chapter 7)*. Many intelligent people still believe that projective methods produce valuable psychographic information that couldn't be obtained otherwise.

Validity complaints aside, motivational research did have an important positive effect on the market research community at large: It showed the inadequacies of demographics and traditional statistical research methods alone. Once accustomed to the colorful, more humanized findings offered by the motivationists, researchers couldn't go back to using only cold, impersonal numbers to delineate consumer markets. Motivation research showed that the numbers alone were too superficial to tell the whole truth about consumers. Many searched for a new form of inquiry that would wed the technical accuracy of the statisticians with the human insights of the motivationists. That new form became psychographics.

# 2 The Birth of Psychographics: Focus on the Person

*I used clinical psychology to prove that we cannot describe a person simply on the basis of age, income, and marital status, but we also have to describe him by the type of person he is. In a good interpretive questionnaire or open-ended interview, you should find out what are some of the most beloved products somebody owns. Taking myself, for example, you would quickly find out I have a greenhouse and I have on my desk a magazine called* Gardening. *I like to raise plants, and I'm not motivated by showing off. It doesn't do anything for me. I'm expressing my personality by the kind of things I'm doing.*

— Ernest Dichter

*We originally intended it to extend across all the measures of the mind, hitting at the minds and feelings of people—that's what psychographics was supposed to be—interests of the mind. Originally, we divided psychographics into two areas: the benefits aspects—product-related interests—and lifestyles. Lifestyle information does as well or even better than focusing on product characteristics in certain categories where emotions are more deeply involved. When people yell out a brand of beer, they're saying something about who they are—when they say "Old Iron City," that's a little bit different than saying, "Heineken."*

— Russell Haley

*Psychographics is the use of psychological, sociological, and anthropological factors, such as benefits desired (from behavior being studied), self-concept, and lifestyle (or serving style) to determine how the market is segmented by the propensity of groups within the market—and their reasons—to make a particular decision about a product, person, ideology, or otherwise hold an attitude or use a medium. Demographics and socioeconomics are also used as a constant check to see if psychographic market segmentation improves on other forms of segmentation including user/nonuser groupings.*

— Emanual Demby

*It is a creative tool that gives you a feeling for people you don't know personally.*

— Joseph Plummer

T HERE IS NO one single person or event that can be credited as the originator of psychographics. The history of science is marked by instances in which people in various parts of the county or world simultaneously venture into similar new territories unbeknownst to each other. The beginning of psychographics is another case in point. Widespread dissatisfaction with simple demographics and disillusionment with motivational research, coupled with the increasing accessibility of computers, gave many researchers the raw material they needed to begin quantitative studies that attempted to measure qualitative elements such as personality traits, motivations, and psychological attributes. The groundwork was laid by the end of the 1950s, in part through several published papers.

In September 1958, Dichter's Institute for Motivational Research published a 45-page monograph titled *Typology*. In the booklet, Dichter outlined the value of classifying the people who make up markets into separate groups—typologies—according to how their "personality traits, social and economic levels, attitudes, motives, or clusters of characteristics...apply to a specific type of purchase behavior." Dichter makes several related points: a person purchases different products depending upon his degree of satisfaction and his self-image; the self-image is a complex combination of attitudes toward self and others that varies depending on the role being played; the types of products a person buys reflect self-image; products in which more of the ego is involved, like clothing and cars, are more reflective of ego than low-involvement items like pencils:

> *Another way of expressing this all-important concept is: everything a man does tends to reflect some characteristic aspect of his self. Some acts reflect more of the total self, some less. None will capture the total man, but understanding the self-expression involved in a particular behavior pattern provides us with the tools for making a more successful product or service.*
>
> *When an advertiser understands those 'typical aspects of character and self-concept' which operate in the purchase and use of a product, he can modify and improve his product to meet the special needs of the personality types represented in his market, rather than a simple breakdown of the market by social and economic groupings.*

It is interesting to note the similarity between Dichter's concept of typology and later definitions of psychographics. The major difference seems to be Dichter's dogged adherence to motivational techniques. Later in *Typology*, he outlines how to use projective techniques such as depth interviews to segment markets into personality types.

In the same year, Daniel Yankelovich published an article in *Printers' Ink* in which he called for an end to disagreements between researchers over "technical problems of size and character of sampling." Yankelovich suggests wedding the best of quantitative and qualitative research. This is the first mention this author can find of the idea that the two types of research could be blended to produce even more valuable consumer insights:

> *(These) false distinctions between qualitative research and quantitative research...(are) like arguing the relative merits of the saw versus the hammer in carpentry. No one technique is equally appropriate for all problems, and research firms will have all the sound techniques available when needed....And psychological research has increased the technical resources of marketing research tenfold.*

Yankelovich charged that psychoanalytic techniques were misapplied to the consumption of products because the jargon of neurosis was developed for clinical uses in understanding individuals. Using the jargon, he said, made it more difficult to explore the consumer-product relationship. Psychoanalytic techniques, he went on to say, could not help the manufacturer reach his ultimate goal—to increase his share of the market and get more people to buy his product. In order to do that, Yankelovich said:

> *... It is clear today, at least in some quarters, that marketing research that integrates the older nose-counting techniques with the newer techniques of psychological research is the one sure method for implementing the total marketing concept.*

By this time, some academic researchers had already conducted the first studies using psychometric ways of exploring personality and its effect on product choices. These psychometric techniques included quantifiable tests designed to measure psychological variables, such as intelligence and aptitude. In 1959, Morris Gottlieb published "Segmentation by Personality Types" in an American Marketing Association publication, *Advancing Marketing Efficiency*. In 1960, Arthur Koponen published "Personality Characteristics of Purchasers" in the *Journal of Advertising Research*. In the paper, he attempted to correlate consumer behavior with scores from standardized personality inventories, but his results were somewhat less than spectacular.

Yankelovich further articulated his idea of synthesizing quantitative and qualitative research methods in a 1964 article in the *Harvard Business Review*. In this article, he postulates using what he called "nondemographic segmentation" to create clear profiles of target markets. Nondemographic segmentation divided consumer markets by any variable that proved to be linked to demand. It could include product aspects such as value, purpose desired benefits, and aesthetics; and human variables such as a consumer's susceptibility to change, attitudes, individualized needs, or self-confidence. Yankelovich said that demographics should be seen as only one way of segmenting the market. A marketing director should never assume in advance that one method of segmentation would work best, but consider all possible segmentations and choose the most meaningful ones to work with.

Researchers in other realms were also exploring methods to account for differences in product appeal. In a 1959 paper presented to the American Psychological Association, William Wells posited that differences in sales could be attributed to differences in brand images caused by "attitudes, opinions, and beliefs about the properties of a product." This was the precursor to Wells' later "Attitudes, Interests, and Opinions" paper that formed the basis for psychographic research.

In this early paper, Wells also said that the expressive values (the personal and social aspects of the product image) could be measured by using adjective check lists, a technique often used in personality assessment. In personality assessment, subjects are asked to choose from lists of adjectives (friendly, lazy, phony, interesting, brilliant, cultured, etc.) to describe themselves. Wells suggested that this technique could identify consumers' images of the users of various brands. The degree of similarity or difference would help determine why they did or did not use the brand. Another technique Wells suggested is a bi-polar rating scale, which allows people to rate something by choosing a degree between two opposite adjectives, such as intelligent vs. stupid or rich vs. poor. This paper is significant, because scaler rating systems later became the basis of measurement for psychographic studies.

By the mid-1960s, researchers in both academia and the commercial world were delving into psychographics. Many were using the psychometrician's "pen and pencil" inventories (intelligence, personality, and aptitude tests) to explore personality, in relation to purchasing behavior. These studies involved adjective checklists or questionnaires with long lists of attributes or statements. Borrowing from these methods, psychographic studies asked consumers to rate attitude statements on a five- or seven-point scale ranging from strongly agree to strongly disagree.

## Who Was First?

The term "psychographics" with its current meaning didn't enter the marketing lexicon until 1965. The first published use of the term was in the November 1965 issue of *Grey Matter*, a Grey Advertising publication sent as a new-business vehicle to all major advertisers in the country. Russell Haley, who headed Grey's research effort at the time, recalls that the word was created at an editorial meeting as a way to describe current agency research. Grey had been using demographics for segmentation, but found that it was hard for creative people to understand. "We thought if we could group people by their interests, then by their demographics, we'd be able to help creative people write copy that spoke to those people directly," Haley says. "We originally intended it to extend across all measures of the mind, hitting at the interests and feelings of people." Later that year, Haley used the term in a speech before a large audience of researchers.

Emanual Demby, a veteran researcher who started his career in the late 1940s with Dichter, also claims to have coined the term by combining psychology and demographics on the spur of the moment one day in 1965. Demby was in the office of a Detroit ad agency with Jack Connors, then-publisher of *Holiday* magazine, who went on to become publisher of *Travel & Leisure*. Connors asked Demby to describe the research he was about to do for the magazine, and Demby spontaneously replied, "psychographics."

Demby says that the research project for *Holiday* identified the Creative Consumer and was the first national probability sample of psychographics. To identify the Creative Consumer, Demby used a creative-passive continuum and looked at the correlation between lifestyle and self concept to build a segmentation model. At one end of the continuum was responsiveness to new products or purchasing creativity; at the other end was passivity or resistance to new products.

Demby built two segments to predict early buyers of new products. People who socialized and went out frequently were heavy users of new products, premium brands, and media, especially print media. They were also likely to travel (especially by air) to drink, and to give parties. Demby used Q factor analysis (inverse factor analysis) to group consumers on the creative-passive continuum. In writing about the study later, Demby said that even the two-segment model allowed him to identify key behavioral and attitudinal differences between demographically and socioeconomically similar media audiences. He found that the audience for *Time* contained more creative, early new-product purchasers than did the audience for *Newsweek*. Demby's study was typical of many early psychographic studies in that its questionnaire was designed to form a general descriptive profile of consumers.

The 1960s were a period of growth and experimentation in psychographic research as researchers gained expertise with the new technique. As academic articles appeared criticizing personality traits as predictors of behavior, theories were borrowed from other social-science disciplines. Diverse personal factors (demographics, values, product needs) were isolated and run through multivariate analysis to see how and if they correlated with behavior. Thanks to computers and new programs, researchers could now crosstabulate and search for correlations among hundreds of variables.

Some researchers, influenced by psychology, looked at ego concepts such as self-esteem and satisfaction and their relation to purchasing. Others, influenced by various social scientists, looked at social class and the status afforded by various brands. Still others, influenced by David Riesman's theory of social character, looked at whether people were "inner directed" or "outer directed." And then there were those, like Russell Haley, who saw the key to consumer behavior in the types of benefits they expected from the products they bought.

## Benefit Segmentation: Focus on Product

At the same time that Demby's style of general psychographic profiling was evolving, Russell Haley at Grey Advertising was developing another segmentation model. He said it predicted buying behavior better than merely descriptive demographics or volume segmentation that identified heavy users. Haley did a benefit segmentation for Procter & Gamble and first wrote about his new technique in 1961.

Haley said previous types of market segmentation failed because they relied on factors that described consumer behavior rather than looking for factors that caused the behavior. Haley said his "benefit segmentation" was much more useful than personality constructs because it related more directly to the reasons people desired the specific products they bought. "Benefits which people are seeking in consuming different products are the basic reason for the existence of true market segments," wrote Haley.

To illustrate his point, Haley segmented the toothpaste market into four groups: the sensory segment, who bought according to flavor and product appearance; the sociables, who bought the product that promised the whitest teeth; the worriers, who wanted decay prevention; and the independents, who bought based on price factors. Though some benefits may appeal to several segments, Haley said it was the relative importance of each benefit that mattered most.

Haley emphasized that benefit segmentation was to be used in concert with traditional and other segmentation methods:

> *Once people have been classified into segments in accordance with the benefits they are seeking, each segment is contrasted with all of the other segments in terms of its demography, its volume of consumption, its brand perceptions, its media habits, its personality and lifestyle and so forth. And by capitalizing on this understanding, it is possible to reach them to talk to them in their own terms, and to present a product in the most favorable light possible.*

This meant the researcher had to measure consumer value systems and consumer attitudes about various brands in the product category, as well as traditional and psychographic variables. Benefit segmentation was operationally very complex and required computers and sophisticated multivariate attitude measurement techniques. The value of benefit segmentation is that it redirected the focus of psychographic research on the product or category.

## What Is Lifestyle, Anyway?

By the late 1960s, psychographic research was widespread, but there was no consensus about its definition or even the correct term to use. It was alternately called psychographic, attitude, values, or lifestyle research. The changing terms may have reflected the expanding scope of psychographic research. In the beginning, it was a quantitative method of segmenting consumers by personality traits. By the early 1970s, it included lifestyle, which broadened the scope considerably. The first national lifestyle study was done by William Wells, then of the University of Chicago, under the co-sponsorship of Market Facts Inc. and the Leo Burnett Company.

For insight into the reasons for the rise of lifestyle research, all we need to do is look at the social upheavals of the 1960s and early 1970s. In the short span of a decade, society's norms were turned upside down. A questioning of established values began among the young, and before long spread to society at large. Instead of getting married and starting families, many young people rejected traditional lifestyles and began "tuning in, turning on, and dropping out," as Timothy Leary advised.

Women altered established life patterns and began leaving marriages, going back to school, and entering the labor force en masse. The traditional family—man, woman and 2.5 children—splintered as divorces rose. Many adopted alternative lifestyles by staying single, living with friends, or simply postponing marriage and children indefinitely. As the mass market dissolved, it became more difficult for businesses to figure out who their customers were. Lifestyle research evolved out of psychographics as a means of understanding this new social disorder.

Lifestyle research was based on the concept that we all carve out our own individual lifestyle patterns as we make our way through the decades. The concept of the lifestyle pattern in psychological theory goes back to Alfred Adler, an early disciple of Freud, who later rejected Freud's emphasis on biological drives. Adler, who placed more importance on social factors as the basis for personality development, hypothesized that people strive for superiority. The concept of lifestyle gained the attention of marketers in 1963 when William Lazer defined it as "a systems concept. It refers to a distinctive mode of living in its aggregate and broadest sense.... It embodies the patterns that develop and emerge from the dynamics of living in a society."

The foundation for lifestyle research was a paper titled, "Activities, Interest, and Opinions," by William Wells, a professor of psychology and marketing at the University of Chicago's Graduate School of Business, and Douglas Tigert of the University of Toronto. The 1971 paper was based on work carried out in the late 1960s and outlined once and for all what psychographics and lifestyle research included. It became one of the articles most often cited by subsequent researchers in the field, and their Attitudes, Interests, and Opinions (AIO) variables became the standard by which many later psychographic researchers designed their survey instruments. Wells' and Tigert's AIO system measured consumer behavior in terms of:

1) how they spend their time,
2) their interests—what is important to them in their immediate surroundings,
3) their opinions—how they view themselves and the world around them,
4) their basic demographic characteristics.

One well-known lifestyle researcher was Joseph Plummer (now director of new business development with DMB&B). He constructed an international psychographic segmentation model while at Leo Burnett and worked with Wells (who was a consultant for Burnett) on the first lifestyle study. In a paper published at the time, he said lifestyle research was the marriage of market segmentation and lifestyle patterns into a single system. Plummer defined lifestyle as:

> *...everyday, behaviorally oriented facts of people as well as their feelings, attitudes, and opinions. It tells us things about our customers that most researchers did not really attempt to quantify in the past, when the focus was on the product or on widely used measures of classification such as demographics.*

Plummer published the first article officially using the term "lifestyle" in 1970, in which he outlined his work identifying lifestyle patterns among bank-credit-card users. Plummer now says that his research picked up on William Wells' research and what was being done at Purdue University by Douglas Tigert and Frank Pessimer. "Our first survey simply looked at the differences between heavy users, light users, and nonusers of a product category using correlation analysis," Plummer says. Eventually they decided to try a new technique, Q segmentation, which had been the topic of Plummer's graduate work. "That's when the whole idea for lifestyle segmentation came about," he says. "We started describing groups of people as individuals and creating profiles of these individuals."

In the beginning, these profiles were put together from bits and pieces of photos from magazines. They started out with photographs from *Life* magazine and added scrap art from the library to create the individuals who emerged from their lifestyle data. Later, they created professional photographs of the people who represented the groups. "It was based on research, but they weren't real individuals," says Plummer. "It really helped the creative people to visualize the kind of people we were talking about."

Lifestyle analysis was soon being used for many of the agency's other clients. In pioneering work for the packaged-goods industry, Burnett used lifestyle analysis for Schlitz to find out that people who drank a lot of beer were "real macho people who lived life to the fullest and didn't take any crap from anybody," Plummer says. Out of that research came the "Grab For All the Gusto You Can" campaign that boosted the brand's memorability so well during the 1970s.

When Procter & Gamble was developing a new laundry soap, lifestyle analysis was one of the many research techniques used to determine who the market for the new product would be. The lifestyle research found that there were five attitude groups among American housewives—Practical Women, Convenience-Oriented Women, the Economy-Minded, the Traditionals (or Mrs. Tide), and the Experts. The heaviest users of laundry detergent, they discovered, were young women with large families who didn't want to be chained to the laundry room. After considering all the research, the agency recommended that P&G reposition its faltering Cheer brand as an all-temperature product that was easy to use. Soon Cheer was the second-best-selling detergent on the market.

## Psychographic Variations

The problem of defining psychographics recurred throughout the early 1970s. Although lifestyle research evolved out of psychographics, there were those who suggested that the two be separate. Some said the term psychographics should be reserved for mental aspects of the consumer—attitudes, beliefs, opinions, personality traits—while lifestyle should be used to refer to consumer activities or behaviors. Since this would have added an unnecessary layer of complication on an already-complicated technique, psychographics is still considered to include lifestyle.

The most widely published definition of psychographics was written by Demby in a presentation for the American Marketing Association in 1974. He said psychographics had three levels:

1) Psychographics is the practical application of the behavioral sciences to marketing research;
2) It is a quantitative research procedure that is indicated when demographic, socioeconomic, and user/nonuser analyses are not sufficient to explain and predict consumer behavior;
3) It seeks to describe the human characteristics of consumers that may have bearing on their response to products, packaging, advertising, and public relations efforts. Such variables may span a spectrum from self-concept and lifestyle to attitudes, interests, and opinions, as well as perceptions of product attributes.

By 1975, Wells had observed no less than 32 separate definitions in 24 different articles on psychographics. In an effort to identify some common ground, he reviewed the types of psychographic studies prevalent at the time and identified five different types of psychographic studies.

### PROFILE BASED ON "LIFESTYLE" DIMENSIONS

In this type of study, the profile is drawn from a large set of general lifestyle items. People are asked about their demographics, product and media usage, and psychographics. The questionnaire includes questions about the use of 100 products, magazine reading or television viewing, and the extent to which they agree or disagree with about 300 Activities, Interests, and Opinions (AIO) statements, such as "I like hunting," "I like danger," or "There should be a gun in every home." Then the results are crosstabulated against a dependent variable. In Wells' example, heavy users of shotgun shells (those who spend more than $11 a year) are compared with those who don't buy shotgun shells. The researcher looks for those demographic, product and media usage, or AIO statement variables that discriminate between the user and the nonuser of shotgun shells.

*Figure 2-1  Life Style Dimensions*

| ACTIVITIES | INTERESTS | OPINIONS | DEMOGRAPHICS |
|---|---|---|---|
| Work | Family | Themselves | Age |
| Hobbies | Home | Social Issues | Education |
| Social Events | Job | Politics | Income |
| Vacations | Community | Business | Occupation |
| Entertainment | Recreation | Economic | Family Size |
| Club Membership | Fashion | Education | Dwelling |
| Community | Food | Products | Geographic |
| Shopping | Media | Future | City Size |
| Sports | Achievements | Culture | Stage of Life Cycle |

*Source:  Joseph Plummer,* Journal of Marketing, *January 1974*

## PRODUCT-SPECIFIC PSYCHOGRAPHIC PROFILE
The target group is identified by the psychographic items that discriminate between it and the rest of the population. Then the target group is profiled based on a limited set of product-relevant dimensions. Wells describes a study that looked at the product benefits sought by Pinto buyers. They were found to respond favorably to items such as "I wish I could depend on my car more," and "I am more practical in car selection," while they rejected items such as "The kind of car you have is important as to how people see you." This went contrary to the current Ford ad campaigns that portrayed the car as carefree, small, and romantic. Ford repositioned the Pinto to appeal more to practicality, and the model subsequently sold very well. The new product-specific information on Pinto buyers allowed the automaker to put forth a message that would appeal more effectively to people who were similar to current Pinto owners.

## PERSONALITY TRAITS AS DESCRIPTORS
In this type of study, the dependent variable becomes an area of concern. Wells uses for an example a report on "Ecologically Concerned Consumers." The dependent variable is degree of ecological concern, which was analyzed against 20 independent variables: 7 demographic characteristics, 12 personality traits from standardized personality

inventories, and an extra variable—perceived consumer effectiveness: a person's degree of power. The independent variables were evaluated using analysis of variance to see which discriminated between people with high and low ecological concern. Ten variables survived and were input into Multiple Classification Analysis to determine how they correlated with the degree of ecological concern. Answers to the personality-scale questions were then synthesized into four higher factors that correlated with ecological concern: perceived consumer effectiveness, tolerance, understanding, and harm avoidance.

This study differed from the others in two ways: rather than considering all of the psychographic items individually, it summed them into four higher abstract qualities. In addition, rather than crosstabulating all of the independent variables, it linked the independent and dependent variables by multiple regression. Wells says these differences make this type of study more abstract, but less redundant than those that crosstabulate all the uncondensed raw data.

## GENERAL LIFESTYLE SEGMENTATION

This study involves a very large, nationally representative sample and a questionnaire consisting of hundreds of questions on demographics, media and product use, and psychographics. The psychographic section is further analyzed either by R and Q factor analysis or by cluster analysis to clarify respondents into relatively homogeneous groups—to form a typology. Wells uses the example of a Newspaper Advertising Association study done in 1973. The study administered a 300-item questionnaire to 4,000 people. Eight distinct male groups emerged ranging from "The Quiet Family Man" (8 percent of total males) to "The He-Man" (19 percent of total males). Wells notes that this type of study differs from the first three because it doesn't assume that all users of newspapers share common traits. Instead, it seeks to identify different segments among the target audience. As a result, the heavy users of certain products or media may be concentrated in two or more very different segments. This can cause a problem in trying to identify attributes that differentiate the two user segments.

## PRODUCT-SPECIFIC SEGMENTATION

Instead of basing the segmentation on general psychographic items, this type of study focuses on product-specific items. Wells outlines a stomach-remedy segmentation done by Joseph Pernica. Pernica created a list of 80 product-related items, including attitudes toward treatments, beliefs about ailments, symptom frequency, and end benefits provided by different brands. Typical psychographic items were rewritten to focus on the product, so that "I worry too much" became "I get stomach problems if I worry too much." Pernica reduced the 80 items to 13 by R factor analysis. Scores on the 13 surviving items were input into Q factor analysis to group the respondents into homogeneous segments. The study identified four groups: Severe Sufferers, Active Medicators, Hypochondriacs, and Practicalists. The advantage of this segmentation is that it is able to discriminate among brands and their users better than general segmentations can.

Despite the differences in methodology and content, Wells found that all of the above psychographic studies shared two common qualities. They attempted to move beyond demographics by adding extra dimensions to the questionnaire. Some added two extra variables, some several hundred. For some, the variables came from standardized personality tests or attitude scales; for others, the new variables were "homemade." Another common trait he found was that they all used quantitative techniques—precoded, objective questionnaires that were easy to administer either by the respondents themselves or by survey interviewers. Wells came up with this definition:

> *...psychographic research can be defined as quantitative research intended to place consumers on psychological—as distinguished from demographic—dimensions. Because it goes beyond the standard and the accepted, it offers the possibility of new insights and unusual conclusions. Because it is quantitative rather than discursive, it opens the way to large, representative samples of respondents and multivariate analysis of findings.*

## The Emergence of True Psychographics: Subscriber Profiles

Many of the significant national studies done before 1970 were done for publishers of various magazines. Publishing companies were among the first to undertake large-scale psychographic studies because they saw them as a valuable way to find out about their readers' lifestyles and interests for both advertising and editorial purposes. Psychographic profiles could show advertisers that their appeals were reaching target audiences and could help editors better meet subscribers' needs by providing the kind of reading material that most interested them. These media giants also had the research budgets necessary to finance costly large-scale psychographic studies. The following were considered major breakthroughs in psychographic research:

- Emanual Demby identified "creative" and "passive" subscribers in a study for *Holiday* magazine.

- Clark Wilson studied the relationship between homemaker living patterns, product consumption, and magazine readership. He found that living patterns accounted for 30 percent of the variance in product purchasing and up to 25 percent of the variance in magazine readership. He also identified groups such as "the happy housekeeper," "the venturesome shopper," and "the beauty conscious."

- In two studies spaced six years apart, *Harper's* and *The Atlantic* asked subscribers and their neighbors—people with similar demographic profiles—about cultural, household, and leisure activities. Their "People Next Door" study came up with a profile of subscribers that found them to be involved, active people, "people acutely conscious of the world about them—people who care enough to want to change what they feel needs to be changed."

- Douglas Tigert and William Wells studied the media climate for 53 magazines using their 300 Activity, Interest, and Opinion statements. Their goal was to find out how advertising copy could be improved to more accurately reflect readers' lifestyles. They found distinct psychographic profiles for different magazines. Differences were most acute between married male readers of *Reader's Digest* and *Playboy*.

- *Life* magazine and W.R. Simmons identified consumers' "self" versus "ideal" image personality profiles. In this national study, they asked respondents to evaluate 20 positive and 20 negative personality traits in terms of whether they possessed the traits (the self image) or wished they possessed the traits (the ideal image). After assessing the discrepancy between the two images, researchers came up with a third dimension, the "need deficiencies" of the respondents. The study also identified purchasing patterns for 150 products and gave them catchy names such as "The Push-Button Woman," "The Eye-Dentity Seeker," "The Weight-Watching Worrier," and "The Aromatic Male." When these product usage patterns were related back to the trait ratings, they provided meaningful insight into why people purchased the way they did.

Despite the slick titles, all of the above studies shared a basic purpose—they painted understandable human portraits of complex consumer markets. As Joseph Plummer discovered when he and his research team first pasted together photo-collage lifestyle profiles of people, this new way of analyzing information made the numbers real to agency creative people. It bridged the gap that mass marketing had created between the sellers of products and the people who made up the markets for those products.

Psychographics had evolved from a narrow focus on personality attributes to a broad-based inquiry into all aspects of consumers' lives. It also had begun to include the product and media-related factors inherent in lifestyle research. By the mid-1970s, as Russell Haley had envisioned, psychographics truly did encompass all measures of the mind.

# Part II

## Psychographics Realized

# **3** *Portraits of America: The Original VALS*

*Typologies are best used imaginatively rather than mechanically. People are too complex to be wholly ensnared in any conceivable typology. For example, an individual may represent different motivational groups in various domains of his spending....*

*Hierarchical typologies have one especially useful property that is not often recognized: their stages are nested. This means that an individual must "grow through" one stage before reaching the next. Clearly, this attribute reflects the fact that our typology is based in large part on the maturation phases that personality theorists say we all experience. The upshot is that each of us has inside all the stages through which he or she has passed.... This is why people see themselves in many parts of the typology.*

—Arnold Mitchell
Consumer Values: A Typology, *June 1978*

T HE FIRST and most widely accepted syndicated psychographic segmentation system, the Values and Lifestyles Program of SRI International, was a product of the far-reaching social shifts of the 1960s. It answered a demand from American businesses for some way to make sense of the ground-breaking shifts in social values and the potential effects on consumer behavior. A marked decline in demand for large automobiles, financial services, and women's foundation garments had made it clear to many companies that something strange was happening on college campuses. Even more bizarre was that these odd-ball notions were filtering down to Main Street.

The 1950s was a time of conventional demands from a stable mass market of consumers who purchased in predictable patterns. The economy was stable, and American men were able to marry, buy affordable housing, gain a foothold on the corporate ladder, and start building families. Their children wanted for little and became accustomed to the idea that their lives would be even better than their parents' had been. Most women accepted their roles as homemakers, mothers, and helpmates for their husbands.

By the time the children born during these boom years reached college in the 1960s, however, the economic future was starting to dim and the country was mired in an undeclared war that was not only unpopular, but to many, immoral. Many young people became disillusioned with their parents' idea that life was about following rules and material gain. They rejected established norms and struck out on life paths markedly different from those of their parents.

This groundswell of change eventually spread throughout society and ultimately resulted in profound changes in the way all Americans lived. Women rejected their traditional homebound roles and were entering the labor force in increasing numbers. Many Americans started to do surprising things. They dropped out of the race, lived in communes, got divorced, took lovers, came out of the closet, went back to college, and did other things that would have been cause for social ostracism in the 1950s.

In *New Rules*, Daniel Yankelovich likens these changes to shifts in the tectonic plates beneath the Earth's crust, so profound that they affected Americans at every socioeconomic level. People went from living life as it unfolded to searching for fulfillment. "It is as if tens of millions of people had decided simultaneously to conduct risky experiments in living, using the only materials that lay at hand—their own lives," he writes.

These societal shifts would have profound ramifications for American businesses. American consumers were becoming harder to figure out. They had become moving targets, and demographics were no longer enough to distinguish prospects from nonprospects. Two 35-year-old married men with roughly the same occupations, incomes, and educational levels could have widely varying lifestyles and widely different product needs. Brent was a social climber who bought everything from cars and furnishings to food and wine as status symbols, while Michael was into transcendental meditation and had a solar-powered log house complete with a composting toilet.

The burgeoning variations among Americans were enough to cause widespread anxiety all along Madison Avenue. A whole generation embraced individualism and rejected the basic tenets of capitalist American society. American business needed a better way of understanding consumers and why they did or didn't buy. Psychographics provided a scale that could distinguish Brent from Michael by measuring their varying attitudes on status or spiritualism and relating those attitudes back to their product choices.

The first national psychographic studies were done for major media companies, but before long, other industries became interested in the new technique. Since customized psychographic studies were expensive and their uses limited, research firms began all-purpose national studies that could provide background on American consumer attitudes for a variety of businesses. Chicago's Leo Burnett and DDB Needham Worldwide were the first agencies to develop large-scale psychographic studies for their own proprietary use. The link between these agencies was William Wells, then a professor of psychology and business at University of Chicago. Wells was hired as a consultant by Leo Burnett, and in 1969 (under the co-sponsorship of the University of

Chicago, Burnett, and Market Facts) he and Douglas Tigert, working with Burnett's Joseph Plummer, developed the Burnett Life Style Study. The study was the basis of the Activities, Interests, and Opinions (AIO) statements Wells and Tigert wrote about in 1971. In 1974, Wells joined Needham, Harper and Sterns, and started the NHS Life Style Study the following year.

Now the property of the merged agency, the DDB Needham Life Style Study provided information used in developing SRI International's Values and Lifestyles (VALS) Program. When Arnold Mitchell began work on the VALS program he consulted with Wells, Plummer, and Haley, among others.

The Life Style Study conducted by DDB Needham's Chicago office is important to mention here because it is the longest-running psychographic study next to The Yankelovich Monitor (see chapter 4). Like the Monitor, it is one of the few studies that gives researchers rare continuous data necessary to quantify actual changes in American attitudes over time. The Life Style Study is based on annual mail surveys of 4,000 American men and women. The questionnaire is a classic example of Wells and Tigert's AIO framework and has provided the basis for many subsequent surveys. Because it was specifically designed by an advertising agency to provide insight into how and why people buy and to solve clients' specific problems, it contains the most comprehensive collection of data on specific use of products, brands, services, ownership and purchase of major durables, and media habits. But because it is DDB Needham's proprietary study, we will reserve detailed discussion for Chapter 6, "Psychographics in Advertising."

## The Original VALS

SRI International was formed in 1946 as the research arm of Stanford University. The organization, which became independent in 1970, provides research and consulting expertise on a contractual basis to businesses and governments around the world. Riding around the well-landscaped 65-acre grounds, one gets the sense of being on a college campus that is curiously devoid of students. But housed in SRI's massive building is the broadest and most diverse pool of research and consulting talent in the world. SRI now employs 3,000 people in 110 disciplines, ranging from the physical, life, and social sciences, to engineering, economics, and international management.

SRI's staff conducts advanced research in more than 300 fields, from crash-testing cars to working on the government's Star Wars program and other top-secret defense-related research. About half of SRI's work is done for the U.S. government; the other half is for commercial or industrial businesses and other governments. Forty percent of its contracts come from international clients on all continents.

Considering the overall organization, the Values and Lifestyles (VALS) Program is a very tiny part of SRI. The organization places far more emphasis and bases its reputation on the engineering work it does for governments. The VALS program employs only about ten full-time people. Ironically, it has attracted more media attention than any other single program, enough so that the vice president of marketing still calls it the "shining star of the business group." In the decade it has existed, despite some shortcomings, the VALS program has been significant indeed. The original VALS introduced the mainstream business community to the concept of psychographic segmentation. This chapter will deal exclusively with the original VALS Program. The VALS 2 Program, which was released in 1989, considerably changed the intent, methodology, and philosophy of the program. The newest VALS is discussed in detail in Chapter 5.

## Mitchell's Masterwork

For the uninitiated, the original VALS was a typology of the American population developed by futurist Arnold Mitchell and introduced in 1978. There was nothing narrow about the original VALS, which was at the same time its strength and its weakness. It was designed to provide insights into how Americans were changing and was intended for use in diverse fields, including government, sociology, psychology, and business. In the end, VALS was criticized for being too broad to be of much use in determining why consumers bought the products and services they did.

Mitchell's original intentions were ambitious. He says in his book on the program, *The Nine American Lifestyles*, "(VALS) seeks to enfold the individual, the marketplace and the society into an interlocked system that reveals both how a change in one area is likely to affect all other areas and how the typology can be used for systematic forecasting changes in the sizes and properties of the groups." Put differently, it took on the formidable task of fitting 230 million Americans into nine groups defined by their values and demographics. It also claimed that those groups would be constant enough to predict various types of behavior, one of which was purchasing.

Mitchell was one of the first people hired by Stanford for its Long Range Planning Service in 1948. An alumnus of Amherst, he had done graduate work in English at Columbia. He had virtually no training in the social sciences and often described himself as a poet. He started at SRI as a technical writer, but due to his gift for making complex ideas accessible, he eventually became a futurist with an established reputation for making cogent predictions about future trends.

Though Mitchell's academic training was somewhat incongruous, his work on consumer values and their effects on spending patterns goes back to the early 1950s. He wrote dozens of proprietary reports for SRI on the subject, most notably a 1967 paper with Mary Baird that first adopts Abraham H. Maslow's celebrated "needs hierarchy." Maslow theorized that as a person matures, he or she goes through five sequential stages: Survival, Security, Belonging, Esteem, and Self-Actualization. Once people satisfied their physical needs, the theory goes, they could move on to more abstract needs like love, social affiliation, power, and enlightenment. Mitchell and Baird identified values that could accompany these stages and extrapolated on the effects that massive shifts of an aging population could have on business and society.

Then came a 1973 book that was Mitchell's first attempt to develop an original theory about social change. He devised a system of "ways of life" that addressed the problems he had with the hierarchical nature of Maslow's theory. "If I am at level 3 and you are at level 4 (and I know it)," he writes, "it's hard for me not to despise you because of your superiority. And you, of course, have a marvelous put-down at your disposal!" The "ways of life" idea modified the structure, depending on how far the person was from the cultural mainstream. There were six groups, with Preservers, Takers, and Escapers on one side of center and Makers, Changers, and Seekers on the other. Pictured as a circle, the Escapers and Seekers were side by side on the bottom and the Preservers and Makers on the top. The Movers were seen as the higher-order evolving group that melded the best of all groups. This idea would carry through to become the basis of the Integrated group in the VALS typology.

In 1977, Mitchell and Duane Elgin described an emerging lifestyle they called "Voluntary Simplicity." The article appeared in *The Futurist* and suggested that many Americans were starting to live a style that was "outwardly simple and inwardly rich," in which they strived for frugality, conservation, natural things, and inner growth. The article generated such a surprising amount of attention that it convinced the decision-makers at SRI that it was time to put the Mitchell Values and Business show on the road. Mitchell, Elgin, and Marie Spengler, who succeeded Mitchell as the director of the VALS Program, traveled around the country conducting seminars on the implications of changing consumer values for businesses. Out of these seminars emerged the idea for a three-year program to be called Values and Lifestyles. But due to the outpouring of interest, VALS was launched as a separate program in 1978 with 39 corporate sponsors.

It must be noted here that, up to this point, it was a theory without any numerical basis. The first VALS survey wasn't conducted until 1980, although by that time the program was already being sold as a full-blown national typology that could typify Americans by common values to predict how they were likely to act as citizens and consumers. By 1984, 79 corporations had signed on, and funding for research had reached $2 million.

## The Typology

The VALS typology was intended to explain the nature of changing human values. It postulated that human growth was not random, but an ordered sequence progressing from the relatively simple, immature states to more complex, higher-order needs. That idea came from Maslow, but Mitchell expanded upon it by applying it to consumer behavior and suggesting that the extent and speed of growth is entirely dependent on the nature of the individual. He writes: "Some unusual people grow and change many times throughout their lives. Others change hardly at all with the decades. Most experience one or two periods when what is most important, most compelling, most beautiful shifts from one comprehensive pattern to another. These are the times when a person's values change—and lifestyles are transformed."

Not only did VALS contend that personal growth and change was a dynamic and orderly process, but Mitchell believed basic personalities could be divided into two different categories: those who were inner-directed—for whom the principal driving forces of life came from within; and those who were outer-directed—who respond to signals, real or imagined, from other people and base their lives on visible, tangible, and materialistic goals. This theory was gleaned from the inner- and other-directed personality theory first postulated in *The Lonely Crowd,* by Riesman, Glazer, and Denney in 1950. Riesman's term "other-directed" was changed to outer-directed in the VALS typology.

Up until 1980, VALS was largely speculative, drawing upon data from the Census Bureau and the Bureau of Labor Statistics. But no theory can stand on its own, and Mitchell soon set out to back it up with quantifiable data. That was the purpose of the 1980 field study. The VALS staff conducted a major mail survey, sending an 85-page questionnaire containing a battery of more than 800 questions to a national sample of more than 1,600 Americans aged 18 or older living in the lower 48 states. The sample was generated by random-digit dialing techniques. After being contacted and agreeing to receive the survey, 79 percent of the respondents returned completed questionnaires.

The survey generated more than one million data points, including information on media usage, eating and food preparation, household assets, and product use. Respondents were asked what cleaning products or brand of margarine they used; what credit cards they owned; about their checking accounts, IRAs, and mortgages; and whether they owned waterbeds, cameras, or decorator telephones. Did they have pets, and if so, what kind—dogs, cats, birds, or mice?

But the algorithm for classifying people into VALS groups was based on their responses to 36 questions, including several demographic items and a variety of general and specific attitudinal questions. On the attitudinal questions, a six-point scale was used: Disagree Strongly, Disagree Mostly, Disagree Somewhat, Agree Somewhat, Agree Mostly, Agree Strongly. The exact algorithm has never been revealed by VALS, but some of the original questions were:

- *Financial security is very important to me.*
- *I want to live every moment to its fullest.*
- *I'd say I'm rebelling against the way I was brought up.*
- *I believe that "industrial growth" should be limited.*
- *Generally speaking, most people are trustworthy and honest.*

- *Everything is changing too fast today.*
- *In general, it's more important to understand my inner self than to be famous, powerful or wealthy.*
- *My greatest achievements are ahead of me.*
- *I believe a woman can work outside the home even if she has small children and still be a good mother.*
- *I like to think I'm a bit of a swinger.*
- *I would rather spend a quiet evening at home than go out to a party.*
- *The purchase and use of marijuana should be legalized.*

The VALS typology consisted of four major groups, and the nine lifestyles were divided among them. They were arranged in a bulb shape with the Need-Driven groups making up the bottom, the Outer- and Inner-Directed groups making up either side, and the Integrated group at the very top:

| | | | Combined Outer and |
|---|---|---|---|
| **Need-Driven** | **Outer-Directed** | **Inner-Directed** | **Inner-Directed Group** |
| *Survivors* | *Belongers* | *I-Am-Mes* | *Integrateds* |
| *Sustainers* | *Emulators* | *Experientials* | |
| | *Achievers* | *Societally Conscious* | |

The nine lifestyles have been well-documented in several readily available sources, so we'll make only a cursory examination here and go on to how they have been applied. (See Mitchell's *The Nine American Lifestyles*, Macmillan Publishing, 1983, and *Personal Values & Consumer Psychology*, by Robert Pitts, Jr. and Arch G. Woodside, Lexington Books, 1984.) What follows are the lifestyle groups described by Mitchell in the first VALS report in 1980.

**NEED-DRIVEN**—(11 percent) poverty causes them to deny rather than express values.

SURVIVORS (4 percent) are the oldest (median age 66) and poorest (income $5,000-$7,500) of the VALS groups. Poorly educated, only half finished high school and one-third completed the eighth grade. As a group, they tend to be depressed, withdrawn, mistrustful, rebellious about their situation, lacking self-confidence, and dissatisfied with life. Their focus is on not slipping any further into poverty, rather than on getting ahead. They escape their bleak reality by watching a lot of television. Most are retired, and 80 percent are widows. They are conventional, conservative and traditional, shaking their heads at the speed of change in the outside world.

SUSTAINERS (7 percent) differ from Survivors in that they are younger (median age 29), have higher incomes ($11,000), and hope to move ahead to a better life (80 percent say they look forward to better things). They are angry, distrustful, rebellious, anxious,

*Figure 3-1 The VALS Typology*

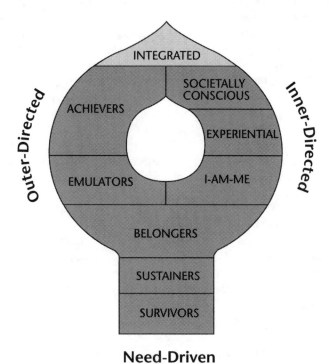

Need-Driven

*Source: SRI International*

combative people who feel mainstream America has left them out. They have large families, and over a quarter of them are living in nontraditional families whose heads are divorced, separated, or living with an unmarried mate. Many are unemployed, and 13 percent are Hispanic. They mistrust the system and have less trust in politicians and corporations than any other group. Yet they view themselves as financially adroit, and many make extra money by illegal or barely legal means. They are more self-confident and ask more of their world than do the Survivors. They feel financial security is of utmost importance, and many will move up to the Outer-Directed groups as they mature. Attitudinally, many are already Outer-Directed, but their poverty requires them to live a needs-based existence.

**OUTER-DIRECTED—(68 percent) happiest of Americans make up the values mainstream.**

BELONGERS , the largest group (35 percent of the population), are so-called because their affiliation needs are high. They strive to fit in and conform at all costs and care deeply about what the neighbors think. They believe in the status quo and aren't suspicious or fearful. They are middle-class, traditional, "moral," and family-oriented. Most are white (95 percent), and many are housewives (30 percent) who are middle of the road in everything from their levels of education to their incomes and ages. They tend to live in small rural towns or open country. Their contented existence is rarely touched by the cruel realities of the world. Instead, they read romance novels and watch a lot of television, especially soap operas. They often abstain from alcohol, have strong traditional values, and feel that mothers should be unselfish, forgiving, and stay at home. They are markedly more supportive of authority figures than the lower groups, and they have the finances to plan for the years ahead. They are happiest when they feel like an insider and find the most comfort when surrounded by the familiar.

EMULATORS (10 percent of the population) are younger (median age 27) and constantly striving to be like those who are richer and more successful. Both men and women are ambitious, competitive, ostentatious, and unsubtle. They like to work hard, but their ambition to rise in social rank is based on superficial knowledge of what it takes to get there. They are the most likely of the groups to have gone to technical school, and many have attended but not graduated from college. This stage may be a key resting place for upwardly mobile members of minority groups. The group has the second highest proportions of blacks and Hispanics after the Sustainer group. This group is mistrustful of "The Establishment" and doubts the system will give them a break. They have very low self-confidence and a poor self-image. They distrust governmental leaders and institutions and are lowest in self-ratings of happiness.

ACHIEVERS (22 percent of the population) are at the pinnacle of the Outer-Directed path. They work hard and are self-reliant, successful, driven people who are the supporting pillar of the system.They are likely to be corporate executives, skilled professionals like doctors and lawyers, or financially established scientists, entertainers, or artists whose goals are fame and fortune. They are the vanguard consumers of all the groups, with their higher-than-average incomes ($31,000) and large assets (almost half with over $100,000 in assets). Twenty percent are self-employed. They tend to live in the suburbs, and 87 percent own their own homes. All this success allows them to feel good about themselves and the status quo. They are staunchly Republican, conservative, and do not seek change. They are in their early 40s, and more than 95 percent are white. One-third are college graduates, and many attended graduate school. They are the Establishment, with little concern for air pollution or tolerance for nontraditional women's roles.

**INNER-DIRECTED—(20 percent) boomers looking inward see higher social concerns.**

I-AM-MES (5 percent) the youngest (median age 20) of the inner-directed groups are overwhelmingly students and male (only 36 percent are female). This is a stage of transition from outer-to inner-directed thinking and is marked by seemingly contrary values and behaviors. This group is at the same time conforming and innovative, contrite and aggressive, demure and exhibitionistic, self-effacing and narcissistic. They are coming to grips with their individual values by rebelling against the established values of their Achiever parents. In the process, they are learning new interests with new interior rewards and in the process redirecting their life goals. They express their emerging identities through flamboyant dress and conspicuous behavior. Many have not devoted much thought to societal issues but rather are involved in being and acting. They are energetic, daring, and love anything new. They love to challenge their minds with intellectual or cultural activities as well as their bodies with physically demanding games and social pursuits. Once the new way of life is found, it seems to evoke a permanent change in that the I-Am-Mes of 10 or 20 years ago still maintain the essence of the values of their youth.

EXPERIENTIALS (7 percent) are the thrill seekers of the VALS typology. They grab out for vivid, direct personal experiences with both hands. Some relish issues and ideas, others are intensely hedonistic, and still others climb mountains, shoot rapids, or skydive to satiate their thirst for life. For them, to be truly alive is to be involved with people, events, and ideas. Some Experientials represent the core of the "voluntary simplicity" idea in that they are immersed in exploring their own inner depths through spiritual inquiry and mysticism. They are uninhibited, impulsive, independent, and self-reliant. Many are artistic and in tune with the subtle nuances of living. Some will expand their thinking and move on to more global, activist, and mission-oriented goals down the road. Mostly, they are in their late 20s, highly educated, and working in professional or technical positions with average annual incomes of about $24,000. Self assured and well adjusted, they don't need the peer approval or social status that their younger I-Am-Me counterparts do. Politically liberal, they believe in the rightness of nature and prefer natural and organic products. Experientials are happy because they believe that life is a constant growing process and that they are improving as each day brings fresh insights.

SOCIETALLY CONSCIOUS (8 percent) are concerned about making the world a better place through their actions. They believe that humans should live in harmony with nature, not try to dominate it; that small is beautiful; that spiritual aspects of life are more valuable than material things; that nature has its own order; that each person should do what he can to right societal wrongs; and that a simplicity in lifestyle is something to strive for. As a group, they are older (average age almost 40), 39 percent have attended graduate school, 59 percent hold professional or technical jobs, and their average income exceeds $27,000. They are activists and their activism takes many forms, from petitioning on consumer issues to fighting for environmental conservation to living socially responsible, self-sufficient lives. They are most likely to purchase environmentally conscious, natural, organic, and biodegradable products; recycle; ride bicycles to work; carpool; and install solar heating in their homes. They are a self-assured, prosperous, and powerful group that vocally wields its clout with both government and corporations.

**COMBINED INNER/OUTER-DIRECTED—the best of both worlds.**

INTEGRATEDS (2 percent of the population) are a very rare breed of human with an innate sense both of what is appropriate or necessary and of their own abilities. They have matured to the point that they can put together the decision-making ability of the Outer-Directed with the insight of the Inner-Directed. They have developed a balanced style of thinking and behaving that allows them to lead when necessary and follow when appropriate. They weigh the consequences before acting, can be flamboyant or subtle, and can see the big picture as well as the nuances and the potential for things not going according to plan. They have a kind of inner completeness or strength that draws others in and inspires emulation. They are open, self-assured, expressive, and able to balance the drive to accomplish with close interpersonal relationships. They are both observers and creators, and they believe in themselves and their abilities. They don't care about conspicuous consumption or the trappings of success, because they have already attained what they feel is most important—self respect without ego or selfishness. Demographically, they are older—in the middle or upper age groups— highly educated, more white and male than female or minority, and married with incomes of $30,000 and more. Their political views run more to the center than either the conservative Achievers or the liberal Societally Conscious. Many have graduated from years as successful Achievers or Societally Conscious. A small portion are younger people who have been fortunate enough to find themselves early in life.

In 1981, SRI fielded a second survey (this one of 2,100 adults) to further refine the system for classifying people into VALS types. By then, SRI had decided that it would be better to farm out the product and media use aspect of the survey to organizations that specialized in such things. By 1982, VALS had set up links with Simmons Market Research Bureau and soon after that with Mediamark Research Inc., which categorized the 15,000 respondents to each of their surveys (now 20,000) by VALS type. This allowed researchers to see which VALS groups tended to use hundreds of different brands and product categories, which magazines they read, and what their other media habits tended to be. These links made it possible for researchers to find out, for example, whether Experientials or Societally Conscious were more likely to be heavy users of Tabasco™ sauce or whether more Achievers or Belongers read *Architectural Digest*. These links were said to provide important clues about what advertising approach would be the most effective in reaching target audiences.

## Market-Based or Not?

The decision to contract out the most directly commercial aspect of the new typology may have been one of the strategic flaws in the original VALS to be revealed by the decade's end—that it was not market-oriented enough. Some observers pointed that out early on. In a 1984 paper on VALS, Rebecca Holman of Young & Rubicam wrote:

*SRI's decision to delegate the product and media survey aspect of VALS types to other organizations undoubtedly derives from its organizational identity. SRI sees itself as a social science organization primarily concerned with human evolution and growth, personal maturity and the future of man within extant socio-political structures. As such, the more pragmatic concerns of many of the VALS subscribers, namely how to market goods and services more effectively, are of less interest to SRI.*

Ironically, it would be these pragmatic concerns of subscribers and the inability of VALS to satisfy them that would necessitate a complete overhaul of the VALS program by the late 1980s. SRI began development work on VALS 2 in 1987.

## Shifting Structure

If VALS was less than effective in predicting product choices, did it accomplish the wider purpose for which Mitchell had intended it? Could it predict the value shifts that would occur in the population? Mitchell offered four possible future scenarios, ranging from hard times to "bouncy prosperity," in the 1981 report "Values Scenarios for the 1980s." In constructing the scenarios, VALS researchers drew heavily from the resources of SRI's "futures group," the Strategic Environment Center.

The "best guess" scenario projected that the proportion of the Need-Driven groups would drop from 11 to 10 percent—Survivors still 4 percent and Sustainers down to 6 percent of the population. The ranks of the Outer-Directed would drop to 60 percent from 67 percent—Belongers down to 30 percent, Emulators stable at 10 percent, and Achievers down to 20 percent. The Inner-Directed groups would increase from 20 to 22 percent of the population—I-Am-Mes to 6 percent, Experientials up to 9 percent, and Societally Conscious up to 11 percent. The Integrateds would rise from 2 to 4 percent of the population.

In the "best guess future," Mitchell foresaw the rise of "national integration," which would "give the country a direction, a purpose, and a unity so notably lacking in recent years." This integration would be led by Achievers who had graduated to the Integration stage. "By 1990 and the early 2000s," he wrote, "we expect the nation to have had enough success that it will, economically and emotionally, be able to refocus attention on nonmaterial aims." This, remember, was written in 1980—a striking portent of the new environmentalism and "green consumer" that would emerge in the 1990s.

Did the original VALS accomplish its aim of giving government and business planners a theoretical crystal ball? Perhaps so. But by the end of the 1980s, the Belongers were still the largest group by far, making up just under 40 percent of the population. Although forecasting the shifts was infinitely interesting from an academic standpoint, it also illustrated the highly theoretical nature of the original VALS. Many subscribers found themselves asking just how they were supposed to use this stuff. It was hard for businesses to understand, let alone apply, the permeations and shifts among the groups through time.

## Using VALS in the Early 1980s

VALS hit the market with such a media splash that it wasn't long before major magazines were trumpeting the triumphs of this powerful new way of understanding Americans. One of the first publicized successes was the Merrill Lynch lone bull campaign of the 1980s. In the late 1960s, Ogilvy & Mather put together a Merrill Lynch campaign that showed a herd of bulls thundering across a plain with the slogan, "Bullish on America." It conveyed reliability and patriotism. Upon analyzing that approach in light of the VALS types, researchers at Young & Rubicam found they were inadvertently appealing to the wrong group of people. The herd mentality and the patriotic undertones of the ads, it was said, worked better on Believers than on the self-assured and successful Achievers the firm was trying to corral.

The 1980s were approaching and the company felt it was time for an image overhaul. By 1979, Young & Rubicam, one of the charter VALS subscribers, had taken over the account and put together a new campaign around an Ogilvy & Mather idea, "A Breed Apart." In the new ads, a lone bull wandered through the deserted canyons of Wall Street, took shelter in a cave, or sat perched majestically on a mountaintop against a brilliant sunset. The ad content emphasized imagination, innovation, and instinct, rather than the stability so evident in the past campaign. The new campaign was designed specifically with Achievers in mind. It was strategically intended to appeal to growth-oriented investors who felt their success was a result of independent thinking and a pull-yourself-up-by-the-bootstraps philosophy. The new approach was also timed perfectly to capitalize on the start of the longest bull market in the nation's history and the growing mood on Wall Street that it was worth a little personal risk to get a piece of the ballooning pie.

"We all love to see America grow, but the heavy investor wants an investment firm that's going to help him get a share of that growth," said Dr. Joseph Plummer, then Young & Rubicam's executive vice president for research, in a speech at the University of Illinois at the time. "Our strategy shift to 'A Breed Apart' was clearly emotionally on track with the Achiever target audience."

Plummer, who had left Burnett's Life Style Study behind when he joined Y& R in 1979, became one of the original VALS most ardent supporters. VALS proved itself with the Lynch campaign, he said. A year and a half after the campaign was launched, the recall score (the percent of Americans who say they remember an ad) shot up from 8 to 55 percent and Merrill Lynch had gained two market share points on the New York Stock Exchange.

VALS was seen by many as the answer to their research prayers. "It's a whole new dimension for us," Plummer told *The Atlantic Monthly*. "Before VALS we didn't really have a sense of who the consumer out there was. Now we know how they live and what they buy—and why they buy it." And by 1984, Plummer wasn't the only research executive who was publicly praising VALS.

VALS quickly became the hottest new tool in the market researcher's grab bag of tricks. In addition to the original 79 sponsors, many leading advertising agencies, top advertisers, and Fortune 500 companies eagerly signed on for the new service. Within four years, 250 different corporations had used the VALS program in some way, and there were 171 regular subscribers or "members," each paying between $20,000 and $150,000 for VALS. For their money, they received reports and videotaped presentations explaining the typology, a quarterly full-day training session, consultation and inquiry privileges with VALS staffers designed to integrate VALS immediately into ongoing projects, and the opportunity to attend an annual conference to find out how others were using the program. For an additional fee, subscribers could enroll in the Leading Edge Program, which provided them with an annual survey on attitudinal trends and industry forecasts.

Like the earlier psychographic studies, VALS found that specific magazines attracted widely different audiences. Achievers tended to subscribe to *Time* and *The New Yorker*, while Belongers liked to read *Reader's Digest*. VALS even attained such a state-of-the-art image that it became a selling point by itself. In 1984, the *National Geographic* ran a full-page ad in *The New York Times* with the headline, "The National Psychographic" over the text: "According to VALS, 80 percent of our readers are in the three most desirable groups—Achievers, Societally Conscious, and Belongers."

Some top U.S. advertising agencies, such as Ogilvy & Mather and J. Walter Thompson, began trying to use VALS to help them place advertising spots within the television shows most likely to reach their targets. They found, for example, that daytime soaps were watched most heavily by Survivors, Sustainers, and Belongers, groups who are at home with their televisions on during the day. Achievers, on the other hand, could be reached through sports or news shows, while the Societally Conscious (if they watched at all) only tuned in to critically acclaimed dramas or documentaries and issue-oriented shows on PBS. VALS never became more than a minor factor, however, in media selection, which is still done largely via standard Nielsen numbers sometimes supplemented by Simmons or Mediamark data.

Soon VALS established another link, with geodemographic systems such as Claritas' PRIZM, which brought VALS to the zip-code level. PRIZM is a computerized database that breaks down small geographic areas in the U.S. (such as zip codes, states, counties, census areas, or postal carrier routes) into 44 different lifestyle groups based on similarities in demographics and product use of the residents. The linkage makes it possible to see, for example, whether a particular zip code in New York has more Societally Conscious or more Achievers and the specific neighborhoods where they're likely to reside. (See Chapter 13 for more about geodemographic cluster systems.)

The beauty of VALS for many of the original users was that it helped them to see their particular customers as people with identifiable values and aspirations. By administering the abbreviated 30-question VALS Lifestyle Classification System, they could analyze their own customers by VALS types. Then they could see how their customers' psychological profile compared with the national population, the local market, or the competition's customers.

Many firms used VALS to carve out unique niche markets in increasingly competitive industries. In the early 1980s, when the soft-drink market consisted of Coke and Pepsi neck and neck for first place and everybody else last, Dr. Pepper introduced the campaign, "Hold Out for the Out of the Ordinary—Hold Out For Dr. Pepper," emphasizing individualism and aimed specifically at the Inner-Directed VALS groups. Dr. Pepper executives were determined to win that market, even if it meant losing the entire Outer-Directed Belonger group. "We currently see 30 percent of the young population as Inner-Directed; it's the most rapidly growing segment. Our projections indicate Inner-Directeds will make up 60 percent of that population by 1990," a Dr. Pepper brand manager told *Marketing & Media Decisions* at the time. Dr. Pepper's more recent "Be A Pepper" campaign, showing people moved to break out of the crowd after tasting Dr. Pepper, continues to use an approach targeted at self-assured, Inner-Directed consumers.

VALS was a new way of viewing the marketplace and a way that seemed to be working for a growing number of companies selling everything from beauty aids to wine:

• VALS played an integral part in getting Timex off on the right foot in the home health-care market. Timex wanted to find the likely market for three health devices—a home blood-pressure monitor, a digital scale, and a digital thermometer. VALS researchers identified Achievers and Societally Conscious as the potential market because of their penchant for high-tech innovative products; their concern about health, especially preventive health care; and their tendency to buy high-end gifts. Ads were developed showing an attractive and successful-looking Achiever couple striding off the tennis court. Before a year had passed, Timex had captured 34 percent of the electronic blood-pressure monitor market, compared with 9 percent for its nearest competitor. Timex executives attributed the ad campaign's success to VALS.

• *Reader's Digest* used VALS to help Clairol more effectively reach its customers through ads in the magazine. Ads were designed to appeal to both Outer- and Inner-Directed groups. They pictured a well-dressed presenter in classic profile with the text: "Color and condition that should have been yours can be. Make it happen. Sells the most.

Conditions the most." Outer-Directeds would appreciate that Clairol was popular. Inner-Directeds would like that it allowed them to "make it happen" and take control.

• Ads for Folonari wine showed the company's spokesperson, Pernell Roberts, tieless, taking jug wine out of the refrigerator. This appeal targeted the Inner-Directeds, who were seen to be so self-assured that they didn't care about the prestige of corks as long as the wine tasted good. They also were identified as the group most likely to be big wine drinkers and to try new brands because they used their own judgment and weren't afraid to take risks.

• Seattle's Recreational Equipment Inc. used VALS to find out who its customers were and how they used its products. They found that nearly half of customers were in the Societally Conscious group. The company redesigned its stores in earth tones to be more attractive to the core customers. They also put out a catalog that featured models with longer hair, beards, moustaches, and other 1960s-inspired accoutrements.

• San Antonio real-estate developer Ray Ellison Homes used VALS to get a handle on its clientele. It surveyed 5,000 home buyers in its market and asked them about their opinions on landscaping and wallpaper, as well as giving them the VALS attitude questions. The company found that Belongers, Achievers, and Societally Conscious were the groups most likely to buy its homes. Through focus groups with members of the three groups, the company found that certain types of interior and exterior features appealed more to certain groups. When an Achiever women saw a tiled country kitchen, she said she'd never have the time to clean all that tile. The tile in the luxurious master bedroom, however, didn't bother her. One was associated with work and the other with relaxation. The company reviewed its houses and put together models designed for each of the three groups. Societally Conscious liked energy efficiency, while Achievers went for the status-raising appearance of special facades, luxurious carpeting, and high-tech security systems. Belongers were attracted to traditional decors and comfortable homes populated by loving families.

VALS has been instrumental in the formation of hundreds of other new product launches or advertising campaigns. The California Egg Commission used it to help reverse sliding egg sales. Jell-O used it to pull in Belonger women with a cute appeal emphasizing the jiggle. A San Francisco HMO used it to draw in Belongers with a more group-oriented appeal. New York Telephone used it to reach smaller businesses. Cesar Chavez and the United Farm Workers used VALS and geodemographics to craft a direct-mail fundraising appeal to the Societally Conscious. MasterCard used VALS in designing its "Master the Possibilities" campaign. The ads featured interviews with John Huston, André Previn, and Twyla Tharp, mentioned the card only in passing, and targeted the Inner-Directed groups. Grape Nuts ads, showing handsome young people eating cereal alone in shining morning light, were directed at Experientials with their "Morning Is Your Time" tagline. With VALS, cereal-eating became a spiritual quest, and eating Jell-O became a way of having fun.

## The Decline and Fall of VALS

The research community's honeymoon with VALS, however, was destined to end, and end it did on a rather sour note. By about 1986, criticisms became more widespread, and even long-time friends of the program began to question its applicability. Among the criticisms were that VALS was simplistic and too general, that it was too theoretical and its developmental psychology origins were not really applicable to consumer markets, that it was really just demographics in disguise, and that there were too many similarities between the groups and not enough homogeneity within each group to make them useful as consuming models. Others said that, with Belongers making up more than one-third of the population and the Integrateds accounting for a miniscule 2 percent, the system was too unbalanced to be valuable for identifying markets. Marketers further challenged the usefulness of identifying Survivors and Sustainers at all. Since they were so poor, they reasoned, they could hardly be considered choice consumer targets.

By the end of the 1980s, there was more disillusion than enthusiasm in written accounts about VALS. We'll go into more detail about the disillusionment in Chapter 5, which discusses VALS 2. Suffice it to say for now, the winds of market research fashion had shifted, and by 1987, SRI researchers were looking for ways to revamp Mitchell's original typology to address the concerns of critics and clients.

One thing the critics of VALS failed to acknowledge was that VALS, whatever its inadequacies, had partially accomplished what it had set out to accomplish. Mitchell had conceived of it as a theoretical tool for understanding changing societal values in general terms. Its use as a consumer model was auxiliary and postulated almost as an afterthought. The most important effect the original VALS had on the collective market research community can still be seen today in the expanded variety of new methods and techniques now being used to understand consumers' emotions and mental processes.

VALS, like other early psychographic tools, was valuable in that it showed researchers a new way to think about markets and gave creative people a way to understand the distant human beings that make up markets. VALS was important because it was the first experience many executives of America's largest corporations had with psychographic segmentation. VALS instructed corporations in the specifics of psychographics segmentation—a technique many adapted to their own industries and research departments. VALS, while by no means the only such tool or the best, was certainly the one most publicized by the mainstream press.

In the final analysis, VALS succeeded as a long-range planning tool. What's more, some of its predictions have come true. In his 1974 report, *Consumer Values,* Mitchell warns about the paradox of the new affluence. Although the society will be more affluent in 1990, he says, these new consumers will not respond to the mass market appeals that worked in the past. They will have the personal income to spend as they like, but many will be morally opposed to unchecked consumerism and companies and products that pollute the environment. Some will continue to buy, but they will be educated and sophisticated enough to be much more selective in their spending habits.

Inherent in that statement was the promise of rich rewards for those clever merchants who could unravel the secret of what makes the younger generation buy. To do that, Mitchell said, businesses would need to take a more person-oriented approach, marketing in different ways to different groups: "The central problem in advertising will be how to sell to values increasingly geared to processes, not things. Sales appeals directed toward the values of individualism, experimentalism, person-centeredness, direct experience, and some forms of pleasure and escape will need to tap intangibles— human relationships, feelings, dreams, and hopes—rather than tangible things or explicit actions."

In 1974, the idea that intangibles were worth tapping was still a relatively controversial one. In 1990, it is standard advertising procedure, and the most successful agencies have developed proprietary methods designed to fix on consumers' emotions. The early 1980s turned into a mass consuming binge, and that may have been partly because Madison Avenue learned about the importance of intangibles so early and well. Whether or how much VALS contributed to that lesson is not as important as the fact that the marketing successes of that period came in the wake of the mainstream awareness of psychographics. And for many researchers, this awareness came in the form of new psychological frameworks provided by tools such as VALS and the Yankelovich Monitor. If nothing else, these and other early psychographic systems gave American businesses a new microscope with which to study the people who made up their markets and paved the way for a new generation of higher-order psychographic research that would be designed to solve specific marketing and business problems.

# 4 The American Pulse: Yankelovich's Monitor

*Since the social revolution of the 1960s, marketers have increasingly accepted the idea that an understanding of changing social values is as important to successful marketing as the traditional study of demographic forecasts and economic outlook. The move to the "marketing approach," a widespread policy shift which began in the 1950s, meant that it was not sufficient to understand consumer needs, attitudes, and behavior in the specific product category being marketed. Rather, the marketing approach demands knowledge of and sensitivity to the consumers as a total entity: who they are, how much money they can spend, and increasingly, their life goals, concerns, beliefs, taboos, that is, their social agendas.*
— *Florence Skelly*
**Journal of Consumer Marketing, *1983***

A S AMERICA ENTERED the 1970s and the tectonic plates of social and cultural change were grinding away at established ways of living, the market research firm of Yankelovich, Skelly & White saw opportunity amid the confusion. With such profound changes going on, social scientist Daniel Yankelovich and researchers Florence Skelly and Arthur White saw that corporate America desperately needed some way to test the American attitudinal environment. Yankelovich, Skelly & White came out with the Yankelovich Lifestyle Monitor in 1970 as a way to chart changing societal attitudes and their impact on businesses.

In 1990, the Monitor celebrated 20 years of operation. Though the owners have changed, new trends added and others deleted, it remains the longest-running psychographic study in the country. It also still provides many of America's largest advertisers with vital information about the changing attitudes and values of consumers for use in new-product development and creating advertising strategies, as well as for long-range planning.

The overriding focus of the Monitor is attitudinal. It quantifies consumers' feelings about a whole range of issues—time, money, family, self, institutions, change, emotional life, stress, and the future. It also provides demographics and some media and purchasing behaviors.

There is a widespread misconception among many in the commercial research community that the Monitor is similar to the Values and Lifestyles (VALS) Program of SRI International. These two studies are similar only in that they both seek to measure the attitudes of Americans, and that they are the only syndicated national psychographic studies. In both purpose and method, however, the Monitor and VALS are very different. While VALS is a large-scale psychographic segmentation scheme designed to identify similar groups in the real marketplace, the Monitor is an environmental scan, intended to provide general insights into emerging social trends.

## The Origins

The Monitor was a product of the growing body of evidence compiled by Yankelovich et al. that fundamental changes were happening in America. While doing market research for major corporations during the 1960s, Daniel Yankelovich and Florence Skelly noticed that attitudinal changes were having profound effects on certain industries. Many businesses were surprised to find that while they had been immersed in competitive maneuvering, their markets had begun to shrink. Back when American consumer tastes were more uniform, businesses had become accustomed to making improvements or developing new products or features in reaction to what competitors were doing.

American consumer tastes began to change, and whole industries watched perplexed, as long-established markets eroded. One of the industries hit hardest was ladies' foundation garments. Playtex asked Yankelovich, Skelly & White to identify the reason for the marked downturn in the girdle market. "I remember they were boasting about more stitching in the Playtex girdles as a point of difference with the competition," Yankelovich remembers. "What we found was that there was a profound change going on. People were thinking about a more natural look, and they regarded girdles as artificial and hampering and anti-freedom." While Playtex and other foundation garment manufacturers had been worrying about each other, the customers had decided the product no longer fit their needs.

A similar shift was happening in the automobile industry. The manufacturers were totally involved in each other and paid limited attention to what the customers wanted—until they noticed their sales falling. Yankelovich says the hierarchical nature of the General Motors line reflected manufacturers' attitudes of the time. "The line went from Chevrolet, to Pontiac, to Buick, to Oldsmobile, to Cadillac, with stepped-up features, price, and status," Yankelovich remembers. People just starting out bought a Chevrolet, and when they got a little bit more money, they moved up to a Pontiac. Then when they became middle managers, they bought a Buick or an Oldsmobile. And the true mark of success was being able to afford a Cadillac. "Detroit felt that it was the law of nature, that the world was organized according to this status hierarchy," Yankelovich recalls. The automakers' mistake was in thinking this pattern would last forever.

Yankelovich's study for Chrysler found that people's reasons for buying cars were changing, while the manufacturers' approach was staying the same. Many consumers had switched from buying cars for status to buying them as a means of personal self-expression. A study for Ford showed that the Thunderbird, which was not a part of the Ford hierarchical model lineup, was the original self-expression automobile. "People were buying it to make a statement and express their individuality, not as a symbol of their status," Yankelovich said.

This is not to suggest, he says, that status is no longer a motivation for auto buying. On the contrary, status is still a major motivating force for many of the people driving around in Mercedes and BMW models. The point is that Detroit took a fatally long time to notice the writing on the wall and to realize that growing numbers of consumers preferred smaller cars over big gas guzzlers, as well as cars that expressed their individuality and their separateness from their parents and from the establishment. Long before Japan cornered the compact-car market, Yankelovich and others had advised automakers to introduce new lines with a greater variety of models, so that consumers who wanted smaller, personal cars would have more choices.

Studies for other companies led Yankelovich, Skelly & White to study financial services, leisure time, and personnel recruitment and management. They also did a study on the changing values of youth for *Fortune* magazine and CBS Television. They found a decline in the Protestant work ethic among the young that would have profound effects on how future Americans would save, invest, work, and spend their leisure time. "We were picking up signs that the social fabric was changing, and it was fraught with implications for industries as diverse as automobiles and food," says Yankelovich.

By 1968, YS&W had begun development work on the Monitor. They observed and read everything they could and pooled all relevant information. Some of their most useful insights came from studying popular culture, literature, and music. "We listened to popular music and noted what it was saying," remembers Skelly. "The Beatles 'Let It Be' became our trend, Away From Self- Improvement. A lot of other groups had the same message around that time—that you're wonderful just as you are."

Based on their research, they devised a list of trends concerning Americans' changing attitudes about everything from the nation and the world to themselves, their homes, and their families. Some trends were at first noticeable only among Americans under age 30, while others affected "middle America." Most trend information in the press up to that time was based only on observation. YS&W's idea was a milestone because it proposed taking an annual survey that would quantify exactly how Americans were changing.

In its first year, 58 major companies, including Procter & Gamble, American Can, and General Motors, signed up to sponsor the study. Florence Skelly remembers that there was a lot of interest right from the start in the idea behind Monitor. "A lot of the CEOs who were interested in sponsoring this unknown thing called Monitor had children in college," Skelly says. "They knew that something funny was going on. They were terribly interested to see that the national phenomena we were measuring and studying were things they had encountered in their own homes."

The idea behind the Monitor, Skelly explained in a 1970 speech, was to help its clients see how emerging trends affected business and whether there were opportunities they were missing. The Monitor would assess the size and direction of the trend, whether it was confined to a narrow group, or growing and spreading in the population at large. By repeating the survey every year, it could show the relative growth or decline of various trends over time. It would show the proportion of the population that was part of a trend and describe the people in terms of demographics, political attitudes, religious affiliations, ethnic origins, and so on.

## How They Did It

The hardest part of developing Monitor was in developing the interviewing instrument. "It took us a lot of money, hard work, and argument to come up with a valid and workable instrument for measuring and tracking social issues," Skelly says.

What were the right questions to ask, how should they be phrased, and how should they be administered? And once they were answered, how could it be determined whether they accurately measured what they were supposed to measure? The researchers determined early on that it would be impossible to have a "one-item, one-issue" questionnaire because of the nature of some of the trends and the possible embarrassment of the respondents. "Consider the look on the face of a housewife in Peoria, if asked, 'Would you say you are very sexually free, moderately sexually free, or hardly sexually free at all?'" Skelly notes.

The solution was to make the questions structured, rather than open-ended, to reduce respondent or interviewer biases. More than one item would be required for each issue, and they would form a composite score to show the respondent's position on the issue. The questions would be of the three following types:

- Statements that respondents rated as to the extent of their agreement. For example, "If more people were regular church-goers, there would be less trouble in the world today."

- Multiple-choice questions such as, "Which of these types of movies do you enjoy more—a movie that gives you something to think about or a movie that makes you feel strong emotions; happiness, sadness, anger, or whatever?"

- Problematic questions. For example, "Mr. X and Mr. Y are having an argument about the quality of life each would like. Mr. X says he would gladly give up modern convenience for the more natural life of a hundred years ago. Mr. Y says that although things may be more hectic and complicated, life today is more satisfying. Whose side would you be on in this argument?"

In addition, the researchers concluded that it was useful to have one measure of the trend plus several specific examples. They also found that some questions needed introductions or stage settings to allow the respondents to work through their attitudes enough to be able to articulate them.

Once the YS&W task force came up with a battery of possible questions, they began the arduous process of validity testing, which consisted of seven steps:

1. A trial group of people known to represent a wide range of points of view was selected. Each person was rated by experts on a one-to-five scale according to their known points of view. For some, this primary assessment was done by sociologists who conducted in-depth interviews lasting up to five hours.
2. The names and addresses of the people were then assigned to field interviewers who administered the questionnaire.
3. The composite scores based on the questionnaire were computed and compared with the expert rating item by item.
4. The reliability of the expert ratings was measured by selecting a number of subjects and having them re-rated independently by other experts.
5. The items that produced low correlations (less than .5) were suspect. Before discarding them, a followup interview was conducted to identify the reason for the variances.
6. At the same time, the questionnaire was administered to a second set of people, who were asked the reasons behind their answers in taped interviews lasting more than two hours. The reasons were analyzed to see if they were relevant to the issue being measured. In some cases, the researchers found that the question was measuring something entirely different than had been intended. One example was the statement, "There are some circumstances when it is perfectly all right for a man to be unfaithful to his wife." Agreement was supposed to measure movement away from an absolute moral code. Instead, they found that women who disagreed were expressing their concerns about the meaningfulness of marriage.
7. The questions that didn't work were redone based on the reason-why test group and what produced the best feedback in the sociologists' depth interviewing.

Once the questionnaire was revised to meet all validity criteria, YS&W researchers went back and administered it a second time to a much larger sample group. They wanted to make sure the responses to each item were sufficiently diverse that they didn't reflect truisms. They also wanted to be sure that the several questions used for measuring each trend were neither redundant nor unrelated. After this pilot test, the questionnaire was revised again.

At last, the final questionnaire was administered to a national sample of 2,500 Americans in their homes. The final interviews, which lasted around an hour and a half, were conducted in more than 360 locations around the country. Field interviewers also left behind the part of the survey that contained sensitive questions so the respondents could complete it in private and send it back.

When it was first published in 1971, the Yankelovich Monitor measured 35 trends. Among these were:

•Anti-Bigness
•Physical Self-Enhancement
•Physical Fitness/Well-Being
•ScientismTechnocracy
•Personal Creativity

•Away From Self-Improvement
•Living for Today
•Ethnic Orientation
•Social Cultural Self-Enhancement
•Hedonism

•Defocus on Money
•Meaningful Work
•Mysticism
•Sensuousness
•New Romanticism

•Non-Institutional Religion
•Liberal Sex Attitudes
•Blurring of the Sexes
•Acceptance of Drugs
•Anti-Hypocrisy

•Introspection
•Novelty and Change
•Beauty in the Home
•Return to Nature
•Simplification
•Personalization—Rejection of Conformity

•Rejection of Authority
•Tolerance for Chaos and Disorder
•Female Careerism
•Away From Familialism
•Local Community Involvement

The Yankelovich Lifestyle Monitor has gone on to build a client list that has numbered between 80 and 120 corporations. As of this writing, annual subscriptions cost $35,000 the first year and $29,000 for renewal subscriptions. Subscribers receive copies of the public volumes, including a data reference book, a management summary, and economic outlooks for about 25 industries. If they wish, they can also have direct online computer access to the data. The firm's researchers also provide custom analysis and on-site consulting for clients. Some of the longest-term clients include Procter & Gamble, S.C. Johnson Co., Sears Roebuck, Coca-Cola, American Express, R.J. Reynolds, and Nabisco.

## Changing Hands

In 1985, the multinational advertising giant Saatchi & Saatchi acquired Yankelovich, Skelly & White (YS&W). Soon after that, Saatchi & Saatchi acquired another firm, Clancy and Shulman, and decided to merge the two firms. As a result, Daniel Yankelovich and Florence Skelly left to form the Daniel Yankelovich Group (now DYG Inc.) and Telematics, taking about 20 employees with them. The new firm formed by Saatchi & Saatchi, Yankelovich Clancy Shulman (YCS), won the right to use Yankelovich's name and still conducts the annual Monitor survey and syndicates the results. The name was shortened to simply, the Monitor.

## Monitor's Segmentations

One of the reasons some think that Monitor is similar to VALS is that both studies offer segmentations—the population divided into several general groups composed of large numbers of people with similar attitude profiles. The difference is that the VALS groups are designed to identify similar groups in the marketplace, while the Monitor segments are provided to facilitate understanding of the data with no attempt made to categorize buying behavior, brand choice, or media usage by rigid typologies.

YS&W researchers began clustering the data by general attitude similarities in the second year of the study. They had learned the first year that clients' eyes started to glaze over after listening to a presentation explaining 35 trends with 6 slides for each trend. "We felt that our presentation was too long-winded, so our main purpose in clustering the trends and clustering the people who represented trends that seemed to go together was data simplification," Skelly says. "We called them by different names and identified clusters of trends and anti-trends that went together. It made for a much more readily fathomable presentation, because instead of talking about 35 trends, we were talking about 5 groups of people."

The segmentation became so popular with clients that the Monitor researchers feared it was being misused. Skelly described the situation in a 1983 article:

> When Yankelovich, Skelly & White developed social values clusters for the sole purpose of simplifying our Monitor trend data, some clients thought of our values clusters as market target segments—a use light years away from our intentions or marketing experience. By 1974, we saw a new social values cluster emerging: a group we called Aimless. We feared that, despite our cautions, some would take the Aimless as a target segment rather than as a description of the social structure of the country. This could open the door to soap geared for the Aimless, an Aimless car, and so forth, an outcome we really worried about.

Despite repeated statements by the original YS&W and YCS that the segmentations are not to be used as market targets, there still appears to be some confusion among clients. If nothing else, these segmentations illustrate overall changes in American attitudes that Monitor has uncovered over the last 20 years.

The segmentations have changed as main issues of concern have changed. There have been five different segmentations since the study began. In the first, researchers found the population split roughly between those who followed traditional values and those who broke new ground. There were five different patterns of traditionalists versus the forerunners. Attitudes were clearly divided on the issues of credit and change. For example, the traditionalists paid in cash. They thought using credit was wrong and a sure road to ruin, while the forerunners used a lot of credit. Similarly, with the issue of change, traditionalists resisted change while the forerunners embraced it.

Today's segmentation, however, could never run along the same divisions. "If you tried to segment today's population on those issues, you would get mush, because everybody's come to grips with the issues of credit and change in one way or another," says Susan Hayward, senior vice president of Yankelovich Clancy Shulman. The issues of division change frequently. In the early 1980s, attitudes were divided around self-perception and the ability to be a smart, capable consumer. "There was a bunch of people then for whom the consuming process, and with it living, was a game. We called them Gamesmen because they were trying so hard to win," says Hayward. Another group of people, who recognized the need to be a good consumer but didn't have the confidence in their own abilities, were dubbed the Scramblers.

The Aimless was one of the most persistent groups (present from 1976 to 1987). They were iconoclasts wandering through life in a "stubborn pursuit of the experience-laden full life of the Me Generation and its persistent psychology of entitlement." By 1987, even these die-hard remnants of the 1960s had "faced up to reality," lost their idealism, and adopted the more pragmatic values of some of the other groups. Perhaps they were ex-radicals like Gary on the television program "thirtysomething," who stopped living out of their vans, got jobs as teachers, and became parents—still poor, but now indelibly part of the system.

## Neo-Traditionalism

The segmentation used going into the 1990s (1987-1991) has five groups, one of which is split into two smaller groups. The hot issues today have to do with selecting and integrating traditional and new elements into a new personal value structure. "The current social climate seems to be about combining what worked well from the 1960s culture with what worked well from the 1970s," says Hayward. "Each of our current segments has put together a different combination of elements from those two periods to come up with their value system for the 1990s."

The Monitor segmentation is defined according to 200 attitudinal questions in the interview, but the survey also has sections dealing with demographics and product usage, such as ownership of high-tech products like computers, fax machines, and microwaves. Demographics, product preferences, and behavior do not play a role in defining the segments; rather, they are treated as dependent variables and used to provide further insight into the values of the various groups.

These are the six major adaptive patterns that segment the American people in the Neo-Traditionalist era:

TRADITIONALISTS , who comprise 19 percent of the population, have a median age of 48. Less than one-third are college educated, and only 44 percent of the women are employed. They cling very strongly to traditional rules—respect for authority, duty, conformity, and materialism. They resist new products, are brand and store loyal, and are price sensitive. They respond well to the American message and are uncomfortable with technology.

GOOD NEIGHBORS, 19 percent of the population, are younger than Traditionalists, although one-third are retired. Their median income is $24,000, and 48 percent of women are employed. They are a well-adjusted group with a secure sense of self. They believe in living and letting live, but prefer the company of people like themselves. They seek an orderly, stable life and value shared experiences with family and peers. They are strongly influenced by word of mouth and respond well to a "people like me" approach.

REACHERS, 17 percent of the population, are the most ethnic and the least educated, and have the lowest median income ($21,000). Their values combine traditional and progressive elements. They believe in traditional male/female roles, and they work to achieve material rewards, which they see as the definition of success. On the other hand, they like instant gratification, have no long-term goals, are self-centered, and need to project an invulnerable image. They seem to be reaching across the gulf between their aspirations and their ability to achieve them. Underneath it all, they are insecure and seek assurance that they're O.K. As consumers, they are impulsive followers and need to be reassured. Messages from a trusted spokesperson or experts are effective with this group.

NEW ESTABLISHMENT , 21 percent of the population, are often anti-establishment rebels from the 1960s who have now attained a level of material success. They are highly educated and have comfortable incomes. Their median age is 44, and 30 percent are professionals or executives. They still believe in the crusades of the 1960s, but are now more or less content to maintain what's positive about the status quo. They derive satisfaction from creative and work pursuits and don't need material objects as symbols of success. They are confident, have a strong sense of control, and are less dependent than other groups on community or group ties. As consumers, they like quality, top-of-the-line products, but they take them for granted. They are big consumers of time-saving services. Word of mouth from people like themselves is a powerful appeal because they have become fairly isolated from the rest of the population.

The fifth group is the ANGLERS, 24 percent of the population, who are then subdivided into Entrepreneurs (9 percent) and Players (15 percent). Anglers have a strong competitive drive, are involved in the physical self, and preoccupied with the nature of relationships. A lust for life manifests itself in many areas of their lives. They embrace new roles for women and use technology as a problem-solving tool.

The first Angler subgroup, **ENTREPRENEURS** , with a median age of 33, is the youngest of the six segments. They are well-educated professionals and executives. Forty-six percent have children, and 67 percent of the women are employed. As take-charge people, they value education, culture, and creativity, and get personal satisfaction from working and playing hard, as well as from connections with friends, community, and family. They show significant social responsibility and commitments to activism, especially in the environmental area. They seem concerned with coming up with solutions. They are strategic consumers and apply techniques of good decision-making automatically.

The second Angler subgroup, **PLAYERS** , is much less intense than the Entrepreneurs in every area. Their median income is $26,000, 31 percent are college-educated, and 46 percent have blue-collar jobs. They play the game, but don't seem to have the driving desire, or necessary cards, to win. They tend to focus more on short-term monetary goals and prefer spontaneity and excitement to duty and obligation. Since Players lack the self-confidence of Entrepreneurs, they will not be the first on the block to try new things. They use products that bolster their self-image and are responsive to the appeals of experts and celebrities.

The attitudinal winds, however, have shifted, and it is again time to devise a new segmentation. Hayward says the newest segmentation will be out in 1991. There are telltale signs that the current segmentation is no longer an accurate reflection of reality. During the last two years, the demographic differences between the segments have lessened. In 1987, the median age of Traditionalists was around 60, and the youngest group had a median age of around 32. Now the median age gap is shrinking. "Also, there's little connection anymore between the values these groups hold and the behaviors they exhibit," Hayward says. "I'm beginning to conclude that everybody's coming to grips with life as it's going to be lived in the 1990s. It's time to look for some new divisive issues."

## The Changing Monitor

Over the 20 years of the Monitor study, researchers have measured a total of 60 trends at various times. New ones are added as they become relevant, and trends that show no movement for several consecutive years are deleted. One of the original trends deleted in 1986 was "Acceptance of Drugs," which measured attitudes about legalization of marijuana and recreational use of drugs. Public opinion on the topic had turned from cold to frigid by 1986, when the crack cocaine epidemic and its contingent rise in violent crime first started making headlines. "In 16 years, we never got more than 4 percent of the population that was really hot on the idea (of legalizing drugs)," Hayward says. "We left it in for so long just to make sure nothing was starting up or dying down."

The current Monitor measures 45 trends. Most are identical to the first trends, but some have been added and others updated. Brand Consciousness and Concern for Education were added for the first time in 1990. The Brand Consciousness statements will measure whether there is increased interest in well-known brands and why. "One of the things we've said for a number of years now is that consumers have a lot of interest in well-known brands, not for the emotional brand-loyalty reasons, but because a brand is a signal of something that works well and doesn't entail any risk," says Hayward.

The other new trend for 1990, Concern for Education, looks at how Americans think about education. Is it seen as a pragmatic tool for getting ahead in the world or as a way of broadening and deepening one's own individual experience?

Nine trends from the 1970s were dropped in 1990 because they showed no movement or didn't seem to be relevant anymore. These deletions speak volumes about what we've outgrown. One deletion was Liberalization of Sex Attitudes. That trend measured the sexual revolution, but had little relevance in an era tainted by AIDS-induced fear of sex, a time when many singles are electing to remain celibate. Also dropped were: Concern for Mental Well-Being, Mysticism, Social-Cultural Self Enhancement, Scientism/Technocracy, Away From Self Improvement, Search for Community (substituted by Ethnic Orientation in 1990), Acceptance of Purposeless-ness, and Responsiveness to Fantasy.

Five trends of the 1980s were also dropped in 1990: Need for Self-Sufficiency, Hunger for Personal Feedback, Toward Divisiveness, Away From Clutter and Complexity, and Hunger for the Peak Experience.

When Monitor researchers think American attitudes may have come full circle in some areas, they may reinstate earlier trends. In 1990, they reinstated three trends that hadn't been measured since the early years of the study: Sensuousness, Beauty in the Home, and Ethnic Orientation. Sometimes the experiment doesn't work. "I think we're going to lose Sensuousness and Beauty in the Home again next year," Hayward says. "We reinstated them for a couple of years in the early 1980s and then omitted them again because they didn't show much change. We're seeing similar things now, unless we've just picked the wrong years or it's no longer a useful measurement. Attitudes have changed in those areas, and our trends are not picking up the changes."

In cases where the measurement validity of the Monitor statements is suspect, Hayward and her staff come up with new statements to redefine the trend and refine the measurement. Such is the case with the drug issue. Hayward is thinking about reframing the question to measure attitudes about drugs as a social problem. Similarly, the 1990 Monitor includes several updated trends. One that needed updating was the original "Blurring of the Sexes." Its original purpose was to measure the movement toward androgyny. In 1990, that was changed to "Blurring of Sex Roles," which measures changes in the division of household labor, among other sex-role issues. Also updated has been the original trend "Away from Familialism," which looked at attitudes towards communes. In 1986, that was changed to "New Forms of Familialism" which asks about non-related consumer units.

Another update was "Need For Ideological Orientation," which was added in 1977. In 1990 that was dropped and a new trend, the "Need For Religion," was added, which asks if there is a religious renaissance going on now. "After a decade of focusing on the self," Hayward says, "it looks like people now are interested in things outside the self— connections with other people like family and friends, sense of community, participation with a group of people with whom one feels a membership. There's a needle pointing in that direction. It could turn out to be religion; it could turn out not to be. But when you put that together with the new concern for environment, it's clear there's a need for something bigger than one's self. That's what we hope to measure."

## Users and Uses

Monitor is used primarily for strategic planning by the 80 corporations that are current subscribers. These clients include all the Japanese car makers, Sears, Coca-Cola, Spiegel, American Express, AT&T, MCI, and Dow Chemical, among many others. Over the years, the bulk of Monitor clients have been concentrated alternately in various industries. When the Monitor first started, Hayward says, many of the clients were packaged-goods manufacturers. As these companies became more sophisticated in their use of research, some stopped using Monitor because they developed their own in-house studies or relied on similar studies by advertising agencies. "The packaged-goods industry loved us in the beginning because they really needed us," Hayward says. "They needed ways to respond to a consumer who was changing radically in the way they responded to advertising and marketing approaches. We have fewer now because they know all this. They're used to thinking this way now after 20 years, and they have internalized it."

Adhering to the motto, 'If it's not broke don't fix it,' American corporations don't usually go seeking research insights until the industry falls on hard times. Today, the Monitor is seeing more new business from retail and service firms that are trying to gain an edge in an ever-more-hostile competitive environment. "The problem with retailers at the moment is they have no internal structure for using research of any kind," Hayward says. "As an industry, they just don't use it, they don't have the budgets, and they don't have anybody who knows how to use it or how to apply it. But it's an industry that's in terrible trouble, so they know they need it."

One reason some former Monitor clients say they dropped the service was that there was no direct link to product use, and they found it difficult to translate the relatively abstract trends identified by Monitor into possible consequences for sales of their products. Though Monitor researchers attempted for several years to address the product link problem, Hayward says, it was too risky to change the Monitor format. The ideal case would be to link Monitor trends more directly to sales of products by asking respondents about their intentions. This isn't done, but Hayward says some sales trend information is contained in YCS's special industry reports. The Monitor's chief use, Hayward notes, has always been long-range planning, which looks at sales as part of a broader picture. In this application, clients find it valuable to review sales trends over time and analyze them in relation to Monitor findings.

At the strategic planning level, Hayward says, the need for the Monitor will be especially acute in the 1990s, an era in which a follow-the-leader media mentality surrounds the hottest new sensation with hype in the blink of an eyelash. In this media-saturated environment, it can be very difficult for businesses to discern a fad from a longer-term trend. This is the real use for a research tool like Monitor that is based on more than 20 years of historic data. By knowing where we've been attitudinally, business leaders can make better decisions about how attitudinal shifts are likely to affect consumer behavior in the future.

## The Latest Trends

The Monitor has helped researchers predict many significant recent consumption and behavior shifts, such as the move to white and light alcoholic beverages, the moderation of drinking habits, and the changing nature of consumerism: instead of writing to Ralph Nader, people now write to a corporation's chairperson. Monitor researchers also say they were able to forewarn their clients about Americans' reemphasis on ethics and morality and the increasing importance of home as a safe haven.

To distinguish long-term trends from fads, Monitor researchers say they look for the size of the movement and evidence that the issues are truly important to large segments of the population. The larger the groups that are affected and the more connections they find, the more likely it is they are looking at the start of a long-term trend. One example is the long-term moderation in alcohol consumption. Although the beer, wine, and spirits industry hoped this was a fad, it appears to be a permanent change, as these attitude shifts identified by Monitor show:

- The baby boomers, now in the peak years for alcohol consumption, never associated drinking alcohol with maturity as their parents did. They don't like the taste of scotch and martinis and don't think they have to do something distasteful to be a "grown-up." They prefer white liquors, like vodka and tequila, or fine wines and imported beers.

- Alcohol consumption works against the new concern with health and fitness.

- You can't succeed at work by regularly consuming three-martini lunches.

- Baby-boomers now have children to protect and are less tolerant of drunk drivers.

- Parents may also forsake the drink after work for quality time with their children.

- Peer pressure to drink now translates into permission not to drink. The designated driver is no longer viewed as a wimp but as a responsible, caring friend.

Several years back, Monitor analysts predicted that direct marketing was here to stay because they saw it as an antidote to consumers' increasing frustration with clothes shopping. Consumers report they resent spending precious time on what they consider to be a risky and frustrating chore. Monitor shows that while a majority of women say they enjoy shopping for groceries, less than half find it pleasant to shop for clothes. Fully 53 percent of women agreed that "I enjoy buying new clothes, but shopping for them is often frustrating and time-consuming." It is far more convenient to pick up a phone to order and have the item delivered directly to the home. As long as the merchandise looks like the pictures and returns are easy, direct mail is going to be a long-term phenomenon.

Home television shopping, on the other hand, is a fad, according to Monitor analysts. The consumer likes to be in control, while shopping channels require a shopper to sit in front of the screen waiting for a desired item to come up. What's more, there is no guarantee of product quality.

## Hunkering Down

Another major finding of the 1990 Monitor was a marked decline in all the consumption-oriented trends. "Americans are going to stop spending money," Hayward says. "Being trendy, being successful, consuming conspicuously, high-tech interest with new products for the sake of newness, competitiveness, the keeping up with the Joneses that Yuppies were into—all that's disappearing."

Hayward calls it a "hunkering down." People will continue to buy replacement items and items they need or that interest them, but the era of unbridled consumer spending is at an end. What's more, this declining consumption trend does not seem to be a function of economics, notes Hayward, even though economic times are less than ideal. "Even if we went back to the economy of the 1950s tomorrow," she says, "consumers would not be frantically spending money anymore. Not because they're economizing, not because they're afraid of recession, not because they've suddenly decided to save for the future, although all of those things may be happening."

It may be more a case of enough is enough. After nearly a decade of self-indulgence, the morning after is here at last for many Americans. Many baby boomers are becoming parents for the first time, others have changed jobs or simply changed their attitudes, and are cutting up their credit cards. For many, the thrill of buying something new and discarding the old has worn thin. The moment of reckoning is still at hand for others, however. One 1991 survey finds more credit cards were in active use than in any single previous year; credit-card companies were still enjoying huge revenue increases despite the looming recession in the rest of the economy.

## Who's Crying Now?

The critical harbinger of change is dissatisfaction. Monitor analysts have predicted behavior changes by identifying disgruntled groups and areas that show evidence of great dissatisfaction.

For a few years now, Susan Hayward says, there have been signs of significant dissatisfaction among the ranks of working women. The 1990 Monitor identifies even more erosion in satisfaction levels of women that may represent an attitudinal change of monumental proportions. Something similar happened two decades ago when women rejected traditional homemaker roles and entered the work force en masse.

Today, women see that equal pay for equal work is a myth and being a working woman isn't all it was cracked up to be. They have at least three full-time jobs: their careers, their children, and their housework. They give 100 percent at work, then come home and give 100 percent more—doing most of the housework and taking care of the kids until they fall into bed exhausted, only to start again at the crack of dawn. Now they're finally getting mad as hell, and they probably aren't going to take it anymore, says Hayward.

"Women would love to quit working, and in their heads they're going to," she says. In 1990, when working women were asked under what conditions they would quit working permanently, 50 percent of them said they would quit working if they didn't need the money. That's up from 30 percent the year before.

"That's a monstrous increase in just one year," Hayward says. "I think we're looking at a revolution equivalent in terms of social values to what happened in the 1960s. It's going to have ramifications for employers, marketers, the distribution industry, husbands, children, and all the institutions of society."

Another standard part of the survey explores women's attitudes toward jobs. This also showed a substantial shift away from full-time work and toward part-time work. Among women, the portion who agreed that women with children should have a career if desired dropped from 56 to 49 percent between 1989 and 1990. And the portion who agreed that women with children should work only part-time while the children are at home rose from 31 percent in 1989 to 39 percent in 1990. In addition, more women in peak childbearing years, between ages 25 and 34, reported that they were spending more time with their children and bringing work home from the office less often.

The survey has typically shown that women still do most of the cooking, dishes, and cleaning. The only area that showed equal participation between men and women was grocery shopping, but even this trend is not as egalitarian as it seems. In 1990, the survey added a question asking who made out the food shopping list. The majority of respondents said it was the woman. Men may be found in grocery-store aisles, but they're often just there because a woman sent them, says Hayward.

"For a number of years, we've been seeing signs that women were dissatisfied with the way things were and that something might have to change," Hayward says "But this is the first time we've seen these major attitudinal changes in these areas. It's as if the logjam broke and we're going over the edge. Women want to have their lives back."

This attitudinal change is only a precursor to action, Hayward says. What actions? Will women rise up and hold their bosses or husbands hostage until the government supplies better child care or housework is divided equally? No, but they may forsake higher-paying jobs in favor of jobs offering the benefits they need, such as longer vacations, flex-time and child-care support. As women become an indispensable part of an aging work force that has fewer younger workers, this attitude change will require changes in the way America does business, Hayward says.

"Employers who need to attract and keep qualified workers will have to start offering support systems that address the other half of their employees' lives," Hayward says. "They won't be able to expect 14-hour days from them, either, and once women stop doing it, men will begin to think that maybe they don't have to either."

Some may wonder whether this signifies an end to the women's movement. Could employers react by hiring fewer women? Hayward says that may be a knee-jerk response from short-sighted management, but that employers with insight will have to adjust. "Women make up about half the work force," she says. "Either we learn to do with a much smaller work force or somebody changes their minds."

## Post-Boomers

Another group that Monitor researchers say may be a harbinger of change is the post-boom or baby-bust generation. These younger Americans, born after 1964, have had to live in the shadow of the baby boom. They have never really had music, culture, or products of their very own. They came of age in a socially and economically confusing time that offered them no guarantee of success or support and required that they become competitive at an early age. Consequently, they are serious and more interested in protecting themselves financially than in sowing their wild oats.

They court in groups rather than in pairs. Their behavior patterns are unlike any previous generations, and Monitor researchers say businesses may be in for a surprise when they finally start exerting their influence.

The Monitor's theory of social change somewhat resembles Hegel's dialectic process of social change: thesis, antithesis, synthesis. The thesis in this cycle was the 15 years from the end of World War II until 1960, when the Traditional Values System reigned. The early 1960s marked five years of turmoil that began the antithesis stage—people rejected tradition and embraced the opposite. This lasted until the end of the 1970s, when another period of turmoil occurred, involving recognition of realities and pragmatic attempts to deal with them. Since 1986, with the development of Neo-Traditional values, a synthesis has been underway.

The post-boomer group will have a key role to play if this pattern holds true in the future. Monitor researchers theorize that the synthesis will last through the 1990s—its 15-year span. By then it will have become a new thesis, the starting point for a new cycle. The post-boomers, who do not remember the stages of the past cycle, will then be in their early 30s and 40s, and entering more powerful positions. Their influence will be key in deciding how the nation grapples with the huge bill of financing the baby boomers' retirement. The potential revolution may be more pragmatic and goal-oriented than in the past, but Monitor researchers think it will be just as dramatic.

## The Age of Sameness

It's not the same world in the 1990s as it was when the Monitor began in 1970. At that time, historic changes were going on in the American psyche, and some people really believed they were changing the world for the better. Today, the earth has stopped shaking, leaving the status quo pretty much intact. Most people have settled into a comfortable set of values that suits their everyday lives. We're concerned about the mountains of garbage we generate, but nobody wants a landfill in their backyard; many of us can't even bear the inconvenience of recycling. We want to help the homeless and the crack babies, but few offer to take them into their homes. It may no longer be the Me decade, but self-interest is still the number-one underlying motivation. The more things change, the more they stay the same.

"We're looking at ten years of no major upheavals," says Hayward. "There are going to be modifications and adjustments and slight changes in direction, but we're not going to have any upheavals such as we had in the 1960s or the mid-1980s. Now seems to be a time of consolidation and sameness, and building a base on which you can construct whatever lifestyle it is you want. People have one major shared goal, and that is enhancement in the quality of life."

Is Monitor still as useful in an age in which attitudinal changes are measured in minute increments instead of sweeping shifts? It is more important than ever, says

Susan Hayward. It is more difficult today for marketers to discover the crucial nuances that peak consumer interest in their products. "Consumers are not going to spend, and they're not as fascinated with new products as they used to be. If the population is growing at a slower rate and personal income isn't growing, then a business strategy that's built around the expectation of 10 to 15 percent annual growth is going to fail because it isn't out there. That means that protecting your market share, cannibalizing existing market share from other companies, is going to be the only way to grow." And doing that, she says, requires better understanding of consumers' wants and needs through surveys like the Monitor.

Daniel Yankelovich, who started it all 20 years ago, agrees. His new company, DYG Inc., runs a survey called Scan that takes a broader look at how social changes affect business. It assesses, for instance, the impact of social trends on the labor force and the relative social values stance of different countries. At some point, Scan will be an international system used by multinational corporations to evaluate foreign consumer markets. Understanding changing social norms, Yankelovich says, is crucial for marketers today because the nature of the change is so subtle, yet the consequences of a misstep are so much greater. Yankelovich says:

*People are struggling to try to integrate some stable marital family values and at the same time to adopt new lifestyles, dual-earner households and more equality, and it's a hell of a difficult job. It's decisive for many products and services. Take another social change, the way retirement is going. The concept of retirement used to be that you stopped working, and you sat back in a state of disinvolvement and inactivity until you finally died. That concept of retirement is almost totally transformed, with people working part-time and being active and using new technology. Anybody who let their marketing to older people be guided by old concepts of retirement would be bankrupt overnight.*

*I think social change was easier to grasp in the 1960s because you had this revolution against dominant conformity values. There's no revolution going on today, but that doesn't mean there aren't social changes. It just makes it harder to sort it all out.*

# 5 | *Disillusionment and the New VALS 2*

*"When VALS first came out, it enlightened us and described behavior in certain ways that some people hadn't thought of before. But now it makes people think in boxes and categorizes people in ways that aren't really relevant. We can forget we are dealing with unique individuals."*

*"It's really arrogant to think that you could get a fix on someone's psyche and then manipulate it to get them to buy a certain kind of product."*

*"I don't use VALS, and I don't know anyone who got any use out of it."*

*"You have to look at what they buy and then define them by those choices, instead of the other way around."*

*"We all looked at each other and wondered what to do with this."*

*— VALS critics, 1987*

*When VALS 1 was introduced, values were closer to the surface and more reflective of people's behavior as consumers than they are now. But times have changed, and we're now living in an age of diminished expectations, when economic, educational, and other types of resources play a much more important role in how consumers act.*

*— Ed Flesch*
*former VALS project director*

ALMOST AS SOON as SRI of Menlo Park, California, introduced the original Values and Lifestyles (VALS) program, it became the focus of lively debate. Academics in the field of psychology, if they noticed VALS at all, took issue with its unorthodoxy and dismissed it as unscientific. They said the model was based on little actual research, either in a field or laboratory situation; and beyond that, Arnold Mitchell was not a trained psychologist. Other critics used VALS to rekindle the ongoing discourse about the usefulness of values in predicting consumer behavior. Because of various constraints and prior experiences, they argued, people do not always act in ways consistent with their stated values. Academic values researchers, would-be defenders of VALS, had problems with VALS, too. They could not support a program, even a values-oriented one, that shrouded its scoring method in a "black box" of secrecy.

Values researcher Lynn Kahle, an associate professor in the College of Business Administration, University of Oregon, became perhaps the most vocal early VALS critic. "To qualify as science, something must be public," Kahle wrote in a 1984 letter to *Marketing News.* "This principle guides psychology, sociology, astronomy, parapsychology, and other disciplines. SRI, however, has placed itself below these disciplines scientifically by refusing to reveal how respondents are classified into VALS types. Without this information, we cannot praise or condemn VALS with complete objectivity. But we can express displeasure with silence."

## The Value of Values

Despite these criticisms, VALS soon gathered an impressive subscriber list and became the most widely used system of measuring values. During the 1980s, it was praised in the popular press as "revolutionary." But there was an unfortunate aspect to VALS' initial success. The market researchers who were so quick to embrace VALS were also the first to drop it when it became apparent that VALS wasn't a crystal ball that could answer all questions about consumer attitudes. As a result, many became disillusioned with psychographic research in general, when it was the VALS typology that had failed them. One well-known market researcher has since called the original VALS "a public relations triumph, but a research disaster."

Though it was the most visible, VALS was by no means the only values measurement system. Rokeach's Value Survey and Kahle's List of Values also examined the relationship between values and consumer behavior. Kahle's List of Values (published in 1983) probed the psychological characteristics and values of a representative sample of 2,264 Americans. During extended face-to-face interviews, the respondents revealed the values they considered most important. Among these were: self-respect, security, warm relationships, a sense of accomplishment, self-fulfillment, being well-respected, excitement, and a sense of belonging, fun, and enjoyment in life. Kahle says major findings of the study were that "values have a pervasive relationship to how people adapt to their life circumstances" and that values warranted more study than they had received to date.

The work of these values researchers and others suggested that personal values could provide important clues about certain types of consumer behavior, but that the extent of usefulness depended upon the product as well as the usage situation. These were two distinctions that the original VALS had failed to consider.

Critics have correctly charged that the original VALS tried to take on the impossible task of being all things to all researchers. It tried to provide one model that would apply to all consumer behavior—from buying deodorant to buying luxury automobiles. Values researchers agreed that values aren't useful for predicting behavior such as deodorant buying because of the low-involvement nature of the product. Deodorant, like toilet paper or dish soap, doesn't engage the consumer's ego. One is pretty much as good as the other as long as it delivers certain benefits. In buying an automobile, however, one is expressing something about oneself, so it's likely the car purchased will be a reflection of personal values. Is the consumer environmentally concerned? Perhaps they'll buy a Geo that gets 50-plus miles per gallon. Is the consumer more risk-oriented, high-powered, and in control? Maybe a Jaguar will be the car of choice.

VALS suggested that Achievers, Societally Conscious, and all the other VALS types would usually buy in predictable ways. But it soon became apparent that more often than not they didn't. Sometimes time-pressured Societally Conscious moms would buy disposable diapers or mentally exhausted Achievers would veg out in front of the tube with a bottle of beer. Many market researchers discovered that, with some products, the usage situation became the primary determinant of demand. By failing to take product usage into consideration, except in a purely ancillary way, the validity of VALS soon became a major topic of discussion, even in the popular press that had previously extolled its virtues.

## Disenchantment

In the early 1980s, academic articles appeared that described "person-situation" segmentation. This was a way of dividing markets by groups of consumers within usage situations. "As demand results from the interaction of a person with his or her environment, a segmentation perspective that includes both the person and the situation is needed to explain demand and target marketing strategy," writes Peter Dickson, of Ohio State University. Researchers advocating person-situation segmentation saw it as an approach that would refine the behavior-predictive ability of both psychographics and benefit segmentation. In some cases, it was said to be one of the only approaches left that would help increase demand for certain products struggling for survival in an increasingly competitive environment.

One example of an advertising campaign that effectively employed the usage situation concept was the "orange juice isn't just for breakfast anymore" spots of several years ago. In a market that was pretty well saturated, these ads changed the way many consumers thought about orange juice, lengthened the time it was an appropriate beverage to drink, and increased consumption. By looking at the situations in which a person uses a product, researchers gain deeper insight into consumer motivations. They can distinguish, for example, between people who drink beer to socialize, those who drink it to escape from the pressures of the day, and the college jock who drinks it to quench an enormous thirst for fun.

As more researchers recognized that people played different roles in different usage situations (i.e., the Achiever who buys leisure products like a Belonger, or the Belonger who buys personal-care products like an Emulator), the criticism arose that VALS was too general to be useful, because it lacked specific product-purchase data. The MRI and Simmons product data, it was felt, were just too far removed from the original VALS survey to reliably indicate purchasing differences across groups. (The DDB Needham Life Style Study discussed in Chapter 6 is an example of a broad-based psychographic study that makes product and brand data a central part of the survey instrument.)

VALS provided a way of segmenting markets by attitudes and demographics, but marketers who wanted to find out about specific product usage had to go back and do primary research, perhaps through focus groups, to find out how the heaviest buyers of a product used it. That effectively took the research back to where it was before VALS classification, which frustrated some clients and further called into question the usefulness of the VALS system. "The use of psychographics without consideration of the situational context can sometimes become a game of shadow boxing rather than target marketing," wrote Dickson.

Others, like Ernest Dichter ("Whose Lifestyle Is It Anyway?" 1986), decried VALS as demographics in disguise. "The emphasis on values and lifestyles has become very popular of late," Dichter writes, "though it is actually the latest in a long line of attempts to pigeonhole people into different personality types or 'styles of behavior'— comparable in many ways to attempts to distinguish people by census-related variables such as age, income, and marital status." Dichter further charged that underlying idiosyncratic factors, such as a childhood experience of poverty, can throw off the whole VALS system. A person who falls into the Achiever category by superficial attitudes and demographics, he argues, but who experienced childhood poverty may be so affected that his spending patterns may resemble those of a Survivor.

Some consumer patterns change simply due to the "cogwheel effects of lifestyle," Dichter further charges. He points to the increasing demand for mineral water, a change that was not foreseen by either demographers or trend watchers. It may have come about, he says, because increasing numbers of Americans began traveling abroad, where consumption of mineral water is widespread. Lastly, Dichter argues, the dynamic nature of life itself makes classification by lifestyle difficult. "My lifestyle today may be quite different from two years ago.... The motivating factor of my lifestyle is not the absolute amount of my income, but its tendency," he writes. The key question is whether one is ascending, standing still, or descending economically.

## VALS' Validity Attacked

In 1987, *Adweek's Marketing Week* published an article and a series of letters that represented the most negative publicity VALS had received to date. The article quoted research and planning directors at packaged-goods giants like Campbell Soup Company, General Mills, and General Foods as saying that VALS was of little use for identifying buyers. Campbell Soup found their soups were purchased by two diametrically opposite groups, one competitive, affluent, and dynamic, and the other composed of "slobs." General Mills found a similar problem in trying to discern the VALS types of cereal buyers. How does a marketer attract one group while not turning off the other? When General Foods used VALS to examine buyers of Maxwell House coffee, it also had problems with consistency of VALS types for different types of behavior. Achievers in the workplace might act like Belongers in the supermarket.

The article granted that psychographics in general (the Monitor was also mentioned), and VALS in particular, was effective in advertising, if used by creatives to tailor ads to certain target markets. The drawback was that it often required two or three different campaigns and big ad budgets to be successful. One agency research director, who explored the VALS classifications of frequent flyers for a client in the travel industry, found that 90 percent were either Societally Conscious or Achievers, but he didn't have the ad budget to go after both groups.

Another persistent complaint was the discrepancy in the size of VALS groups. Because Belongers made up 39 percent of the population, they frequently represented more sales volume than did the heavy-user group that actually consumed more of the product per person. A breakdown of the yogurt category for General Mills, for example, found that Experientials were 20 percent above average in their yogurt consumption, but because they only made up 3 percent of the population, they only represented 4 percent of total yogurt consumption, whereas Belongers were average yogurt eaters, but accounted for one-third of all yogurt consumption. Many marketers wondered why they should bother with other groups at all if Belongers were always the biggest consumer group?

The article was followed by several letters from executives of market research firms who seemed to revel in attacking VALS' Achilles heel. For psychographics to be truly useful, said one letter, "It has to probe people's attitudes and values that relate to purchase decision of the product (or service) in question, not just investigate generic attitudes and values." Another suggested doing unique attitude segmentations that were category specific, such as examining the preferred brands of buyers with traditional values or high self-esteem versus those with non-traditional values or low esteem. The collective view seemed to be that the more product-specific you can get, the better.

SRI was quick to fire off a rebuttal. Gloria McConnell, then director of the program, called the criticisms "fairly typical examples of VALS bashing," and charged that the critics seemed not to understand how the program worked, or they were blaming VALS for the complexity of the marketplace and their own lack of sophistication in using the system. VALS, she countered, started from a broad base and worked inward to a specific category or brand. Its real value, she said, is that VALS "illuminates specific consumption behaviors on the basis of empirically validated broad psychological principles." VALS should not be viewed as a panacea, she suggested, but as just one of many valid tools at the marketer's disposal. She was, however, silent about the specific criticisms raised in the article and letters: that VALS was just retooled demographics, the uneven size of the VALS groups, and the system's inability to pinpoint changes in buying behavior across groups.

## VALS Overhaul

Shortly after the flurry of negative publicity, SRI announced its decision to begin developing a second version of the system, VALS 2, which would change the original VALS concept considerably. Was the action necessary to save the VALS program? Some observers say the move was spurred by a decrease in VALS revenue. SRI refuses to confirm that subscribership declined during that period. Current program director Susie Wong won't comment on revenue, but says only that VALS 2 subscribership now stands at 350 businesses and corporations.

Wong's appointment to director represents a significant change in the program's organizational structure. Wong has headed SRI's Consumer Financial Decision Program since 1986. In 1989, she was given the additional title of VALS 2 program director. SRI, however, denies that merging the two programs represents a downsizing of VALS. "The VALS program remains the star of our business group," says Dennis Maxwell, SRI's vice president of corporate marketing. The decision to combine the two programs was based on Wong's capability, rather than any problems with VALS 2, he adds.

The decision to update VALS was not sparked by public criticisms, Wong says, but was made because subscribers had been expressing similar dissatisfaction with the program. "As the system, which had been created in the late 1970s, started to age," Wong says, "its predictive power was lessening." Any program based on values has a limited life span and needs to change as the reality it measures changes.

As VALS senior research psychologist Bruce MacEvoy sees it, the inner- and outer-directed dimension of the original VALS had became obsolete. "It was part of the social myth that if you grew up in the 1960s you were inner-directed. You had values, you took drugs, and you were fighting against the system," MacEvoy says. "If you were outer-directed, you were driving around in a Cadillac, wearing gold rings, buying and selling souls, and sending armies to Latin American countries. It doesn't quite work that way anymore."

The original VALS was designed to explain a society dominated by the tastes and values of people in their 20s and 30s. These days, the oldest baby boomers are heading into their 50s, the population is becoming more diverse, and the liberal agenda has caved in, creating a world that requires more than inner and outer direction and Maslow's needs hierarchy to explain it. At the same time, the number of products has proliferated, and the number of media vehicles has exploded. The all-encompassing scope of the original VALS didn't address the new complexity of the consumer marketplace, says MacEvoy. "Because it tried to explain so many things, it didn't explain any single thing very well."

Given such a dynamic business environment, Wong says, it was essential that VALS become an instrument that clients could use to determine the different ways people react to change. VALS 2 does this, according to Wong, by incorporating E. M. Rogers' theory on the "diffusion of innovations" into the new model. Rogers' theory contends that first there must be awareness of an innovation, i.e., that there is some relative advantage to the new item. After the initial awareness stage, a person moves through interest, evaluation, trial, and finally adoption. People move through these categories at different rates of speed: the top five percent are Innovators, who are the first to adopt an innovation. Early Adopters can be up to 12 percent of the population and are ahead of the majority in adopting. There is also the Early Majority (one-third), the Late Majority (one-third), and Laggards (15 percent), who are the last to adopt. Typically, marketers have been most interested in the first two categories because they provide initial sales volume and are viewed as the groups that influence others to adopt new things.

Rogers' theory of innovators and laggards has become a standard measure used in many psychographic studies. The theory of diffusion of innovation is more central to MacEvoy's latest project, Japan VALS (see Chapter 8), than it is to VALS 2. Unlike the first VALS, VALS 2 is not based on any a priori assumptions. Rogers' theory was considered along with the original VALS inner/outer-directed theory and other theories during the pretesting to determine which items would be the most predictive of consumer behavior. "The fundamental thrust of the development of VALS 2 was a validation—a proving of usefulness," MacEvoy says. "We put everything on the table for VALS 2 and tested it equally."

## Development of VALS 2

VALS researchers took pains from the start to guarantee that VALS 2 wouldn't be subject to the same criticisms that had befallen the original program. Most important, they addressed the applicability problem by designing VALS 2 as a business tool focused on predicting consumer behavior, and abandoned attempts to provide a model of societal values. VALS 2 is based on personality dimensions, selected especially for their correlation with purchasing behavior. "We're not looking at their style of relating to other people, their spiritual goals, or their ethnic values," MacEvoy says. "All we want to know is their consumption tendencies."

VALS 2 is a leaner, more focused, problem-solving tool that cannot be criticized as the creation of one charismatic individual. The second version is a product of the collective work of a series of staff members and paid consultants who met between 1986 and 1989. The goal of these meetings was to devise a psychographic system with the appeal of the original VALS, but with a sounder theoretical and methodological basis.

One of the consultants who worked on VALS 2 was Harrison Gough, professor emeritus in University of California-Berkeley's psychology department and famed author of the California Psychological Inventory. "The question before us was: of all of the various aspects of personality, how can we extract what seems to be at the root of this model so that the new model is generated in fact?" MacEvoy says that Gough supervised the selection of the psychological dimensions that would be included in the final VALS 2 questionnaire. Gough, however, says that his role was much more ancillary, and that by the time he finished his consultancy in 1989, no concrete solutions had been found to shore up the problematic theoretical basis of the original VALS program. SRI's own literature states that an early step in developing VALS 2 was to identify fundamental psychological orientations that underlie patterns of consumer preference and choice. It further states that the research team identified three self orientations that are most useful in defining consumer behavior and labeled them "principle," status," and "action."

Francois Christen, the VALS research director who originated the development of VALS 2, has since left SRI to found his own consulting firm, Fair Oaks Group in San Francisco. Christen says that the process of developing VALS 2 was much less systematic than the literature makes it sound. Recognizing that the Achilles heel of the original VALS had been its lack of statistical validity, Christen started by searching for a consultant to help with the development of the new program who had impeccable credentials in the quantitative area. He found Lee Cronbach, one of the country's most respected psychometricians. Dr. Cronbach, now a professor emeritus in the education department at Stanford, has a list of credentials that includes career achievement awards from the American Psychological Association and the American Educational Research Association. He is perhaps best known for his work in personnel classification and validation of psychological testing methods.

"Cronbach introduced me to Harrison, who put me on to John Kamp, a post-doc at the Institute for Personality Assessment at Berkeley," Christen says. " Basically, John and I worked up most of the items (for VALS 2). Harrison sort of looked over our shoulders and gave his comments, but essentially John Kamp and I sat in the café in Berkeley and worked up items or borrowed items from other scales and decided what constructs we wanted to measure."

Once they had a list of constructs, Christen and Kamp set about testing their value as predictors of consumer behavior. "For each construct, we had attitude statements and we looked for behaviors that people with these attitudes were likely to display. For example, maybe the person was a variety seeker. We would ask, 'What behaviors are they likely to exhibit?' Maybe they try new foods regularly or go on vacation to a new place every year. Then we looked for statistical relationships between the attitudes and the behaviors. That gave us criteria against which to validate our scales."

The difference between VALS 2 and the original system can probably best be exemplified by looking at the major human influences behind the two systems. Mitchell, though a visionary, lacked the academic credentials necessary to appease some critics. VALS 2 has Lee Cronbach, who oversaw the compilation of the data and the creation of the VALS 2 consumer segments after Christen left. Cronbach's theories of personnel testing have been used to efficiently group people in the armed services, health diagnostics, and education. Cronbach realized that the same principles could apply in marketing. "Marketers looking out at the U.S. population are looking at a population they would like to recruit," MacEvoy says. "They're trying to do the same thing college admission boards or an army personnel person is trying to do. They're trying to find out who among this mass of people represents the groups that they really should be talking to."

Unlike the original version, VALS 2 is methodologically sound, perhaps even above reproach. While Mitchell devised his inward/outward-directedness theory long before there were field data to back it up, the VALS 2 typology is based on two separate field surveys of more than 2,300 respondents each. The first survey was fielded in April 1987 to develop the segmentation system. The initial questionnaire included 400 attitude items, a large battery by any measure. These 400 attitude items measured 65 psychological dimensions. In addition to innovativeness and inward/outward-directedness, dimensions tested included self-monitoring, approval seeking, excitement seeking, impulsiveness, novelty seeking, image consciousness, narcissism, individualism, selfishness versus altruism, cultural, outdoor and nutritional interests, aestheticism, and materialism.

In a second survey conducted later in 1987, the attitude and interest items were examined in relation to respondents' media behavior and tendency to buy products in 170 different categories. Items that didn't show a higher degree of correlation to consumer behavior than did straight demographics were discarded. Through a process of elimination, the 65 personality constructs were weeded down to 12 and then to 5. The final questionnaire has 4 demographic questions (sex, age, education, and income) and 42 attitude questions rated on a four-point scale—mostly disagree, somewhat disagree, somewhat agree, and mostly agree. Seven questions measure each of the 5 constructs. Some of the items on the VALS 2 questionnaire are:

- *I am often interested in theories.*
- *I like people and things that are outrageous.*
- *I am really interested in only a few things.*
- *I often do something just for the heck of it.*
- *I'd like to spend a year in a foreign country.*
- *It is the luxuries in life that make life worthwhile.*
- *I could stand to skin a dead animal.*
- *I often crave excitement.*
- *I hate getting grease and oil on my hands.*
- *I like my days to be predictable.*
- *I must admit I like to show off.*

*Figure 5-1*

## Comparison of VALS™ and VALS 2™

| | VALS | VALS 2 |
|---|---|---|
| **Development Process** | Intuitive, stemming from years of tracking social trends & consumer behavior | Rational-empirical utilizing SRI's market experience & extensive consumer survey data |
| **Conceptual Model** | Developmental psychology Maslow's needs hierarchy | Personality test theory |
| **Context** | Human maturation Generational change '60s & '70s world view Youth vs. Establishment | Consumer behavior Increasing social complexity Increasing social constraints |
| **Basic Dimensions** | Inner vs. outer direction Needs hierarchy | Action, status & principle orientation Resources |
| **Number of Segments** | 9 | 8 |
| **Segment Sizes** | 4% to 38% of U.S. adult population | 8% to 18% of U.S. adult population |
| **Measured Attributes** | Values | Personality dimensions |
| **Measurement Method** | Social attitude statements (varying levels of emotional sensitivity) | Self-descriptive statements (low level of emotional sensitivity) |
| **Number of Questionnaire Items** | 24 Attitudinal 6 Demographic | 42 Attitudinal 4 Demographic |
| **Richness (Improvement in targeting)** | 100% (standard) | 120% to 130% |

*Source: SRI International*

The VALS 2 questions measure intellectual, status, and action orientation. Gone are the questions in the original VALS with dated references to political issues like the legalization of marijuana and abortion. SRI, however, still will not reveal how the responses are categorized into VALS 2 types. One interesting finding from the VALS 2 tests was the method that emerged for measuring status orientation, MacEvoy says. The best way to measure an individual's need for status was not by direct questioning, but by looking for "somewhat agree" or "somewhat disagree" answers in other categories. "Defining the people who don't really have extreme values in any direction works just as well in capturing the status-oriented person as throwing scales at him that say, 'I worry about how people think about me,'" MacEvoy says. The status-oriented, like chameleons, rarely have strong opinions on anything. They tend to drift to one side or the other, depending on the stance of whomever they are trying to impress.

## Self-Orientation and Resources

VALS 2 groups are classified according to two aspects—their self-orientation and their resources. Both of these dimensions are believed to figure prominently in consumer decision-making. Self-orientation refers to what motivates consumers—beliefs or principles, status, or action. "As consumers, people buy products and services and seek experiences that fulfill their characteristic preferences—that help give shape, substance, and satisfaction to their lives. The patterns of attitudes and activities that help people reinforce, sustain, or even modify their social identities VALS 2 calls 'self-orientation,'" states SRI.

Marketers should take different approaches when dealing with principle-oriented consumers versus status- or action-oriented ones. Principle-oriented people are guided by intellectual matters rather than feelings, events, or other people's perceptions. Status-oriented people alter their behavior to fit their surroundings in a chameleon-like effort to win the approval of those around them. Action-oriented people thrive on new social or physical activities.

The resources dimension is an important part of VALS 2 because it is a different way of evaluating consumers in relation to one another. SRI literature claims the resources aspect hasn't been considered before in consumer theory. Other observers, however, point out that any basic consumer behavior textbook includes a section on the importance of consumers' resources in determining behavior. SRI states that VALS 2 emphasizes consumers' intelligence and achievement, rather than their receptiveness to communications, as is the norm in consumer behavior research. This new approach reflects Cronbach's background in educational testing and sees consumers as task-performers. They are then differentiated according to their respective abilities to perform the task of making a purchase:

> To make a purchase, use a service, and so on, a person must have conceptualized some need as 'requiring' an external product or service; the product or service must be available for purchase; and the person must have the disposable income, time to choose, awareness of outlet, and acceptance of price necessary to make the purchase. Thus, the resources

*dimension reflects consumers' self-understanding, awareness of the real world, and social or economic freedom of action. More specifically, resources consist of the nonpsychological, ascribed attributes (such as disposable income, education, marital status) and the psychological attributes (energy level, self-confidence, awareness of products and media, propensity to purchase) that with self-orientation shape the person's responses to the offerings of the market.*

In VALS 2, the resources measure looks at the ability of a particular group to respond to an appeal to buy. The old VALS system assumed that people's lifestyles were a free expression of their values. VALS 2 recognizes that in today's complex world, a wide range of constraints, from financial to psychological, can prevent a person's values from having free expression in the way they live. The resource dimension measures these constraints. Strugglers, the group with the fewest resources, can be barraged with ads that even call them by name and they still won't buy, because they can't; they don't have the self-confidence, income, or eagerness to buy that other groups do. As MacEvoy explains it, the resources determinant is a kind of pre-screening device to separate the most likely prospects from the least. Resources generally increase from adolescence through middle age, and decrease with extreme age, depression, financial reverses, and physical or psychological impairment.

As the first reports from VALS 2 users come in, it seems the new system is an improvement over the old. If there is a criticism, it comes from those who enjoyed the theoretical loftiness of the original VALS. "The main criticism I've heard of VALS 2," says MacEvoy, "is that it's a little too good technically. It's kind of dry and mechanical, and it doesn't have as much passion and heart as the original VALS system did.

"It's kind of a two-edged sword," he continues. "Lee Cronbach, Francois Christen, and the other people who started it really did everything correctly to make a powerful prediction system. But along the way, they made it into a kind of bureaucratic tool for sorting people, when a lot of the media people, creatives, come to a lifestyle segmentation for its warmth and its color."

Some veteran market researchers, however, say the new system has not addressed one of the critical flaws of the original: it is still true that only a small portion of the market for any product will fall into any one segment. Marketers will still be faced with a tough decision: market to only part of the market and risk alienating a portion of their real customers or execute two or more separate programs to target each VALS 2 segment. Since the latter will most likely be cost prohibitive, the marketer is again left in a no-win situation.

## VALS 2: The New Typology

Using the dimensions of self-orientation and resources, VALS 2 has defined eight consumer segments with differing attitudes and behavior patterns. The groups are fairly balanced proportionately, ranging from 8 percent to 16 percent of the population, so that each represents a viable consumer target.

The VALS 2 framework looks like a rectangle arranged vertically by resources and horizontally by self-orientation. The resources dimension is set up as a continuum with the groups with fewest resources on the bottom and the groups with abundant resources above. Above the rectangle are Actualizers, the group with the most resources. Strugglers, the group with fewest resources, is below. These extremes do not fall squarely in any of the self-orientation categories. Each group in the middle, however, exemplifies one orientation over another.

*Figure 5-2  VALS 2 Types*

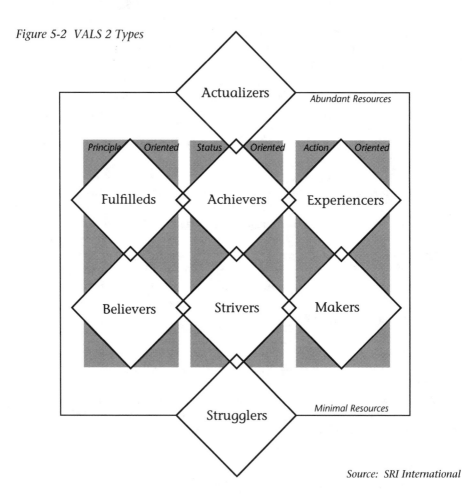

*Source:  SRI International*

**Actualizers:** (8 percent of adult population) Highest income. Abundant resources and self-esteem allows them to indulge in any of the self-orientations. Successful, take-charge individuals, Achievers are interested in personal growth and exploration. They are sometimes motivated by principle and sometimes by a desire to effect change. Image, while important to them, is more an expression of their cultivated tastes and personal character than a status symbol. They are the established and emerging leaders of the power structure, but they still seek new challenges. Their range of interests is wide. Social issues matter, but they also like to enjoy the finer things of life.

*Demographics:* Their median age is 43, and their median income ($58,000) is the highest of all groups. Fully 95 percent have at least some college education, and 68 percent are employed in white-collar jobs. Most (72 percent) are married, and 59 percent are male.

**PRINCIPLE-ORIENTED** consumers try to behave in ways consistent with their world views.

**Fulfilleds:** (11 percent of adults) Mature, satisfied, comfortable, reflective people who value order, knowledge, and responsibility. Well-educated and informed, most are professionals or recent retirees, interested in broadening their knowledge. They are content with their families, careers, and station in life, and their leisure activities center around the home. They are moderately respectful of the status quo, institutions of authority, and social decorum, but keep an open mind. Fulfilleds base decisions on strongly held principles and consequently appear calm and self-assured. Their incomes give them consuming flexibility, but in general they demand functionality, value, and durability in products.

*Demographics:* Their median age is near 50, and their median income is $38,000. Most have a college degree or more. Many are at the peak of their professional careers, and one-fifth are retired. They are the group most likely to be married.

**Believers:** (16 percent of adults) Conservative, conventional people with concrete beliefs based on traditional, established codes—family, church, community, and the nation. Often, their moral codes are deeply rooted and literally interpreted. They follow established routines centered around the home, family, and social and religious organizations. Though modest, their education, income, and energy are sufficient for their needs. As consumers, they favor established brands.

*Demographics:* Nearly 75 percent are married, and most have grown children. Fewer than 10 percent have more than a high school degree; half did not complete high school. Over one-third are retired, mostly from blue-collar jobs. Twenty percent are homemakers. Median income is $21,000,

**STATUS-ORIENTED** consumers seek a secure place in a valued social setting.

**Achievers:** (13 percent of adults) Much of their self-definition comes through career successes. They like to feel in control of their lives and value structure, predictability, and stability over risk, intimacy, and self-discovery. They are deeply committed to work and family. Work gives them prestige, material rewards, and a sense of duty. Their social lives reflect this focus and are structured around family, church, and business. They respect authority and the status quo and live politically conservative, conventional lives. Image is important. As consumers, they favor established products that demonstrate their success to their peers.

*Demographics:* Most are in their 30s or entering middle age. Three-fourths are married, many with young or teenaged children. Nearly half have a college degree or more, and about half are managers or professionals. About 45 percent are two-earner households, and median income is $50,000.

**Strivers:** (13 percent of adults) Unsure of themselves, Strivers seek motivation, self-definition, and approval from the outside. They look to the opinions of other people to determine what they should be and do. Money is the measure of success for this group, who often feels cheated by their limited resources. In striving for security, they are deeply concerned about the opinions of other people. They like style and are easily bored and impulsive. They emulate those with more impressive possessions, but generally fail to pull it off.

*Demographics:* Most are in their 30s. Only 25 percent have more than a high school degree; half work in blue-collar, sales, or service jobs, while 25 percent are unemployed. Median income is $25,000, more than half are married, and nearly a quarter live with other relatives. They are the least likely to have surpassed their parents' standard of living.

**ACTION-ORIENTED** consumers like to affect their environment in tangible ways.

**Experiencers:** (12 percent of adults) Young, vital, enthusiastic, and rebellious, this group is still in the process of forming its life values and patterns of behavior. They seek variety and excitement, savoring the new, offbeat, and risky. They are quick to get enthusiastic, but equally quick to cool. They are ambivalent about political issues and uninformed. Experiencers combine an abstract disdain for conformity and authority with an outsider's awe of others' wealth, prestige, and power. Sports, outdoor recreation, exercise, and social activities provide outlets for their abundant energy. They are avid consumers and spend large portions of their income on clothing, fast food, music, movies, and videos.

*Demographics:* Most are in their 20s and living with other unrelated adults—just one-third are married. Fewer than 20 percent have completed college, and many are in or temporarily out of college. Their median income is about $19,000, but due to shared living arrangements, their disposable income is high.

**Makers:** (13 percent of adults) They are the craftspeople and do-it-yourselfers of the world. They are practical people who value self-sufficiency and possess the constructive skills necessary to attain it. Their lives revolve around family, practical work, and physical recreation, with little interest in the outside world. Makers experience the world by working on it—building a house, raising children, fixing a car, or canning vegetables—and have the sufficient energy, skills, and income to successfully carry out their projects. Conservative and respectful of government authority and organized labor, Makers are suspicious of new ideas, but resentful of government intrusion into individual rights. They are unimpressed by material possessions other than those with a practical or functional purpose (e.g., tools, pickup trucks, or fishing equipment).

*Demographics:* Their median age is 30, and their median income is $23,000. Two-thirds are married, many with children. Three-fourths have only a high school education or less, and most of the rest have technical or junior college degrees. Most are employed in blue-collar or services jobs.

**Strugglers:** (12 percent of adults) live constricted lives. Chronically poor, ill-educated, low skilled, without strong bonds, aging and concerned about their health, they are often despairing and passive. Because they are so limited, they show no evidence of strong self-orientation but are focused on meeting the urgent needs of the present moment. Their chief concerns are for security and safety. Strugglers are cautious consumers. They represent a very modest market for most products and services but are loyal to favorite brands.

*Demographics:* Two-thirds are women, fewer than half are married, and virtually none have more than a high school education. More than half are over age 60, and many have age-related health problems. Two-thirds have incomes below the poverty level ($12,000 in 1987).

## Snapshots of Consumers

The descriptions of the groups above only go so far in introducing users to the new VALS 2 groups. As one long-time user put it, "You've got to get in there and live with these people to really understand them." To personalize the groups more, SRI provides a videotape, called "Consumer Portraits," that shows the people represented by the eight VALS 2 groups. The VALS 2 information packet also included snapshots—written profiles of eight archetypal consumers. Here are four examples to illustrate how the groups' attitude differences translate into differences in tastes and behavior.

### ACTUALIZER SNAPSHOT: MICHAEL AND SANDY
Michael, 48, is the chief financial officer of an art supply distribution company. He has a master's degree in finance and is married to Sandy, 46, his second wife. They have one

child, Jennifer, 18, who just entered college. Sandy is a lawyer, specializing in adoption and family law. Sandy and Michael take their careers seriously and feel good about their success. Michael is expecting a promotion to treasurer of the parent company. The promotion will probably mean spending a year in London, something they have always wanted to do. Sandy plans to use the year off from her law practice to write a handbook for adoptive parents on the legal aspects of the adoption process.

Michael and Sandy feel they have a full life. Michael volunteers at the local museum, and Sandy has raised funds for a congressional candidate whom she believes combines a conservative fiscal philosophy with an enlightened social outlook. Michael and Sandy believe that most elected official take narrow, backward positions on issues like abortion and homosexuality owing to ignorance and fear.

Sandy and Michael have a special interest in wines. She has taken courses on wine, and he has built a cellar in the basement. They belong to a wine society and attend biweekly tastings. Michael and Sandy do a good deal of weekend traveling and try to get to France every other year for a combined vacation study trip through the wine country. Their interest in wine complements a love of fine food and restaurants. They have an impressive collection of cookbooks and cooking videotapes, and they frequently use a small television and VCR in the kitchen for cooking lessons. For Michael and Sandy, socializing with friends is an important part of their lives. They frequently invite friends to their home—close friends for spur-of-the-moment casual dinners and a wider circle for parties that are known for their creative themes and exquisite food. To balance their gourmet dining habits, Michael lunches on yogurt and fruit and tries to keep in shape by belonging to a gym near the office and working out or running at least three times a week.

Michael and Sandy love jazz and classical music. They enjoy reading—both fiction and nonfiction—and they subscribe to a variety of publications such as *The Wall Street Journal, Architectural Digest, Smithsonian, Food & Wine* and *The Atlantic*. They are sophisticated shoppers who think carefully about what they buy, such as Michael's Swiss watch and Italian suits. Together, Michael and Sandy have furnished their home with country antiques and watercolors. In their activities and their possessions, as Michael puts it, "we believe in quality, we pay attention to aesthetics, and we look for opportunities to expose ourselves to new ideas."

## FULFILLED SNAPSHOT: JOAN AND BOB

Joan is 55 years old and has been married to Bob, 58, for 30 years. They met in college. Bob finished his bachelor's degree in business and went on to develop a career with a large construction company, where he is now vice president and general manager. Joan and Bob have two children, Jeannie and David. Jeannie is 23 and about to complete her nursing degree. David is 27, married, and working as a landscape architect. Now that the children are grown and on their own, Joan has retired from her 27-year career with a small bank.

Joan and Bob live a quiet, stable life that centers around home, church, and personal interests. Joan and Bob take pride in their home in which they've lived for more than 20 years. The house is large and eclectically furnished. Bob likes antiques, oriental rugs, and landscapes; Joan prefers contemporary furniture and abstract sculpture. Joan has supervised the integration of these elements into an attractive and comfortable mix. Both Joan and Bob are avid readers. Bob prefers historical novels and business-oriented best sellers. Joan prefers biographies and travel writing. They both enjoy classical music and invested recently in a new stereo system, including a compact disc player. Although neither watches much television, they rarely miss "60 Minutes." Bob sometimes watches "Face the Nation," and Joan usually turns on the network news before bed.

Joan and Bob attend neighborhood church services at least once a month. Although neither talks much about religion, both have strong personal beliefs. They look to the church principally as a place where old friends and families can come together. Having lived in the same neighborhood for so many years, they value the church as an important and enduring part of the community.

Joan and Bob have thought carefully about their life decisions. In Joan's words, "We've stood up for what we believe in—even when it's not so popular—although we're generally pretty conservative." They take their responsibilities seriously; voting is a good example. Joan and Bob always take time to find out where candidates stand on the issues, and they vote accordingly.

Joan and Bob take good care of themselves. They eat well, buy good clothes, and select things that will last. In Bob's words, "They cost a little more but make good sense in the long run." Although they go out only occasionally, they enjoy eating in a favorite French restaurant on special occasions. Their kitchen is well supplied with top-quality utensils and appliances, including a large food processor, a juicer, and a yogurt maker. Bob and Joan both enjoy wine with dinner, which Bob selects at a local specialty shop. They tend to stay home on weekends, working in the garden, reading, or just "puttering around the house."

They own a new Mercury Sable and a ten-year-old Volvo station wagon, both of which are immaculately clean and perfectly maintained. They bought the new car for a long-planned extended vacation trip—a four-week drive through the Southwest to visit Indian ruins and indulge Joan's growing interest in photography. They especially enjoyed the many hours of driving because it gave them an opportunity to talk and reminisce about their life together. As Bob says, "We've built a comfortable life for ourselves. We've worked hard at maintaining a good marriage and raising a family, and we've made a real contribution to our community. All in all, we can feel very satisfied with what we've done."

## STRIVER SNAPSHOT: ANITA
Anita is 33. She was divorced seven years ago after two years of marriage. She is employed as a secretary by a paper-box manufacturer and finds her work dull. She hoped for a promotion to office manager shortly after starting with the company eight years ago, but lost hope and interest after another secretary got the position. In Anita's words, "I guess nobody said life was going to be a picnic, although some people do seem to have all the luck." She envies her coworkers' wardrobes and buys a lot of trendy clothes to keep up with them.

Anita just moved into a small apartment in a new suburban singles apartment complex with a pool and other recreational facilities. She has furnished it with colorful framed posters and a new sofa, but still hasn't scraped together enough money to buy the new bedroom set she fell in love with at the local department store. Because the rent is higher here than at her last apartment, she also had to pass up buying a Pontiac Firebird that she really wanted. She is getting by, albeit unhappily, with her five-year-old Chevy Nova.

Anita spends many evenings at home watching television—usually a movie on one of the cable channels or sitcoms like "Who's the Boss" and "Moonlighting." She listens to the rock radio station that's giving away trips to Florida. In the summertime, she sometimes plays softball in a league with friends from the office, finishing the evening over pizza and beer. She has little interest in community issues and doesn't vote, although she considers herself a Democrat since most of her friends are.

Anita would like to quit smoking and lose weight, and plans to join a dieting program. She thinks she may join a spa as soon as her Visa bill is paid off, but regular clothing purchases keep her credit balance high, and she never seems to get caught up. She plays the lottery regularly in the hopes of making it big. "Having more money would make a big difference in my life," she says.

## EXPERIENCER SNAPSHOT: KEVIN
At age 24, Kevin is a single, high school graduate who works in the data processing department of a large computer company. Although he has no career plan, his job pays reasonably well, providing Kevin with more than enough income to cover his portion of the rent on an apartment he shares with a friend from work. The remainder is spent on entertainment, clothing, and socializing.

Kevin is rarely home. He has several favorite clubs where he and his friends go to hear live music, and he goes to rock concerts frequently. He eats out almost every night, often trying new restaurants and new foods. Franchised fast-food outlets are favorites, as well as Chinese and Mexican restaurants. Kevin has a favorite bar, famed locally for its selection of more than 100 beers from around the world. Kevin and his friends pride themselves on having tasted and ranked every one.

Kevin thinks of himself as an adventurer. He has taken several Club Med vacations because he likes the idea of going somewhere exotic. Last year, he took a two-week bicycle trip with five of his friends. He enjoys sports and often plays racquetball on the weekends (he owns a graphite racquet) or joins friends for a casual game of basketball. He plays on the company volleyball team, which last year placed second in an amateur league competition. Kevin's new sailboard has replaced his ten-speed bicycle as his current prized possession. He windsurfs almost every weekend at a lake about 30 minutes from his home. When Kevin is home in the evening, he likes to watch television—adventure shows like "Miami Vice" are favorites.

Although not much of a reader, Kevin picks up magazines like *Bicycling, Rolling Stone,* and *Omni* at the newsstand. Although he feels no strong political affiliation, his political opinions tend to be conservative, combined with a resentment of taxes and government intrusion on individual rights.

Kevin drives a two-year-old Mazda RX7, which he has equipped with special alloy wheels and an elaborate stereo system. Kevin is proud of his appearance. He looks healthy and athletic, and dresses in casual but carefully selected clothes. He buys designer jeans, trendy sweaters and shirts, and high-quality athletic gear. His apartment is sparsely furnished. Although he intends to hang up a few posters or pictures, he never seems to get around to it.

Kevin doesn't spend much time worrying about the future. "No way am I ready to settle down," he says. "I make a decent living, and when I get off from work I want to have fun!"

## How to Use the Typology

Like the original VALS, VALS 2 attempts to provide a clearer understanding of consumer segments for targeted marketing. Although it is perhaps most effective in developing and targeting advertising, it also has been used in new product development, sales and promotions, strategic planning, and human resources.

In any application, the first problem is how to identify the VALS groups that are heavy, medium, light, and nonusers of the brand or category in question. To do this, a subscriber might administer the VALS 2 questionnaire to a sample of consumers. If that's not possible, another way to break down use by VALS 2 types is to look at syndicated survey data from Simmons or Mediamark. Both surveys categorize the users of thousands of products by VALS 2 types. For example, if an analgesic company was trying to apply the VALS 2 typology, the result might look something like this:

*Figure 5-3  The Ibuprofen Market by Brand*

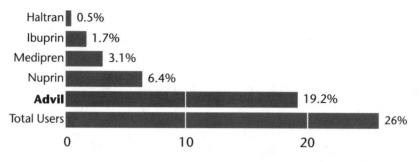

Source: *SRI International*

According to syndicated data, Advil is the market leader in the ibuprofen category, with 19.2 percent of the market. Nuprin is a distant second, with a 6.4 percent market share. Among the total adult population, about 26 percent use any ibuprofen at all.

If the maker of Nuprin was trying to increase market share, the next step would be to examine the relative VALS 2 breakdowns for users of each brand. The breakdowns might look something like this:

*Figure 5-4  Nuprin Users by VALS 2 Type*

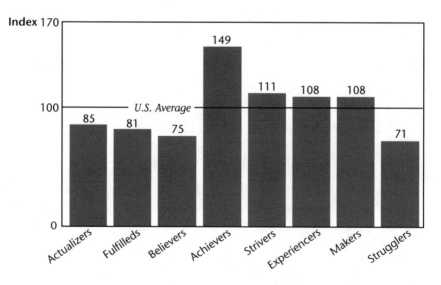

Source: *SRI International*

*Figure 5-5  Advil Users by VALS 2 Type*

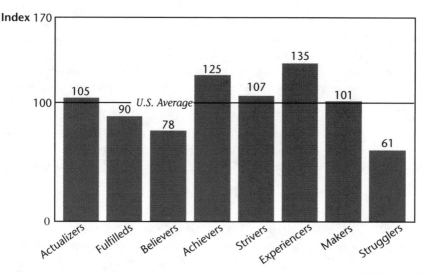

*Source: SRI International*

The graphs show that Experiencers, Achievers, and Strivers are most likely to use Advil, while Achievers, Strivers, Experiencers, and Makers are likely users of Nuprin. One interesting point is that Nuprin has a lower usage index among Actualizers and Experiencers than does Advil. (An index of 100 represents average usage.) To make any type of decision, the manufacturer now needs to know which VALS 2 types account for the greatest volume of ibuprofen usage.

*Figure 5-6  Headache Remedies and Pain Relivers: Use Levels for Two VALS 2 Types*

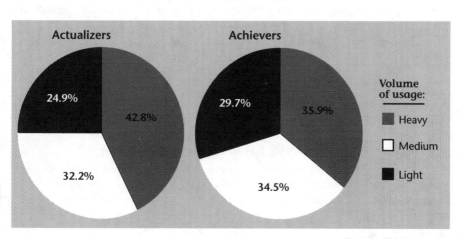

*Source: SRI International*

Since nearly 43 percent of Actualizers are heavy users of pain relievers, the makers of Nuprin should be curious why their brand shows below-average usage in this group. Another glaring question is why the Achievers are 49 percent more likely than average to be users of the brand, but less likely to be heavy users of the category. These two facts suggest that something about Nuprin attracts more Achievers, and something about Advil attracts more Actualizers. Nuprin might want to analyze its presentation in light of the competition to find out where the flaws are and alter its approach to tap into the potential of the Actualizer group.

But how can agencies or manufacturers determine what it is in their presentation that works or fails with various groups? To make it easier for subscribers, the VALS staff has come up with lists of words and images that are most likely to appeal to each VALS 2 group.

## Words and Images

What makes one word or image attract or please, and another word or image offend? The answer has much to do with the attitudinal orientation of the individual. One established theory in advertising copy research is that the most effective advertising talks to the target audience directly, using the words and images with the greatest relevance for the people in that audience. This might mean using words or images that reflect the target's self-image or even their aspirations. That's where it gets tricky. Common sense and intuition can determine some of the most obvious approaches, but the subtle turn-offs are often a matter of nuance.

Go back to the snapshots of VALS 2 types. A jeans manufacturer attempting to target Michael and Sandy would obviously not show a group of rowdy people in a bar playing pool and drinking beer. The advertiser might, however, show people in a tasteful wine bar sampling an especially interesting new varietal. That's common sense. What would be harder to determine is exactly the tone the ad should have and what words to use. This is where the VALS 2 words and images become useful. Compare the words and images that work for Actualizers, Fulfilleds, and Experiencers.

### Actualizers

| WORDS | TUNE-INS | TURN-OFFS |
|---|---|---|
| variety | people in charge | helplessness |
| excellence | happy, active, successful people | poor quality |
| change | responsible citizens | inferior workmanship |
| intelligent | non-traditional roles | formalized religion |
| personal freedom | people who are involved | ultra-conservative |
| environmentally responsible | global issues | establishment |

## Fulfilleds

| WORDS | TUNE-INS | TURN-OFFS |
| --- | --- | --- |
| confident | mature, married couples | anything radical |
| responsible | grown children/grandchildren | extreme extroverts |
| organized | intimate circles of friends | loud "salesman" types |
| intelligent | successful career men | heavy metal or rock music |
| reliable | authority figures | uninformed people |
| reasonable | civic situations | narrow-mindedness |

## Experiencers

| WORDS | TUNE-INS | TURN-OFFS |
| --- | --- | --- |
| excitement | exotic | ill health |
| sense/sensual | pushing to the limit | inactivity |
| new | hedonism | formalized religion |
| innovative | self-discovery | overweight people |
| successful | the environment | boring conventional people |
| intelligent | active sports | and situations |

This is only a partial list, but it illustrates the common threads that can be used to weave a common appeal to different groups. The groups above, though very different, all react positively to the word "intelligent." On the other hand, the images of civic situations that would appeal to the Fulfilleds might also work with the Actualizers, but would be a definite turn-off to Experiencers.

An advantage of the VALS 2 system is that it is designed to be more flexible to make targeting different groups easier. The segments are interconnected, and neighboring types have similar characteristics that can be combined in varying ways to suit particular marketing purposes. Instead of being limited to two or three predefined combinations, marketers can target two or more segments at a time by creating any of more than a dozen combined groups, depending on the marketing objectives. In other words, the structure of VALS 2 makes it easier to capitalize on commonalities between two or more seemingly different groups.

Actualizers and Fulfilleds are one possible combination. They share a heightened social awareness and are more concerned and active where social or environmental issues are concerned. Both are also intellectually curious, well informed about world events, and are the most tolerant of other races and political points of view. They make up the prime market for natural foods, health foods, media reporting on public affairs and the arts, educational TV, and products deemed less likely to harm the environment.

Actualizers and Experiencers are also a good combination. They are both innovative, impulsive, and experimental, thriving on risk, variety, and the unpredictable. They try to make their lives exciting and express their individuality whenever they can. They are the prime target for trend-setting, innovative products. They are also likely to be a good market for new restaurants, new foods, new sporty cars, imported beer, and anything new the entertainment industry can offer—from movies to popular music.

Other possible combinations include: Fulfilleds and Believers, Achievers and Strivers, Experiencers and Makers, and Believers and Strugglers.

## What You Get

The VALS program costs between $12,500 and $50,000 a year, depending on the size of the firm subscribing to the service. A giant packaged-goods company like Procter & Gamble would be charged the highest rate, while a smaller company would pay considerably less. For their money, subscribers are licensed to administer the VALS 2 questionnaire. SRI analyzes the data and VALS-types the respondents. The subscription also includes special industry reports, consumer surveys, and consulting services. The SRI Leading EDGE reports keep tabs on emerging issues like aging and environmentalism, all related back to the VALS 2 framework.

As shown earlier, VALS 2 groups coupled with syndicated survey data from Mediamark and Simmons can show businesses the VALS types of product and media users; but firms need to subscribe to those databases to gain access to the information. The National Family Opinion and NPD Group consumer panels are also typed by VALS 2 groups.

VALS 2, like its predecessor, is also linked to several geodemographic databases. (See Chapter 13 for more on geodemographic systems.) This allows a business to identify the VALS 2 groups that predominate in neighborhoods around the country. Claritas' PRIZM, for example, can find zip codes with the highest proportions of residents who fit the "Blue Blood Estate" lifestyle. With VALS 2, a marketer can then determine that Actualizers, Fulfilleds, and Achievers are the main VALS 2 types living in these zip codes.

## A Case Study

A psychographic segmentation system like VALS 2 is probably at its most powerful when used to identify the images and messages that appeal to targeted consumers. Most researchers would also agree that it provides the most insights for high-involvement products such as clothes and automobiles. Another product that engages the consumer's ego is beer. Della Femina, McNamee WCRS Inc. based a successful 1990 ad campaign for Pittsburgh Brewing Company on insights gained from VALS 2.

The Pittsburgh Brewing Co. asked Della Femina to find out why sales of its main brand, Iron City beer, were declining, and to create an advertising and promotion package that would stimulate sales. John Mather, director of market research, said the brand had been a fixture in Pittsburgh for more than 100 years. The first problem was to identify what was going on in the marketplace. Quarterly tracking indicated that the brand was losing sales in two areas. The core market was growing older and consequently drinking less beer. More alarming, many younger male beer drinkers were completely bypassing the brand in favor of newer brands. "We knew demographically the situation of these two key markets, but because beer drinking is tied to a lot of emotion and imagery, we needed some help there."

Mather, a longtime user and supporter of the original VALS and now VALS 2, wanted to find out which VALS 2 types consumed the brand. He used Simmons data linked to VALS types and found out that he was dealing with Makers, Believers, Strivers, and Experiencers. "Makers were the dyed-in-the wool consumers of the brand, along with their parents, Believers," Mather says. "Then there were the Strivers, who were abandoning the beer, and the Experiencers, another very big younger market, who were totally rejecting it." Simmons data also revealed that the Experiencers had the highest volume of total beer consumption, followed by the Strivers. Mather said it was clear that the brand needed to do something to find out why it was failing to attract the younger Strivers and Experiencers.

"We went out and did some in-depth focus groups prescreening for VALS types and beer consumption," Mather says. "We explored their beer drinking in terms of when, where, and how much they consumed, and the reasons. Then we looked at a lot of the imagery of the various beer brands using sorting techniques." The picture sort is a projective technique that has been altered for commercial research (see Chapter 7). It consists of a deck of photos showing pictures of different types of people and is designed to pinpoint subjects' self-images in relation to their images of the brand. Subjects choose pictures of the people whom they think use the brand, along with pictures of people most similar to themselves.

Mather also looked at semantic stimuli—language and semantic cues—associated with VALS types. "The whole idea was to try to form an image for the beer that was more in line with the younger segments," Mather explains. "The Striver is status-oriented, so we looked at the beer in terms of its status connotations. The Experiencer is looking for a new experience and the promise of taste and change, so we looked at the beer in terms of that."

Another image became a crucial consideration — the evolving image of Pittsburgh in the minds of younger consumers. Iron City's more than 100 years of brand equity in the Pittsburgh market turned out to be both a problem as well as a potential advantage. Because of its long legacy, Iron City's brand image was closely associated with the old Pittsburgh of smokestacks, sweat, and steel workers — a Pittsburgh with which younger drinkers no longer identified. Focus groups revealed that the younger Pittsburgians still took pride in Pittsburgh, but it was a different city for them. It had bounced back with a revitalized economy and an influx of new businesses. It wasn't all smokestacks and steel mills anymore. It still worked hard, but it knew how to have a good time. "They were saying, 'Like the city, we have new lives now. We're going forward, but we'll never forget our past,'" Mather says.

Della Femina now faced the problem of altering Iron City's image to fit the new Pittsburgh, without turning off the dyed-in-the-wool Iron City customers—the older Makers and Believers. Mather's team recognized that the existing image of Iron City could be a plus. They decided to retain the elements of hard work and civic pride that were already part of the Iron City image, while turning up the fun and excitement factors.

The resulting ads juxtapose images of old Pittsburgh with familiar live images of the new vibrant city. Mixed in are shots of young Striver and Experiencer types working hard at having fun. The music is, "Working in a Coal Mine," with new words "working on a cold iron." "We incorporated some of the old and the new, then we superimposed men having fun, playing baseball and basketball, water skiing, and partying. It connotes a hard-working and hard-playing city."

The ads have run on the radio stations that Experiencers and Strivers listen to, and on the television stations and programs they are most likely to see. In the first month of the campaign, sales of Iron City rose 26 percent, and initial tracking suggested that increased consumption among the younger Striver group is a big reason for the improvement. Mather says he can't tell conclusively yet whether sales among Experiencers are picking up, but he believes the ads are reaching their targets.

VALS 2 helped Della Femina get a picture of the market segments the brand was missing. The typology, combined with other techniques, also provided the insight into Experiencers and Strivers that allowed the agency to communicate with them. "It gave us the clues we needed to go in there and try to relate to these people," Mather says.

Mather warns other researchers however, that VALS 2, like any research tool, requires some commitment from the user. "How effective it is depends on the individual user. You've got to make at least a two-year commitment to try to understand these people, the groups, and their exposure." He also says that switching from the original VALS to VALS 2 has taken some adjustment. "I used the original for ten years. It was part of my life. " he says. "But I'm becoming very familiar with this one now, and I think it really does move closer to the actual motivation for purchasing. With high-imagery goods, like a beer, having the self-identity aspect of VALS 2 gives you a very close linkage."

# Part III

# Applying Psychographics

# 6 *Psychographics in Advertising*

*Psychographics is a way of getting to know a customer on a one-to-one basis. You move someone from the next desk to the next room and you can still talk to them, but you lose a little bit. You move them into the next building and you can still call them on the phone, but you lose a little bit more. Today, it's hard to understand customers because we're just so far removed. We don't have enough people to sit down with them one-to-one, so instead, we have to look for things to bridge that distance.*

*—John Mather*
*Director of Marketing Research, Della Femina*

K NOWING CUSTOMERS' PSYCHOGRAPHICS is perhaps the most essential part of effectively communicating with them. Not surprisingly then, the most sophisticated psychographic research is being done for major advertisers. Psychographics is an essential part of advertising research, because it shows advertising creatives at whom to direct their words and images and identifies the messages that are most likely to appeal. Combined with media information, psychographics can help media managers place ads in the programs or publications that reach the target audience most efficiently.

The scope of psychographics is perhaps broadest in the advertising field. For advertising purposes, psychographic research has to encompass not only all the variables that influence the types of products or services consumers buy, but also the factors that affect the success of the communication process. Both purchasing and communicating are extremely complex processes, as changeable and multilayered as the human beings at the center of it all.

Free will, psychological, social, and economic factors combine to complicate the problem of understanding consumer behavior. A person might decide to buy a certain product as a direct function of individual needs, values, or lifestyles. These aspects can also determine the specific product benefits the person wants from the goods and services he or she buys. The added uncertainties of the communication process—

whether or not an individual pays attention to the advertising message—also pivot on personal attitudes, values, and needs.

Advertising researchers face a paradox when doing psychographic research. The work must be broad enough to include all this information, but it must also be specific enough to uncover unique attitudes, emotions, and images involving the specific product or brand. Most advertising research executives say, therefore, that the best psychographic insights come from using a combination of quantitative and qualitative research. Some use qualitative techniques such as focus groups and in-depth interviews to uncover attitudes about the product, then turn to broader-based survey data, such as segmentations, to back up the insights gained during qualitative work. Others gain broader insights first, then narrow the focus to the product category, then to the brand level.

Whether qualitative or quantitative research is used, and in what order, is less important than whether the research process covers all pertinent areas. A summary of what should be included in advertising psychographic research was published by Ruth Ziff, an early proponent of psychographics, who had a long and distinguished career in advertising.

*Figure 6-1  Components of Psychographics in Advertising*

| Psychographic Variables | Product/Brand Data | Individual Data |
|---|---|---|
| **Personality Variables** | **Product Usage**<br>Frequency, Occasion | **Demographics**<br>Personal, Family |
| **Life Style Variables**<br>Personal, Family | | |
| **Needs/Values**<br>Functional, Aesthetic<br>Emotional, Situational<br>Self Image | **Brand Usage**<br>Frequency, Occasion | **Media Data** |
| **Benefits Desired**<br>Functional, Aesthetic<br>Emotional | **Brand Perceptions** | |

*Source:  Ruth Ziff,* Lifestyles and Psychographics, *1974*

# Research in an Age of Cost Cuts

When psychographic segmentation first appeared in the 1970s, the advertising industry was its first and most enthusiastic proponent. But in this world where success or failure often pivots on the originality of an idea, hot new research tools come and go as quickly as waves disappear on a shore. Much like a designer's ongoing pursuit of the next fashion sensation, the advertising researcher is always on the lookout for the newest "magic yardstick" that will provide exclusive insights into customers. Large-scale psychographic segmentation schemes were once embraced as the latest essential marketing tool. Although the newness has faded and some have abandoned such broad inquiries as too expensive, psychographics in various forms is still the core of much advertising research.

Lifestyle studies may have faded into the background in favor of "newer" or sexier techniques. But this is the nature of the beast. For the advertising industry, the constant search for the state of the art is a matter of survival. It's more important than ever to be on the leading edge, or at least to appear closer to the edge than the next agency. At this writing, total advertising expenditures were still rising—amounting to $130.6 billion in 1990. Increasingly, however, major advertisers are asking for proof that those monies are not being wasted.

Going into the 1990s, corporations are less willing to devote vast portions of their hard-won resources to advertising, the efficacy of which many view with skepticism. Major advertisers are consolidating their accounts into one or two agencies instead of several; they want more accountability and they want more efficient advertising for less money. This has resulted in tough times for advertising, especially for anyone involved in research. Among the $2.4 billion market research industry in general, overall revenue growth stagnated after 1989. For advertising agencies, the picture has been even bleaker. The American Association of Advertising Agencies reports that pretax profit margins fell 38 percent at larger agencies (with annual income of $13.5 million or more) between 1978 and 1988.

Agencies and research firms have responded by slashing costs, all too often by decimating their research departments. Research staffs and budgets at agencies like J. Walter Thompson and packaged-foods giants like Pillsbury have been cut by up to 50 percent, according to the trade newsletter *Inside Research.* In the wake of these research purges, many agencies find themselves crippled—incapable of conducting the broad quantitative research they once did. Perhaps some of what has been cut was unnecessary fat, but there seems little doubt that cuts have resulted in research that is somewhat simpler, quicker, and perhaps dirtier.

All across the advertising industry, research executives report that psychographic segmentation studies are being done less often. Many cite expense as the reason: it costs anywhere from $50,000 to $150,000 or more to do a reliable quantitative study of consumers' attitudes, interests, and opinions. Others say that they no longer use broad psychographic studies because they can get more useful psychographic insights through other means. For example, scanner sales tracking data make it easier to learn who buys what and in what quantities. Some agencies combine scanner data with small-scale psychological probes to zero in on the psychographics of actual users of the product or category. In the next chapter, we'll discuss some of the other means being used to gain psychographic insights, including redesigned projective techniques and new computerized emotional probes.

The first half of this chapter outlines four different types of broader-based segmentations used at several major agencies. The latter half of the chapter focuses on the longest-running major quantitative psychographic study from an advertising agency, DDB Needham's Life Style Study. Several agencies have psychographic segmentation schemes that they use in international marketing—most notably Backer Spielvogel Bates' Global Scan and Young & Rubicam's Cross Cultural Consumer Characterization. These systems are discussed in Chapter 8.

DDB Needham's Life Style Study is discussed in detail because it may be the best example of what is meant by a classic, broad-based psychographic study. First, though, let's examine two attitude segmentations: N.W. Ayer's study of the baby boom and Grey's exploration of mainstream America.

## Diversity Among Baby Boomers

In 1986, N.W. Ayer released a psychographic study of baby boomers, 25-to-44 -year-old adults. The study was done to offer greater insight into a group that many marketers were treating as attitudinally homogeneous. Ayer's segmentation identified four distinctly different cliques within this commercially influential generation, known as "The Power Group":

• **Satisfied Selves**—optimistic, experiential, achievement-oriented. They are well-educated, well-paid professionals and managers. Very positive self-image. Keenly optimistic about life and themselves. Innovative, take risks and travel frequently, both for business and pleasure. Leaders of change. Excellent targets for new ideas and technology.

• **Contented Traditionalists**—home-oriented, socially very conservative. Also self-assured, but personally and socially conservative. Because of their strong traditional values, they are most resistant to change and wish "women's lib" had never started. Strongly endorse "Buy American" because it is familiar to them.

• **Worried Traditionalists**—anticipate disaster, traditional values. View the world as a terrifying place. If there is anything to worry about—keeping their jobs, being mugged, or having a satisfactory relationship with their spouse—they are more likely than any other group to show concern. Very poorly defined self-image. Tend to use brands as a way of communicating who they are and to achieve status. Emulators of change. They don't lead, but once they see a fashion they are quick to copy.

• **60s in the 80s**—aimless, unfulfilled, no direction in life. They are the flower children who never left the 1960s. They never seem to find the job they want and have no apparent goals.

"The Power Group" study surveyed a representative sample of 600 Americans aged 25 to 44. The 700-item questionnaire took about 90 minutes to complete and dealt with attitudes toward life, personal relationships, self-image, media habits, as well as purchase usage for 70 categories and hundreds of brands.

Ayer researchers discovered a wide range of behavioral differences and product preferences within the baby-boom group. The types of headache remedies used by Worried Traditionalists were different from those used by Satisfied Selves. The Satisfied Selves watched upscale 'in' programs, while the Worried Traditionalists leaned toward blood-and-guts cop shows.

Marketers who understand the attitudinal differences within "The Power Group" can avoid painful pitfalls, says Fred Posner, Ayer executive vice president. "When Gary Hart was campaigning, he believed that the baby boomers were politically nonaligned," Posner says. "In reality, they are more conservative and Republican than the total U.S. population; they helped elect Reagan."

"Similarly, marketers who pursue the 'Yuppie' market are chasing shadows. They're a marketing myth and probably represent at best only 4 percent of the U.S. population," Posner says.

Baby boomers comprise 33 percent of the total U.S. population and about 50 percent of all adults. Because of their sheer numbers, this generation will affect what goods are produced and what form they take well into the next century. But viewing them as one entity is a serious mistake. "There is no one baby-boomer group with one set of goals," Posner says. Satisfied Selves like to go out and mix, drink and travel, while Worried Traditionalists rarely go out and prefer to entertain at home. Satisfied Selves are more open to new products, while Traditionalists are more likely to be brand loyal. The study has formed the core of many of the advertising strategies used by Ayer's clients today.

## Grey Studies Grownups

Grey Advertising, one of the originators of psychographic research, still maintains a large consumer research operation. The agency does regular broad-based surveys focusing on large-scale societal issues. In 1986, the agency identified two segments in the 21-to-50 age bracket: UltraConsumers and Traditional Consumers. In 1988, a Grey study found three consumer groups in the 50-plus bracket: MasterConsumers, Maintainers, and Simplifiers. The latest Grey study is called "America's New Grownups." It segments the American mainstream into four groups: Vanguard, Rear Guard, Fledgling, and Old Guard.

Grey began the study "Households of the 1990s: America's New Grownups," in an attempt to fill in the gaps in the advertising industry's understanding of mainstream America. Going into the 1990s, Grey people noted that two types of advertising seemed to dominate the marketplace. On one hand, there were the "bright and trendy" spots aimed at hip consumers, and on the other, were retro ads that looked like scenes from "Father Knows Best" and attempted to play on consumers' increasing interest in home and family relationships. Grey researchers felt sure that the 1950s sitcom view of American life wasn't relevant today and that marketers were confusing values, which remain constant, with attitudes and lifestyles, which are constantly changing. The agency's in-house organ, *Grey Insights*, put it this way: "While a working woman of the 1990s may value marriage and family life just as much as her mother did, her attitude toward herself and her place in the world would be very different from her mom's." The study attempted to segment Mainstream American households by critical life priorities and feelings about coping with time.

Grey researchers administered 90-minute interviews to a sample of 477 American adults (age 18 and older) in major metropolitan areas. The survey was directed at the primary householder, the one who runs the home—buying groceries, planning meals, delegating chores, etc. The sample represented all U.S. households and included single parents, childless career couples, and traditional families.

According to the "Households of the 1990s" study, there are four major attitudinal segments in mainstream America with broadly different ideas about life and the use of time:

• **The Old Guard**—These householders (24 percent of survey, holding 17 percent of the aggregate income) are the oldest, with 44 percent over the age of 65. They enjoy a tranquility that is reminiscent of America in the past and hard to find among the rest of the groups of today.

• **Fledglings**—This is the youngest, smallest, and least affluent segment (19 percent of survey, with 14 percent of income). They are intent on getting their lives going— starting careers, attending school, or trying to have social lives. Generally, they live alone or as single parents and spend most of their energy trying to manage their households on their own. They have yet to acquire the maturity, financial stability, or support structure necessary for well-managed lives.

• **America's New Grownups**—The bulk of households in the survey fall into this group (57 percent of survey with 69 percent of income). There are two distinct attitudinal segments within this group—the **Vanguard** (32 percent) and the **Rear Guard** (25 percent)—which differ mainly in the degree to which they strive to have it all. The Vanguard want even more then the Rear Guard to have time in their lives for spouses, kids, career, friends, intellectual development, hobbies, fun, relaxation, physical fitness, and time to be alone.

America's new grownups are the householders of today. They are devoted to self-fulfillment, but their need for emotional connections with others are increasing. They retain some of the priorities of their younger days—performing well at work, being healthy and fit, and feeling good about themselves; and they still need to feel satisfied with their achievements and lives. But at the same time, they are showing an increasing need for loving relationships with their families and a developing sense of responsibility and recognition of consequences. Since many are new parents, raising well-educated, well-adjusted children is a new priority for them as is maintaining close ties with friends and the community around them. It's not surprising then that 37 percent of this group also report that protecting the environment is a greater priority for them in the 1990s.

As illustrated by this ambitious agenda, this group has a greatly expanded vision of the American Dream. The needs of the self are of equal importance to communal needs. Not only do these people want more out of life than any other group, they take it as a given that they will achieve their goals. While they are under considerable stress, they also say that they are extremely satisfied with their present lives and are optimistic about the future.

Demographically, America's new households run the gamut. While 63 percent are in the household-forming 25-to-44 age group, 27 percent are 45 and older. Three-quarters are employed, and 27 percent earn $50,000 or more. The majority (86 percent) are married, and more than half have children. And some 27 percent are college graduates.

Their varied interests keep them extremely busy, but these people also enjoy their time at home. They spent the 1980s busily pursuing careers and using home as a place to get their mail and catch some sleep. In the 1990s, their homes are becoming the center of their lives—a place where they nurture those increasingly important emotional bonds.

The Vanguard households are the least traditional of all households. They are innovators in products as they are in life. The Rear Guard households are run exclusively by women, while one out of every three Vanguard households is run by a man, most of whom are married with children. Here are some of the attitudes of America's New Grownups:

If they only had the time. Above all, time is the most precious commodity for America's New Grownups. Fully 58 percent say they're on the go from morning until night, and 78 percent claim they never have enough time to get anything done. As a result, these people are under a good deal of stress. They are attempting to find better ways to get more accomplished in the time they have. This creates an enormous potential market for services or products that help them save time.

Grey found five basic strategies that innovative Vanguard households use to make the best of their limited time:

**1. Lightening Up.** They are getting more done by doing less of the trivial menial tasks such as cleaning and cooking. There are few clean-freaks among this group. They don't have time to tackle the dust balls under the bed, especially when the other choices are spending quality time with the kids, having dinner with friends, or working out at the health club. These people have learned the basic rule of setting priorities — never do today what can be put off indefinitely. This attitude also makes them prime targets for products that make dreary chores easier, such as Dustbusters or Spiffits cleaning cloths.

**2. Sharing the Load.** Vanguard individuals take an equitable approach to the household workload. In households with two adult heads, both usually share things like shopping, cleaning, and cooking. Everyone in these families pitches in, and kids learn early on how to cope with tasks like grocery shopping, doing laundry, and making simple meals. These people are also adept at doing two things simultaneously, like riding the exercise bike while reading a magazine or watching the news while fixing dinner. These attitudes suggest that these people would be receptive to products like kids' microwave meals and under-the-counter-mounted television sets.

**3. Getting Smart/Staying Smart.** Vanguard householders are information junkies. They like to know everything they can before they get to a store to make a major purchase. This thirst for knowledge makes them great consumers of media. They read everything from movie and restaurant reviews to consumer reports, so they can make the best informed decisions on which competing product to spend their money. Eighty-nine percent consider themselves smart consumers.

**4. Looking for Shortcuts.** They will try anything that allows them to take care of their needs in simpler, faster ways. This makes them big lovers of convenience products. The majority shop frequently by mail and phone. They also buy well-known brands because they see them as another time-saving tactic that makes shopping easier. Products that help these consumers streamline their lives should continue to do well in the 1990s.

**5.Taking Five.** Whether it's five minutes or five days, these consumers always make room for downtime. Taking a break helps keep them going. Some go on vacation; others go for a manicure or work on their bodies. Many are avid participants in sports, whether it be exercise classes or jogging. Just plain relaxing is also a popular way to revitalize themselves. From hanging around the house, taking a nap, renting a video, soaking in the tub, or taking a sauna—Vanguard individuals know the importance of grabbing a little relaxation whenever possible.

Grey's "Households of the 1990s" survey synthesized the demands of America's New Grownups into two factors—quality and access. The demand for quality can be seen in everything from the rich fabrics and subdued colors of today's clothing and home designs to the fine craftsmanship and classic styling now seen in a wide range of consumer products. Access means that companies selling goods and services should make it as easy as possible for customers to buy. Shopping is no longer a pleasurable leisure activity for many people. Consumers want to do what's necessary as quickly as possible, so they can spend more time doing what they enjoy.

Grey Advertising's specific findings of studies such as the "Households of the 1990s" are for proprietary use only. The general findings, such as those outlined above, are regularly published in *Grey Insights*, which circulates to clients as well as others in the marketing research community. Grey basically does two types of attitudinal studies, says Barbara Feigin, executive vice president. "We study these over-arching issues (50-plus, mainstream market) that affect American marketers and advertisers in general," she says. "The other type of attitudinal segmentation we do all the time is very much customized to specific brands. It helps us understand which sets of people have which sets of product-related wants and needs, emotionally-related wants and needs, or aspirations as they relate to their brand choices." We'll discuss more about these techniques in the next chapter.

## The Cycle of Life—J. Walter Thompson's LifeStages

The LifeStages program at J. Walter Thompson (JWT) is a societal model based on stages of life—single, married, married without children at home, etc. Although the LifeStage segmentation is more demographically than attitudinally based, it is a program that the agency regularly uses to gain further insights into the possible wants and needs of target consumers.

LifeStages was the result of more than two years of research and development work at JWT in the late 1980s. The actual concept of the lifecycle, however, goes back to studies done by rural sociologists in the 1930s. "Life Cycle and Consumer Behavior" was the topic of a major conference at the University of Michigan in 1954. Since then, the lifecycle concept has become increasingly popular with marketing researchers. In developing their theory, JWT researchers conducted an extensive review and analysis of published materials relating to lifestage or lifecyle theory. These included academic studies in several disciplines including psychology, sociology, and cultural anthropology, as well as materials from trade, news, business, and government publications. To put attitudinal flesh on the statistical bones culled from the literature, agency researchers conducted in-depth, one-on-one interviews with 100 people in various locations— New York, Philadelphia, Los Angeles, and Seattle.

Finally, the agency launched a LifeStage Panel, consisting of 2,100 adults making up a representative sample of the U.S. adult population. Data were gathered on their demographics (including 23 lifestage-specific variables) and their psychographics—79 psychological variables, 24 psychographic dimensions, and 22 lifestage-specific attitudinal variables. There were also questions about their attitudes toward products, eating habits, and detailed product/brand and media usage data.

LifeStages is more than a simple chronology of the aging process, says Peter Kim, senior vice president and director of the Consumer Behavior Group at JWT. "There was one fatal flaw in the previous theories—and that was the linking of lifestage with aging," Kim says. "Today, age is no longer indicative of one's lifestage position. This framework allows us to look at large databases and use different composite demographic variables to identify the various lifestages."

In JWT's LifeStages, one's progress down the path of life is demarcated by certain milestone events, such as marriage, the birth of children, separation or divorce, children growing up and leaving, and the death of a spouse. The segments are based primarily on a combination of age, marital status, presence of children, and whether one lives with parents or independently. Various attitudinal similarities occur in these demo-graphically defined segments, says Kim. Although specific study findings are for the proprietary use of clients, the following general outline of the LifeStages model identifies nine demographic and attitudinal segments in the American population:

• **At-Home Singles**—(median age 22) young singles who still live at home with their parents. They are planning for the future and have a strong desire for greater independence. One-third are in school. They have few doubts about their ultimate success and few cares. They lead active, thrill-seeking lives, are fun-loving and highly social. Nearly two-thirds are employed, and because they have few bills, they have a lot of discretionary income. They drink; go to bars, concerts, and movies; buy sporting equipment and casual clothes; and spend more than average on personal-care products. *Magazines: Rolling Stone, Seventeen, GQ, Mademoiselle, Hot Rod, Road & Track, Muscle & Fitness*

• **Starting-Out Singles**—(median age 26) young singles who have left home. They are urban, socially and financially independent, self-reliant, and assertive. They are just starting their own households and taking on responsibility for their own daily needs. They do their own grocery shopping, cooking, cleaning, and bill-paying. That two-thirds of them live with other people might show that they either can't afford, or are fearful of, living completely on their own. *Magazines: GQ, Muscle & Fitness, Shape, Rolling Stone, Vanity Fair, Cycle World*

• **Young Couples**—(median age 29) young, recently married couples with no children. The happiest of the groups, their lives revolve around their careers. They are self-confident and have high self-esteem. Very much in love, they spend excessive amounts on gifts for each other, such as watches, clothes, diamond rings, neckties, wallets, and humorous cards. They differ from the young couples of yesteryear in four key respects: they are older and more affluent, both partners work, and they are likely to retain a youthful, active lifestyle. They seem to be stretching out this period of their lives before jumping into parenthood. They want to be noticed and prefer personalization, change, and novelty in their products. They are leisure-oriented and participate in sports, but

their product preferences also show a shift toward nest-building behavior—buying homes, purchasing power tools, furniture, crystal, and kitchen sinks.
*Magazines: Glamour, Cosmopolitan, Car & Driver, Field & Stream, Country Living*

• **Young Parents**—(median age 32) married parents whose oldest child is a pre-teen. Their purchase behavior is driven by the needs of their children, who are often young and dependent first-borns. Many are facing the stresses and strains of parenthood for the first time, and they want to do it right. This leads them to do whatever is necessary in terms of housing, juggling schedules, and financial sacrifices to make it all work. Because most are two-paycheck families, they attempt to accomplish all this under severe time constraints. They are trailblazing new sex roles and making tremendous adjustments along the way, all the while asking, "Did Mom do it this way?"
*Magazines: Parents, Working Mother, Family Handyman, Mother Earth News, Inc.*

• **Single Parents**—(median age 41) unmarried parents raising their own children. This group fits none of the usual stereotypes: only 28 percent are black, and fewer than 20 percent are unwed mothers. The majority have been married before, and their present situation is the result of divorce. They are predominantly female, and most are having a hard time financially. While most households today require two paychecks, they have to struggle with one. This, combined with the stress of shouldering the sole and constant responsibility for dependent children, puts a lot of psychological pressure on this group. They have low self-esteem, are unhappy, and feel that life has treated them unfairly. They are present-oriented, alienated, distrustful, and introspective. They struggle with the loneliness of being single at the same time they must bear the responsibilities of parenthood. As a result, they relish the joys of being a parent and are more absorbed in their children's lives than any other segment. They are big consumers of a host of contradictory products, such as baby food, toys, alcoholic beverages, convenience foods, and designer jeans.
*Magazines: Jet, Essence, Soap Opera Digest, Ebony, New Woman*

• **Mature Singles**—(median age 45) older, never married or separated/divorced singles. They are less self-assured, less career-driven, and less interested in social climbing than many marketers believe. Only 2 percent say they would finish first if life were a race. They feel somewhat alienated as they watch their peers who are married and raising families. They are indifferent to career and not into fashions or trends. Compared with other segments, they are unhappy and pessimistic, have relatively low self-esteem, and feel insecure and left behind. They travel, spend a lot of time out of the house, and they drink rather heavily.
*Magazines: New York, New Yorker, Esquire, Playboy, Road & Track, Gourmet, Discover*

• **Mature Parents**—(median age 47) married parents whose oldest dependent child is a teenager or adult. They still face parental responsibility, but their older children (42 percent have adult children at home) can satisfy many of their own daily needs, such

as preparing meals. This gives this group more time to concentrate on each other and begin to function once again as a couple. They go to movies and restaurants and are less harried, beginning to look forward to the time when their children leave the nest. They still spend heavily on their children, but they are now buying different things: swimming pools for summer vacation, typewriters for college term papers, and minicycles or wristwatches for graduation. Just when many have nearly paid for their homes, they find themselves taking out second mortgages to pay for college.
*Magazines: Workbench, Sports Illustrated, Redbook, Fortune, Outdoor Life*

• **Empty Nesters**—(median age 62) older couples whose children have grown up and left home. They consider this a very happy period of their lives and are surprisingly active. Half are employed, 30 percent are retired, and the rest call themselves homemakers. Most saw their children leave six or more years ago and they've been using their time in meaningful and productive ways. They aren't as rushed as other segments. They spend much of their income on "big-ticket" purchases such as motor homes, organs, movie cameras, Cadillacs, and self-cleaning ovens. They are heavily into investments and are quickly becoming the most important leisure segment.
*Magazines: Changing Times, Prevention, Consumer Digest, Creative Ideas for Living, Reader's Digest*

• **Left-Alone Singles**—(median age 70) seniors who have lost their spouse or are separated or divorced. They face their final years without a partner and must confront the spectre of declining wealth and health. Surprisingly, after an initial period of adjustment, most develop a positive outlook on life. They are healthy, relatively happy, doing all the things they put off for years. They like being in control of their own lives and are better off financially than one might think. They have a disproportionate number of financial investments such as treasury notes, bonds, CDs, and money-market accounts—and their living expenses are fairly modest. They are heavy mail-order buyers.
*Magazines: House Beautiful, Prevention, Ladies' Home Journal, Woman's Day, Sunset*

This model is aggregated into three major groups of New Singles, New Couples, and New Parents:

| NEW SINGLES | NEW COUPLES | NEW PARENTS |
|---|---|---|
| At-Home Singles | Young Couples | Young Parents |
| Starting-Out Singles | Empty Nesters | Mature Parents |
| Mature Singles | | Single Parents |
| Left-Alone Singles | | |

The LifeStages model was devised, Kim says, because the agency wanted a method to determine the effects that demographic shifts might have on consumption. "We found lifestage to be a very important predictor of product usage," Kim says. The aging of the population, the middle-aging of the baby boom, and the maturing of consumers in general will create shifts in the LifeStages groups, which will in turn create a fundamental shift in the needs driving the marketplace.

*Figure 6-2  Lifestage Shifts in the Early 1990's*

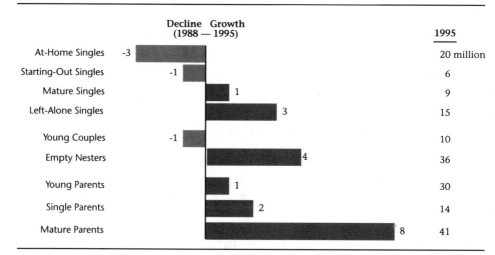

Source: *J. Walter Thompson and the U. S. Bureau of the Census*

For example, Census Bureau projections indicate that between 1988 and 1995, the number of young singles (At-Home and Starting-Out Singles) will decline by about 13 percent, to number 26 million in 1995. At the same time, the older singles market (Mature and Left-Alone Singles) will mushroom by 20 percent, to hit 24 million. In the couples market, the number of Empty Nesters will increase by nearly 13 percent, to 36 million, and the number of Young Couples will shrink.

Other shifts will occur in the teen market, which is currently shrinking but is expected to grow through the 1990s, creating opportunities for smart marketers. There's also good news for single women. By the mid-1990s, for the first time in many years, young men will outnumber the women who are three years younger than themselves (the most popular age-spread for marriage.)

LifeStages literature released by JWT contains little on the attitudinal differences that separate the segments. Other lifecycle theories, however, contend that an age group's outlook on life is shaped by the watershed events they have experienced during their lives. People who grew up during the Depression of the 1930s tend to be more frugal and less willing to use credit. They are now aged 60 and older. When the baby boomers, who grew up during post-WWII prosperity, reach the age when their children are grown and they can once again spend on themselves, their lifelong love of consuming may create a booming market for many new products. Not only that, LifeStages suggests that boomers will redefine and greatly expand the scope of the older market. "Our research indicates that the duration, sequence, and content of American lifestages have changed dramatically in recent years," Kim says.

## Think Tank Prognosticating: Ogilvy & Mather's NEW WAVE

Psychographic inquiries can take forms other than those involving mountains of data manipulated to form segments. Almost every agency has some proprietary way to uncover consumer trends. These studies are psychographic in that they attempt to illuminate how changes in consumers' attitudes influence their lives and their purchasing patterns.

Perhaps one of the most exhaustive trend monitors is Ogilvy & Mather's NEW WAVE™ Program, which is part of the TrendSights division. The NEW WAVE Program is offered as a syndicated service for outside clients as well as other Ogilvy & Mather divisions. It is a state-of-the-art trend-monitoring system that collects information from thousands of sources, analyzes it all, and comes out with a series of regular reports on the American state of mind and how it relates to particular categories or brands. It is a two-part system that includes both environmental scanning and surveying.

NEW WAVE SCAN™ is an extensive scanning service designed to identify the leading edge of consumer change. A network of more than 100 researchers conduct street-level interviews with both consumers and retailers twice a year to monitor the social environment, keeping tabs on everything from new flavors of ice cream to window displays on Rodeo Drive.

This elaborate scanning process is designed to find out what is happening in ten areas: publications, professional newsletters/syndicated data sources, international/domestic new products, food innovations, new menu items, new fashions/styles, pop culture, technological innovations, news events/hot topics, and commercial/cultural developments abroad. This takes place in 11 key bellwether markets around the U.S: New York, Los Angeles, San Francisco, Chicago, Kansas City, St. Louis, Houston, Atlanta, Tampa/ St.Petersburg, New Orleans, and most recently, Seattle.

The other part is the NEW WAVE POLL,™ which is done in alternate years. It is a quantitative survey of 1,000 trend-setting consumers who are given a 40-page self-administered questionnaire. To focus on the part of the population most associated with change, only consumers between ages 18 and 49 are interviewed. They are also approached in trend-setting locations that tend to be magnets for the forerunners of change and innovation, such as stores, restaurants, health clubs and college campuses. The NEW WAVE programs screen participants for trend-setting qualities according to Rogers' Consumer Adoption Curve, which identifies Innovators, Early Adopters, Early Majority, Late Majority, and Laggards (see discussion of Roger's theory in Chapter 5). Only those people found to be Innovators, Early Adopters, and Early Majority are surveyed.

"Our focus is on change, understanding change—its dynamics, who is responsible for it, and what kinds of changes are likely to take place," says Fred Elkind, senior vice president and director of the TrendSights division. "We don't want our data clouded up with people who don't influence change."

The survey is intended to quantify the trend insights gained from the SCAN. The questionnaire includes general items on leisure activities and preferences—everything from favorite movie personalities to length of hair, favorite clothes colors, eating, fitness and media, and vacation habits. The survey also gathers information on psychological attributes (inner-/outer-directed, material vs. experiential vs. spiritual orientation) and attitudes toward product/service dimensions (economy vs. quality, classic vs. novelty). Another part of the survey gauges respondents' acceptance or awareness of new emerging developments picked up in the SCAN.

NEW WAVE differs from surveys that compile and try to correlate disconnected lists of lifestyle factors, behaviors, or attitudes, says Elkind. "We're specifying a particular activity, such as exercising or eating at home, and then we're asking why they do that," Elkind explains. Another novel aspect of NEW WAVE is that it asks consumers to give their opinions on future products. "We're allowing consumers to help us and our clients design the products they want for the future," Elkind says. For example, people are asked about their sports and casual wear styling preferences for the 1990s, completing a checklist of the colors, patterns, and fabrics they'd like to have.

The above is not an exhaustive list of broad-based studies used in advertising: many top agencies either refused to reveal anything about their research procedures or, due to proprietary considerations, couched them in such general terms as to render any discussion useless. The following discussion of DDB Needham's LifeStyle Study should be more valuable. This broad-based annual survey, perhaps the best example of classical psychographic research extant, has been the template for many previous studies. The Life Style Study could be considered the standard against which other major psychographic studies should be measured.

## Classical Psychographics: DDB Needham's Life Style Study

Since 1975, DDB Needham Worldwide of Chicago has been keeping track of what Americans think, do, watch, read, and buy. The Life Style Study is interesting not only for its longevity, but because it contains a lot of detailed information that allows it to function in a variety of ways. It provides insights that help define target consumer groups, and it also helps identify consumer trends.

The Life Style Survey, based on an annual survey of 4,000 American adults, is the longest continuously running psychographic study in the country next to the Yankelovich Monitor. It is based on an annual mail-back survey that consists of more than 1,000 questions on activities, interests, opinions, product use, and media behavior. Because of the specificity of the questions and the large survey sample, the Life Style Study is probably the most highly detailed consumer psychographic database currently available.

The brainchild of William Wells, Life Style is a working example of the concept of psychographic research. Wells outlined the concept in "Activities, Interests and Opinions," a 1971 paper coauthored with Douglas Tigert and often cited by researchers in the field (see chapter 2.) Wells began the Life Style Study in 1975, shortly after joining Needham, Harper and Stearns, and it has been a mainstay of the agency's research process ever since.

Perhaps more than any other piece of psychographic research, Life Style illustrates the potential power of the large-scale psychographic study done correctly. It gives the agency ready information on everything from consumers' levels of self-confidence and daring to what brands of cars and ketchup they buy and what television shows they watch.

At one point in the 1970s, Wells used Life Style data to create consumer segmentation. It identified five male types and five female types. Among them were the Militant Mother, the Frustrated Factory Worker, and the Self-Made Businessman. That segmentation scheme, however, was short-lived. "We discarded it because we didn't find it useful, "Wells says. "If you can get four or five quite different sets of segments out of the same set of data depending upon which method you use," he continues, "it's pretty hard to contend that any one of them is the definitive answer." In addition, the segmentation shared the flaw of all such schemes—it split the market into segments that required separate target-marketing plans.

The constancy of the database, however, is its own reward. Life Style has continued because it has proven itself valuable even without the frills of a glitzy segmentation.

## THE HEART OF LIFE STYLE

Life Style's foundation is a 23-page questionnaire with more than 200 activity, interest, and opinion (AIO) statements and 700 questions on product and media use. The survey is administered to a portion of Market Fact's nationally representative consumer panel, people who agree to record their purchases in diaries to supply the research firm with first-hand consumer data. The Life Style questionnaire is given at random to male or female heads of households, who then have one month to complete the survey and send it back. Considering the length of the questionnaire, Life Style has a high return rate of about 80 percent.

Unlike most other agencies, DDB Needham is quite open about the content of its psychographic questionnaire. Because of this willingness to share what works, the Life Style questionnaire has been the basis of several other well-known psychographic studies, such as the original VALS system. "I had quite a few conversations with Arnold Mitchell and was very much aware of what he was doing," Wells says. "We never held our questionnaire to be proprietary. We gave him copies of our questionnaire, and he used many of the items."

The Life Style Study's AIO section asks consumers to rate the degree to which they agree or disagree with a series of statements. A six-point scale is used, with one being "definitely disagree" and six being "definitely agree." Some of the 220 AIO statements are:

*I have more self-confidence than most of my friends.*
*Our family is too heavily in debt today.*
*Having gray hair makes a person feel old.*
*I am careful about what I eat in order to keep my weight under control.*
*I would rather spend a quiet evening at home than go to a party.*
*Physical strength makes a man more of a man.*
*When I see a full ashtray or wastebasket, I want it emptied immediately.*
*I like to be considered a leader.*
*I wish I could leave my present life and do something entirely different.*
*I dread the future.*
*I get more headaches than most people.*
*I feel I am under a great deal of pressure most of the time.*
*Most people are honest.*
*I frequently get indigestion.*
*A woman's place is in the home.*
*I am a homebody.*
*I am in favor of legalized abortions.*
*I like to pay cash for everything I buy.*
*I wish I knew how to relax.*
*I like the look of a large lamp in a picture window.*
*I like to feel attractive to members of the opposite sex.*
*I don't like to take chances.*
*I am good at fixing mechanical things.*
*I like to buy new and different things.*
*I am afraid to fly.*
*I would do better than average in a fistfight.*
*I like to maintain a youthful appearance.*
*I am interested in spices and seasonings.*
*I support efforts to reduce alcohol consumption.*
*I try to eat natural foods most of the time.*
*Religion is an important part of my life.*
*The use of marijuana should be legalized.*
*I have a lot of spare time.*
*My greatest achievements are still ahead of me.*

*People recognize that I buy only the best.*
*My opinions on things don't count very much.*
*I try to avoid foods that are high in fats.*
*I like to be among the first to see a new movie.*
*The Internal Revenue Service treats taxpayers fairly.*

As the above list shows, the statements measure a wide range of attitudes and opinions. They range from statements that measure personality traits like self confidence and risk taking, to those measuring opinions like stance on abortion or the IRS, to those that relate more specifically to product consumption, such as the statements about headaches, indigestion, and sleeping problems.

The second section of the questionnaire asks about activities during the past year. Respondents check one of seven boxes depending on how often they participated in the activity—never to at least once a week. Life Style asks about participation in more than 250 different activities, including buying a state lottery ticket, going to an exercise class, cooking outdoors, taking a vacation, gardening, bicycling, playing tennis, renting a video, making pancakes, buying fast food, going fishing, staying late at work, attending classes, using toll-free numbers, writing a letter to the editor, and recycling waste. This section also includes questions about sex roles, lifestyles, and grocery shopping. The lifestyle question asks the respondent to choose the best lifestyle: traditional marriage, man-woman equal partnership, or another arrangement such as being single or living with friends. The grocery question asks who does the shopping, how often, and at what time of day.

The products and services section delves into the dark recesses of consumers' pantries, querying them on everything from how often they use liquid detergent and dryer-added fabric softener, to their health coverage, use of credit cards, and which meals are personally prepared and eaten at home. The product-use questions ask respondents to check one of seven boxes depending on whether they used the product not at all, less than once a month, and up to more than once a day. Some questions are more specific such as those identifying particular fast-food franchises like Burger King and McDonald's. Others are more general, such as questions about beverages (light beer, dry beer, wine coolers, and bottled water). Some of the other 400 product categories include over-the-counter medications, candy, health and beauty aids, oat bran, liquor, cake mixes, and dog food.

Life Style also asks about ownership of automobiles and major appliances. It collects data on the number of cars per household, whether they were purchased new or used, and the make and model. Another section queries the intention to make any of more than 40 major purchases in the next four years, including buying a home, 35-mm cameras, cellular car phones, kitchen ranges, color TVs, or obtaining a gold credit card, or IRA/Keogh account.

The media section asks about readership of major national newspapers, newspaper sections, and a wide range of monthly and weekly national magazines. It also records frequency of exposure to several radio formats and various television programs and cable channels. The questionnaire ends with a demographic section that includes marital status, employment, income, and presence and number of children living at home.

## WHAT IT CAN DO
Researchers don't need to know all of this information all of the time, but the large number and specificity of the statements on buying habits, appliance ownership, and product-related attitudes is one important difference that makes Life Style more useful than some other psychographic studies. It allows DDB Needham researchers to define target consumers in several ways.

"We can identify heavy, medium, or light users of a product and then cross-tabulate with other questions to gain more insight," Wells explains. "We might then go a step further and designate the target as heavy users of the product who are especially interested in trying new products and have environmental concerns. We can define the group by a certain set of buying patterns and interests, or we can define them psychographically, e.g., people who are particularly concerned about cleanliness."

Though Life Style has more attitude statements that relate to purchasing, care has been taken that they are not so specific as to apply only to one product or category. Martin Horn, a DDB Needham vice president and associate director of the agency's Delta (marketing) Group explains: "We try to have questions that are broad enough to allow us to profile just about anybody. We don't say something like, 'It's important for deodorant soaps to be mild to the skin.' That's an extremely specific item that would be of value to no one except the deodorant-soap category. But the statement, 'I try to maintain a youthful appearance,' is much broader and could be of interest to Betty Crocker, Clorox, or Dial soap, because it says something about who that person is."

When researchers need specific brand information, they can do a recontact study with all or part of the original panel. This is usually done on a client-by-client basis. For example, a detergent manufacturer might want to go back and ask the people who were frequent users of the detergent category about which brands they use and why. That custom information can then be merged with the general information in the study, so the client can tell that nonusers of the brand are more traditional, drive American cars, are more likely to read the *New York Times*, or differ in any number of ways from brand users.

## CONSUMER PROFILES
Three large agencies merged in 1987 to form the $5 million giant, Omnicom Inc. This megamerger of Battan, Barston, Durstine and Osborn (BBDO), Doyle Dane Bernbach, and Needham Harper Worldwide also produced two large international agencies, BBDO and DDB Needham. Despite the corporate realignment, the Life Style Study

continues to provide insights for much of the agency's research. Horn says it is used for two major purposes: profiling target markets and uncovering consumer trends.

DDB Needham uses its research tools to consistently produce effective advertising. The agency's ads for Bud Light and Michelin were recently voted among America's most favorite by *Adweek's Marketing Week*. The ever-popular Spuds McKenzie consistently scores big with viewers as did the Bud Light "Everything Else is Just a Light" spots, which involve different situations playing on the meanings of the word "light." The Michelin ads hit both men and women in the heart: a baby sits in a tire that circles around the globe to the tagline,"Because so much is riding on your tires." These, like any well-conceived ads, work in part because they know who their target audiences are and successfully speak to them with words and images to which they can relate.

Life Style may not have a direct impact on every ad campaign, but DDB Needham executives say that the Life Style Study is one important tool agency creatives use to get to know their target audiences. Needham's proprietary planning strategy is called "Planning for ROI" (relevance, originality, and impact). Horn says there are five questions that must be answered in any advertising strategy: What's the purpose of the advertising? To whom is the advertising addressed? What benefit will be promised and how will it be supported? What personality should the advertising convey? What kind of media are most appropriate for reaching the target?

"There are a number of ways of learning who the target is and what's important in motivating them," explains Horn. "We'll do a variety of research, both qualitative and quantitative, to answer that question, but one important piece of that puzzle is Life Style, which is usually used to complement all the other pieces. The other pieces tend to be much more focused on the target customer. Life Style takes it a step further and adds a dimension to our understanding of who that person is."

Who are these elusive human beings who consume fast food, travel by train, play golf, or use microwaves? What makes them different from nonusers? What do they want? What do they expect from their products and their lives? The following examples of consumer profiles from Life Style show the insights that can be gained from such a large-scale survey of consumers' activities, interests, and opinions. The profiles in this section and the case study that follows are drawn from *Advertising Principles and Practice*, by William Wells, John Burnett, and Sandra Moriarty, and published in 1989 by Prentice-Hall.

## FAST-FOOD USERS
Life Style defines the frequent fast-food user as someone who eats at a fast-food restaurant at least once a week. Demographically, these people are more likely than average to be single and in their 20s. They most often hold blue-collar jobs and live in the South or Midwest. Politically, frequent fast-food users are both somewhat liberal and somewhat politically alienated, measured by questions like, "My opinions on things don't count very much." As for their other habits, fast-food users are more likely

than average to snack between meals, use convenience foods, and buy high-tech electronics. In their media preferences, they are most likely to read *Working Woman*, *Glamour*, and *Penthouse* magazines, and to watch more television than others, both during the day and at night. In attitudes closely related to media, fast-food users are less likely than Americans are in general to think that advertising insults their intelligence, and are more positive toward advertising.

## MICROWAVE-PRODUCT USERS

Microwave ovens are now in about 70 percent of all households. In one recent national survey, women reported that their microwave oven was the household appliance they used the most. In the 1980s, Life Style identified the most frequent users of microwave products. Demographically, they were women of average age, education, and occupations, but they were more likely than average to have children between the ages of 6 and 12 and household incomes over $30,000. As might be expected, they tended to be working women with busy lifestyles. They more frequently agreed with the statement, "Everyone in our family is on the run." They disagreed more often with the statements, "I have a lot of spare time." They had higher-than-average levels of participation in exercise classes and cultural activities such as attending lectures and classical concerts, visiting museums, and going to movies. They also frequently arranged family outings such as picnics, camping trips, and trips to amusement parks. As consumers, they described themselves as impulse buyers, and said they liked to try new products, shopped at convenience stores, and preferred name brands. They weren't likely to be list makers, coupon users, price checkers, or comparison shoppers.

Their responses to food-related items reflected the hectic nature of their lifestyles. They were more likely to agree that "Meal preparation should take as little time as possible." They disagreed that "Baking shows that a woman cares about her family," and "I like to cook." They also preferred single-serving items because different family members often wanted different entrees. They often used their microwaves for defrosting and reheating and sometimes for foods not specifically designed for the microwave oven. Although they were frequently dieting, they kept more snacks around than most women and were less concerned about restricting salt intake or cholesterol.

Their media habits ran more toward reading newspapers and watching television news programs than for women in general. They preferred home and family magazines, prime-time dramas, detective shows, and cable television. They were also extremely positive about advertising: 80 percent claimed that advertising helped them make better buying decisions.

## CABLE-TELEVISION USERS

As network television continues to lose audience to alternative forms of entertainment, there has been growing interest in finding out who is watching what. Life Style identified two types of adults who purchased cable television in the past year. People who subscribe only to basic cable service differ from those who subscribe to premium pay movie channels like HBO and Showtime, although the groups obviously overlap to some extent. Demographically, recent cable purchasers are younger than average and have more children at home. They also tend to work in professional or managerial positions and have at least some college education.

Many have recently purchased homes or plan to in the near future. They also show a greater-than-average inclination to own or plan to buy things like personal computers, video games, microwave ovens, color televisions, and automatic dishwashers. They consider themselves impulse buyers and are game to try new products, but they are also tough consumers. They are more likely than most other people to return unsatisfactory items.

Entertainment is important to these people and they spend more on it than others do. Their higher standard of living allows them to go to more movies and amusement parks, buy more recorded music, and travel more frequently. Swimming and bicycling are favorite activities, as are attending lectures and going to libraries. They are also more mobile than average, saying they are likely to move within five years. Their attitudes toward advertising are more liberal: they aren't as bothered as others by sex and violence on television. As information-oriented consumers, they are more likely to believe ads that show test results comparing the performance of competing products.

## GOLFERS

Who are those guys in the bright pink-and-green plaid pants out there chasing little balls around every weekend? Life Style found that male golfers share characteristics that distinguish them from the rest of the population. Demographically, they are more likely than average to be over the age of 45, college-educated, and to have household incomes of $30,000 or more. They are also more likely to be retired with grown children. Psychologically, they are self-confident and consider themselves leaders. They are an active bunch, participating in other sports as well as in social and cultural activities. They go to dinner parties, sporting events, museums, and libraries more than average.

As consumers, they are more value-conscious and less price-conscious than most men. They rarely pay cash, shop around for the best price, or pay attention to specials. Their views about television and advertising tend to be liberal; they don't have strong feelings about sex and violence on television, ads for alcoholic beverages, or ads directed toward children.

## TRAIN TRAVELERS

Amtrak used the following profile to help understand its customers and better direct its advertising. Users of train travel are defined as people who took at least one trip of 100 miles or more in the past year. Demographically, they are more likely than average to have a college degree and to hold managerial or professional positions. An active bunch, they participate more often than average in exercise classes. They also enjoy cultural and educational activities such as visiting art galleries and museums, attending lectures and concerts, and going to movies. In their media habits, train travelers are more likely than nontrain travelers to read magazines, and less likely to watch television, except for public television. They are also more likely to buy products of companies that support educational television. Train travelers were also found to be very information-oriented consumers—most likely to shop for specials, do price comparisons, and check in *Consumer Reports* when making major purchases.

Marketing analysts suggested a number of approaches that might be effective given this profile: from the attitude items, they believed these consumers would respond to messages that emphasized the "adventurous spirit" and "heritage of railroads," or showed how the scenery unfolds before one's eyes when traveling by train. These people were also found to like exotic, faraway places, so that was offered as another possible theme. The sensation of speed and the opportunity to meet new people were also possible selling points, according to the target's responses to Life Style.

These profiles lend support to the premise that people who share one type of behavior are likely to be similar in other aspects as well. This idea is at the core of all market segmentation schemes. We are what we think, do, and buy. In our role as consumers at least, we are the sum of all these things.

Such profiles are used in a number of ways. DDB Needham researchers write up the profiles and discuss them with agency creatives. Occasionally, actors will be cast as the person portrayed and videotaped to give an even more vivid picture of the target consumer. The profiles also provide information about the general similarities of a target group upon which to base further research. The next step of the microwave users study, for example, might involve smaller-scale qualitative research to delve deeper into the attitudes microwave users have about themselves, meal preparation, or various brands in the category. Further exploration of the self—images of these women might show that some feel guilty about using microwave food products. An interviewer using projective techniques might then discover that some women used a particular brand of microwave food because it had a wholesome image. The competitor might then decide to emphasize the nutritional value of its brand over simplicity of preparation to attract these guilty users.

Life Style has an advantage over general lifestyle segmentation schemes such as VALS, according to DDB Needham executives. While general systems look at attitudes such as principal orientation or status seeking, Life Style gets closer to attitudes that distinguish a precise group of people—users of microwaves, fast food, golfers—from the rest of the population. "They're trying to infer specific behaviors from general attitudes, and that's a very risky proposition, " Horn says. "We're profiling people who exhibit a specific behavior that is important to that category.

"What we do in Life Style, as should be done in all good research," Horn adds, "is to focus only on those items that are going to be most useful in increasing understanding of the consumer. Some items on the questionnaire may be more useful than others for a particular profile. That's the analysts' job, to determine just what those items are."

## SEPARATING THE TRENDS FROM THE FADS

Another major use of Life Style is to identify changes in general consumer attitudes as they evolve. Life Style has been asking nearly the same questions for more than a decade and a half, which gives it a historical perspective. This allows DDB Needham researchers to point out emerging consumer trends early on.

For example, other studies might discover, as Life Style did in 1990, that 41 percent of Americans think people shouldn't chew gum in public. On the surface, this might seem like bad news for gum manufacturers. Life Style, however, shows that it isn't bad news compared with 1978, when 51 percent of Americans said they disapproved of public gum chewing.

The long-term scope of Life Style also helps distinguish fads from trends. Here are a few trends that have been exposed as fads by Life Style (as released to *Advertising Age* in September 1990):

*Trend or fad?* There's been a religious renaissance.
**Truth:** The portion of Americans who say "religion is an important part of my life" has dropped steadily since 1981.

*Trend or Fad?* No one eats breakfast anymore.
**Truth:** The proportion who say they eat breakfast every day has remained a constant 43 percent since 1983.

*Trend or Fad?* A thousand points of light is a reality. Volunteerism is up.
**Truth:** The percent of Americans who volunteered in the past year has increased only modestly since 1975.

*Trend or Fad?* America is fed up with crime and wants tough treatment of lawbreakers.
**Truth:** The proportion of people who believe the police should use whatever force necessary to maintain law and order is down to 60 percent in 1990, from 71 percent in 1975.

*Trend or Fad?* Families rarely eat together anymore.
**Truth:** Three out of four respondents say the whole family usually sits down to dinner together.

## HOW LIFE STYLE IS USED, A CASE STUDY:
### Blood Center of Southeastern Wisconsin

The Blood Center of Southeastern Wisconsin (BCSW) is a major regional blood center that supplies six counties in the southeastern corner of Wisconsin, an area with 2 million people (one-third of the state's population) and 31 hospitals. Finding an adequate number of donors has become a more difficult task for the self-supporting nonprofit organization as the heavy, smokestack industries of the region have declined. Historically, the center got most of its donations by holding mobile blood drives at plants around the region. During the 1970s, 70,000 jobs were lost in the region, and the BCSW had to start shipping in thousands of units of blood to make up for the shortfall. It was forced to rethink its recruiting policy.

Entirely dependent on voluntary donations, the BCSW had to shift from relying on institutions to recruiting individual donors. This meant it had to begin looking at potential donors as a target market. In 1983, a consortium of 15 blood centers, including BCSW, turned to Needham, Harper & Stearns (now DDB Needham) for marketing help. To help the consortium identify exactly who its target market was, the agency added the question, "How often in the past five years have you donated blood?" to the DDB Needham Life Style Study.

As a result of that one question (added to the storehouse of information already included in the study), researchers were able to suggest changes that made the recruiting process much more effective. For starters, they formed a profile of the typical blood donor and identified the major value and lifestyle differences between donors and nondonors.

Blood donors turned out to have a fairly distinctive style of living. They were most frequently between ages 25 and 54, college-educated, had relatively high incomes, and lived in households with children and a working spouse. They were community-minded and active, regularly attending lectures, going to movies, and playing sports. In addition, they were intellectually curious. They preferred reading to watching television, but when they watched, they preferred shows with some social content such as "Lou Grant" or "M*A*S*H." They got their news from newspapers and radio. They were also more likely than nondonors to volunteer their time and money to help charities.

Life Style information painted a portrait of the person to whom the blood center had to appeal. After reviewing the survey results, center researchers decided to implement the following changes:

**1. Retaining Donors:** The center needed to pay more attention to its long lists of past donors to ensure more repeat donations. Although many donors were eligible and willing to donate again, they considered themselves between donations. Since they hadn't heard anything different from the center, they assumed their services weren't needed. To address this, the center started a major retention program. Nurses were trained in social skills so donors would feel more comfortable. Most important, Life Style revealed that donors were heavy users of greeting cards, so the center began

*Figure 6-3  Profile, Likes, and Dislikes of Regular Blood Donors*

**Regular Blood Donors Are:**
More likely to be male
25 to 54 years old
College-educated
Parents
Financially well-off
Charitable
Community-minded
Sociable
Self-confident
Risk-takers
Busy
Politically and socially liberal
Dieters, concerned about weight
Do-it-yourselfers
Impulsive shoppers (females)
Adaptable to social changes

**Regular Blood Donors Are Not:**
Full-time homemakers
Quiet
Insecure
Afraid to take chances
Troubled by change
Tense
Concerned about nutrition
Interested in health foods
Intensely bothered by sex or
    violence on TV
Unwilling to help around the
    house  (males)

**What Donors Like**
Adventure
Cultural events
Movies
Sports
Shopping
Reading the newspaper
M*A*S*H
TV movies and specials
Middle-of-the-road music
Popular music
Alcoholic beverages
Volunteer work
Reading

**What Donors Dislike**
TV news programs
Traditional family roles
Staying at home

*Source: DDB Needham Life Style Study*

sending thank-you notes to donors after a donation to reinforce the feeling that they had performed a valuable public service.

**2. Family Strategies:** Life Style showed that donors were likely to have children living at home, so center marketers began to develop promotional materials that featured children who had survived emergency situations because of ready supplies of blood.

The center also began to hold blood drives at local high schools, at which students, parents, and faculty members became regular donors. These drives soon accounted for 10 percent of all blood collected in the region.

**3. Education:** The center changed its literature from the previous "cutesy" tone written for the general audience to a serious, information-oriented style more appropriate for the well-educated people who made most of the donations. The center also held focus groups to find out the type of information and the type of presentation that would appeal most to donors. Additionally, the center started targeting their literature to institutions likely to contain potential donors, such as law firms, colleges, and accounting firms.

**4. Work and Income Patterns:** Since most donors belonged to two-earner, financially secure households, the center began sending direct-mail promotions to more affluent zip codes. Staff members arranged with smaller companies to allow employees to visit the center on company time. Finally, the center streamlined the donation process and expanded its hours so that busy working couples would find giving blood more convenient.

**5. Media:** Donors' heavy use of newspapers and radio made these media the most effective vehicles for the center ads. Local radio stations and newspapers were persuaded to carry public service messages. Television, however, was not neglected. Donors had high viewership of the show "M*A*S*H," so the center approached actor Alan Alda, one of the show's principle characters, to film donation appeals. Alda agreed, and the resulting spots became unusually effective recruiting appeals.

**6. Leadership:** Donors tended to see themselves as leaders, so the center made this knowledge work for it. It instituted a program that asked previous donors to act as "leaders" to encourage friends and family members to donate blood as well.

As a result of these changes, the BCSW ultimately had so much blood on hand that it was supplying 6,000 units to other centers by the mid-1980s. Its fixed sites had become so successful that they provided nearly two-thirds of all blood collected, a higher percentage than any center in the country. The retention program proved effective, as did the leadership program. One promotion, for example, appealed directly to 1,200 people, but produced more than 2,200 donors because of friends and family members brought in by regular donors. The center was so satisfied with these results that it planned to update its Life Style information every three years, to monitor any potential changes in the target donor audience.

As the case above illustrates, Life Style is based on a large enough sample and contains enough detailed information to make it a useful resource for many different organizations and businesses. The addition of specific questions can increase the application of the Life Style study even further. But Horn is quick to point out that Life Style is only one of a battery of tools DDB Needham uses. "If you were building a house, you wouldn't use just a hammer because that's what you happened to have," Horn says. "Life Style is an important proprietary tool that no one else has. If it makes our house better, then we'll use it. But it's not necessarily the only thing we use."

In the next chapter, we'll look at some of the other tools that are gaining increasing acceptance at both the agency and the corporate level.

# 7 *Motivational Revival: From Mining Emotions to Bonding With Brands*

*Over the years, research really has had to extend itself to cope with the marketing challenges of today. When Grey began doing attitudinal research in the mid-1960s, communications about packaged goods were mostly about product features, function, and performance benefits—innovations that made the product different. The job of advertising was to make it clear to a particular segment of people who were interested in a particular feature and benefit that this company had one and here's how it worked.*

*Today there's much less differentiation between products because of broader manufacturing expertise and marketing know-how. The challenge now is about intangibles: how can we tap into some of the emotional needs and benefits people are looking for? How can we really connect with consumers' aspirations and understand the role a product plays in consumer's lives and psyches that might go beyond exactly what it is and what it does in factual terms? I think research has had to challenge itself to push its own tools and techniques to be able to measure some of these intangibles.*

*— Barbara Feigin*
*Executive Vice President*
*Grey Advertising Inc.*

**M**OTIVATIONAL RESEARCH is still alive and flourishing in the 1990s. The Freudian connotations have largely disappeared—researchers don't advise shaping gas pumps like breasts anymore—but many researchers report that their use of psychological research tools is up today from ten years ago. Major manufacturers and their market researchers are probing consumers' subconscious minds using everything from the one-on-one interviews and projective techniques once favored by Ernest Dichter to new high-tech tools that scientifically pinpoint consumers' emotional responses to brands and advertising.

Many factors combined have contributed to an increasing interest in motivations. Most important are the external and internal economic pressures on the advertising industry and the introduction of new technology. As advertisers look for ways to economize in a tight economy, they want their agencies to deliver better advertising for less money. And in the packaged-goods industry there's better information on actual sales coming from scanner data now, so it's easier to concentrate research efforts on the people who actually use the category or buy the brand.

In an effort to deliver more effective advertising for less money, many advertising agencies have scaled down and streamlined. They've scaled down research departments to reduce costs, and they've streamlined research efforts to focus in on actual customers. Instead of doing wide attitudinal segmentations of the whole population, more are using scanner data and syndicated services to focus on the people who consume most of the brand or category. At this level, psychographic research can concentrate on key consumers—identifying the psychological, attitudinal, and emotional factors that motivate them.

Another reason for the resurgence of motivational research is that the costs of failure are infinitely higher today with a proliferation of products competing for the same consumer dollar. *Gorman's New Product News* reports that there were 13,244 new products introduced in 1990, up 80 percent from 1985. But with more manufacturers extending lines to capture ever-smaller niches of the market, many of these products are indistinguishable from one another. That means advertisers can no longer sell them according to salient product features or innovations. "Sony used to take a patent out on an innovation and advertise the hell out of it," says Paula Drillman, executive vice president of McCann-Erickson." Today if they have it for three weeks before everyone else gets it, they're lucky. Now we're in a constant battle for who can say it *better*."

Products that fail to differentiate themselves from the rest are destined for the scrap heap. Between 70 and 80 percent of all new products fail, largely because the market for them was miscalculated in some key respect. Take Colgate's FAB 1 Shot, for example. Though this combined laundry detergent/fabric softener had potential, it had captured barely 0.1 percent of the market four years after its 1987 launch. Why? Because market tests were done based on the incorrect assumption that families would be the key market for the product. FAB 1 Shot, however, comes in individual packets, making it more appropriate to convenience-seeking single people than to families with huge washloads. That failure meant losses for everyone concerned, especially for market researchers and advertisers. These days, manufacturers are demanding more account-ability and axing researchers or agencies that fail to get results.

At the same time, consumers themselves are becoming more sophisticated. Bombarded by a cacaphony of competing advertising, they often simply tune it out. Today's ads have to grab attention fast. Consumers are also less inclined to take advertising claims at face value and more inclined to read labels for themselves. Faced with the proliferation of more or less similar products, many consumers buy established brands they have known and trusted for years. People make brand choices for a lot of different reasons. They buy the brand that makes them feel most excited, most comfortable, or most secure. In short, they're buying branded products toward which they feel some kind of emotional affinity.

Studies support the theory that people emotionally bond to the brands they buy. One study by Leo Burnett in Chicago found that commercial icons like the Keebler Elves, Charlie the Tuna, and the Pillsbury Doughboy owed their long-lasting appeal to emotions. "They speak to the heart of the category, the emotional truth of why people buy the category in the first place," says Josh McQueen, executive vice president, director of research at Leo Burnett USA. "Emotions are very event-specific, which is extraordinarily important for advertisers." Commercials, after all, can depict the events that trigger emotions.

These days, every major agency recognizes the importance of emotions and has some kind of process for identifying the essences of brands, exploring consumers' emotional ties to them, and designing strategies around them. Focus groups, one-on-one interviews, projective techniques, and ethnography are considered *qualitative* in that they describe rather than measure and are non-statistical procedures dependent on human interpretation.

Some are going one step beyond these traditional qualitative methods. Leo Burnett USA is one of several firms that has developed a way to measure emotions more precisely. Burnett has an interactive computer program called Emotional Lexicon™ that casts the computer in the role of neutral interviewer and quantifies the previously unquantifiable—consumers' emotional responses to brands and advertising. The final part of this chapter will discuss some of the latest tools designed to measure consumer intangibles.

It is beyond the scope of this book, however, to discuss in detail every new method and projective technique and all the variations used by every agency or market research firm. This chapter is only intended as a summary of some of the newest and most familiar qualitative techniques and some of the ways they are being used in market research today.

## Getting Below the Surface: Projective Techniques

Market researchers discovered early on that they couldn't directly ask consumers why they buy and expect to get the truth. Paul Lazarsfeld outlined this problem in a 1935 article called "The Art of Asking Why." About ten years later, Ernest Dichter and others employed the depth approach, using one-on-one interviews and projective techniques borrowed from psychoanalysis in an attempt to get around the consumer's rational mind *(see Chapter 1)*. "Knowing one's own motivations is one of the most difficult things because we try to rationalize," Dichter says. "Most of us try to explain our behavior in an intelligent way, when very often it is not."

Projective techniques can be as useful to the market researcher as they are to the clinical psychologist, although the problems may be somewhat different. In market research, the questions are often about seemingly trivial things like whether a consumer prefers the color of a box of Tide over a box of All. The consumer may not particularly care about the color of the packaging, but he may still prefer a blue box over a yellow one for reasons of which he is unaware. He may be over-cooperative and express the opinions or attitudes he thinks the researcher wants to hear. Or he may withhold negative or socially unacceptable impressions. Projective techniques are designed to circumvent this over-thinking and get at the core of truth below the surface.

Some psychologists use a lake analogy in speaking of the human mind. Everything above the surface of the lake is the conscious, and everything below the surface is the subconscious. At the very bottom, in the lake bed, is the most deeply hidden and inaccessible material that makes up the unconscious.

It is more or less accepted today that consumer psychologists have little to gain by probing the unconscious, because those profound elements of the human psyche probably have little to do with why people buy. Many buying motivations are found at the conscious or pre-conscious level. In other words, the emotions and motivations that pertain to purchase behavior reside just below the surface "where the trout swim," says Dr. Tom Snyder, developer of Emotional Sonar™, an interactive computer program designed to measure these emotions.

Tools like projective techniques get around the defense mechanisms that prevent an individual from accessing the material that resides at the pre-conscious level. Freud defined projection as an ego defense mechanism, similar to repression, regression, and rationalization, that allows an individual to relieve anxiety by attributing its causes to the outside world. Projective techniques allow an individual to project onto ambiguous external stimuli (items that can be interpreted in a variety of ways), their feelings, impulses, and attitudes. The external stimuli may be pictures about which the subject is asked to make up a story or incomplete sentences that the subject is asked to complete. The theory is that, given the ambiguous stimuli, the person will call up material from his own pre-conscious or semi-conscious need/value system. An important point is that the stimuli be ambiguous enough to keep the subject from realizing the purpose of the study, so that his responses are not influenced in any way.

Clinical psychologists have sought insights into the subconscious through projective techniques, such as Rorschach's ink blots, sentence completion, and Thematic Apperception Tests since the 1930s. One famous early projective study was done by Mason

Haire in 1950. Haire wanted to discover what housewives thought about instant coffee and why. First, subjects were asked directly, "Do you use instant coffee?" If they replied "No," they were further asked, "What do you dislike about it?" Most people said they disliked the flavor. Haire, however, believed that this was merely an easy way to dismiss the interviewer, so he devised a way to dig deeper.

Two shopping lists were created with items like, "two loaves of Wonder bread, two potatoes." The lists were identical except that one listed "one pound Maxwell House coffee (drip grind) and the other listed "Nescafé instant coffee." The subjects were asked to characterize the women who prepared each list. The participants revealed the real reason they didn't use instant coffee when they decribed the Nescafé user as lazy, not a good wife, not thrifty, and a poor planner.

Even today, projective techniques that uncover consumers' real perceptions about brands are a critical part of advertising research. Most agencies today have methods to identify consumers' images of the brand being studied, competing brands, and how those images match with the consumer's self image. Researchers today believe that brand names and companies have personalities or public images, and that understanding those relative images is essential. Consumers, they believe, buy goods and services that match their self perceptions. Going a step further, consumers buy products that represent who they *aspire* to be.

## IDENTIFY THE IMAGE: PICTURES AND STORIES

One of the most widely used projective techniques is the Thematic Apperception Test (TAT). The TAT was developed by Harvard psychologist Henry Murray as a way of investigating fantasies. Originally, it consisted of 30 cards showing paintings and drawings. The subject was asked to make up a story about the picture, saying what is happening now, what has just happened, what will happen in the future, and what each character is thinking and feeling.

In marketing research, TAT pictures can be modified to address a specific marketing problem. Most agencies and research firms use a modified TAT, or have developed their own slightly different version of the technique, and use it to understand how consumers view brands or categories.

Grey Advertising has developed a technique similar to the TAT. It's called the Pictured Aspiration Technique (PAT), and it gets at how a brand fits into consumer aspirations or "the me I want to be." Consumers sort a deck of photos on a scaler rating board according to how well the pictures describe their aspirations. In research done for Playtex's 18-hour bra, this technique revealed that the product was out of synch with the aspirations of the potential customers. "They chose a set of pictures that expressed the me they wanted to be as very energetic, slim, youthful, and vigorous," says Barbara Feigin, executive vice president. "But the pictures that they used to express their sense of the product were a little more old-fashioned, a little stouter, less vital, and energetic looking." Out went the "Good News for Full-Fgured Gals" campaign with Jane Russell as spokesperson, and in came the sexier, more fashionable concept, "The Fit That Makes the Fashion."

Batten, Barton Durstine & Osborne Inc. (BBDO) uses a trademarked technique called Photosort™. Consumers express their feelings about brands through a specially developed photo deck showing pictures of different types of people from business executives to college students, says Karen Olshan, executive vice president and director of research services. The subject connects the people with the brands he thinks they might use. A photosort conducted for General Electric found that consumers thought the brand attracted conservative, older business types. To change that image, GE adopted the "Bring Good Things to Life Campaign." Another photosort for Visa found that the card had a wholesome, female, middle-of-the-road image in customers' minds. The "Everywhere You Want to Be" campaign was devised to interest more high-income males. "People desire to be seen as a particular type of person, so they come to use a brand that has a user imagery they subscribe to," says Olshan.

When D'arcy Masius Benton & Bowles Inc. (DMB&B) wanted to find out how teenagers viewed acne for Clearasil, they used a Thematic Apperception Test. The teens supposedly revealed their own feelings about getting a pimple when they described the feelings of a person in a picture who had a blemish. "We got a very clear image that a blemish meant social isolation and differentness and all those things that a teenager fears most of all," says Hank Bernstein, director of consumer information services at DMB&B. The series of commercials developed had a theme of getting back into life as quickly as possible. "We wouldn't have gotten that kind of information if we simply asked them to talk about acne and acne remedies," Bernstein adds.

DMB&B also uses a variation of the TAT in which the subject is shown a picture of a person with a face that is nothing but a blank oval. The subject is asked to tell what the person is thinking and feeling. In a study for Entenmann's bakery products, participants saw a picture of a faceless woman standing at a counter in front of a package of Entenmann's, holding a knife. They told a story of a woman who cut little pieces from the cake bit by bit until it was all gone. The insights from the focus group resulted in the "Splendid Obsession" campaign that features a couple rushing off to a store in a downpour late at night to satisfy their craving for Entenmann's cake.

Some techniques require the participants themselves to draw or create images. Consumers can visually articulate ideas and attitudes that might be impossible to express verbally. Such techniques can reveal surprising insights. One study of the roach killer market by McCann-Erickson used figure drawings to get at what heavy users of roachkillers— downscale women in the South—thought about roaches. Researchers asked these women to draw pictures of the roach. The agency wanted to find out why Raid spray outsold Combat in certain markets even though most users said the ideal product was Combat. (Combat insecticide disks are placed out of sight in cupboards and kill roaches cleanly with little effort by the user.)

The agency did 100 one-on-one interviews. "In a hundred cases out of a hundred, everybody drew or described the roach as a man," says Paula Drillman, executive vice president. "A lot of their feelings about the roach were very similar to the feelings that they had about the men in their lives." Many of the women who were in common-law relationships said of the roach, "He only comes around when he wants food." They got a vicarious thrill out of seeing the roaches die. "These women wanted control," Drillman says. "They used the spray because it allowed them to participate in the kill."

Many researchers, including those at DMB&B and Grey, also use collage techniques in which people are asked to create artwork that depicts their feelings about using the product or category. "We give people materials, sort of like playtime," says Feigin. "They get a set of magazines, magic markers, glue sticks, scotch tape, scissors. Then they're given various and sundry exercises to do. Draw a collage that tells us how you think of healthy skin, or what are the things that come to your mind and tell us a story about them. We use the technique when we're trying to build a creative vocabulary."

A creative vocabulary includes words, ideas, and images that can be used to develop advertising. Grey Advertising includes projective techniques as part of what it calls Tools and Techniques, a process for identifying brand character. "It helps us to develop an appealing character that strikes a strong emotional chord with consumers and creates a bond with consumers so they feel the brand is special and unique and just right for people like themselves," says Feigin.

Other techniques designed to get at images include brand personification (What would Budweiser look like if it came to life and walked into the room?) and anthropomorphization (What kind of animal would the brand be? What part of the body would it be?) One consumer psychologist, Sharon Livingston, president of Solutions Marketing Research in Locust Valley, New York, uses a technique called Category Sculpting™ to identify brand personality. She borrowed the idea from a therapeutic technique called family sculpting, in which one person reveals family interrelationships by creating a living sculpture consisting of other patients posed to represent each family member. In Livingston's adaptation, she has people create extended families of categories such as the deodorant-soap family or the men's shaving-cream family. In the cereal category, Shredded Wheat is a rosy-cheeked, friendly Aunt Sarah, while Lucky Charms is a mustachioed, ne'er-do-well uncle. In the men's cologne family, Drakkar Noir is the hip, yuppie brother who works on Wall Street; Polo is the blond, beach-boy sporty one; and Old Spice is granddad, who's more interested in his dog than anything else.

## PLAYS AND JOURNEYS

In guided imagery, another projective technique, people are asked to participate in various creative right-brained activities, from inventing dialogs between brands and acting out their expectations for a brand to filling in cartoon balloons and going on mental journeys. Guided imagery often puts the creativity of the consumers to work and illuminates new ways of thinking about worn-out products or categories. Livingston, whose clients have included Hallmark, Kodak, and Mennen, uses LookingGlass™ to uncover brand perceptions. Livingston urges subjects to relax and imagine themselves waking up from a nap to find that a full-length mirror has appeared in the bedroom. "Just like Alice, you put your hand up to the glass and it goes right through," Livingston tells her subjects. "You're intrigued, you're off on an adventure, you step through the frame." Behind the frame lies a short hallway with two or three doors at the end, depending on the number of brands being studied. On each door is a brand name. A study of competing bandage brands found a hygienic, well-managed scientific laboratory with scientists in white coats and the smell of baby powder in the air behind Johnson & Johnson's door. Behind the Curad door was a somewhat less sterile, less consistent picture, which reflected problems in Curad's "ouchless" approach. Further probing, says Livingston, revealed that, subconsciously, consumers equated "ouchless" with less hygienic, since bandages won't stick to dirty surfaces.

Another study of Ovaltine versus Nestlé hot chocolate found a Willy Wonka-like land of fun behind Nestlé's door and a 1950s kitchen replete with the scent of baking bread behind Ovaltine's door. Livingston then used Sensations™ to get deeper into the appeal of Ovaltine. Consumers are blindfolded and asked to smell the product. "Because primitive memory and olfactory sensations are both located in the temporal lobe, scent triggers primitive memory," she says. When asked to smell Ovaltine, one woman saw her dead mother coming over a hill, calling to her. Others remembered making soup or ice skating with mother. "One of the things that came out was that people who still use Ovaltine had a lot of experiences with their mothers that they wanted to preserve," she says, "while people who switched to Nestlé had a lot of anger toward their mothers."

N.W. Ayer has used acting workshops to get consumers to dramatize their feelings about brands. In such studies, some consumers have directed orchestras or pretended to be steering a ship, which demonstrates a need for control, says Fred Posner, executive vice president of research. In a study for Laughing Cow cheese, the 7-to-12-year-old members of one workshop got down on all fours and started making laughing "moo" sounds, which could provide fodder for future advertisements.

N.W. Ayer has a trademarked technique called Adversary Groups™, in which users and nonusers of a category confront each other about their respective stances on the category. Typically, there are two teams with five to ten people per side in a room with two moderators. Each side has a chance to try to convince the other to use or to stop using the brand or category. "They'll do their fighting and screaming through two moderators," Posner says. "What we end up with is all the emotions and hidden reasons why people have an affinity toward something and why they reject it. It uses an adversarial structure, similar to the legal system, to get all the issues on the table and to see which are the most persuasive."

Another N.W. Ayer technique is called Balloons™. People are depicted in various situations with dialog balloons, similar to those in cartoons, placed over their heads. The subject is asked to supply the dialog to fill in the balloons. For example, a person might be shown in front of a rental-car counter talking to an attendant behind the counter. The exercise could show different people (business person, vacationing family) talking first to Alamo, then to Hertz attendants. "You get quite a different perception of what the prospective customer is thinking and what the rental agent is thinking that tells you a lot about their perceptions of the company," Posner says.

The Balloons™ technique is a distant relative of the traditional Rosenzweig Picture Frustration Test. The basis of this projective technique, first published in 1945, is a set of 24 pictures depicting two figures with incomplete cartoon balloons over their heads. It's designed to measure reactions to frustration and includes standardized norms for measuring the reactions. For example, a picture might show a waiter and a diner with the waiter saying, "I'm sorry the cook couldn't cook this as you ordered it." The subject would be asked to fill in the diner's response and thereby reveal his or her own reactions to such a situation. Marketers using pictures of product usage situations have found this a useful way to get consumers to reveal brand negatives they might not otherwise reveal.

## PRODUCT BENEFITS

Part of brand character has to do with the benefits a consumer gets from buying the product. Some of these benefits are purely rational, such as clean hair, whiter teeth, or fresher breath. But there are also less obvious benefits, such as feeling carefree when using the brand, feeling attractive to the opposite sex, or feeling more confident when dealing with strangers. Again, consumers need help to reveal the underlying benefits that make them consistently buy Coke instead of Pepsi.

Market researchers have projective techniques that help uncover the successive layers of product benefits. For example, Grey Advertising's Benefit Chain™ is a self-adminis- tered probing technique that involves several layers of carbon paper. On the first layer, consumers write down in their own words the two most important benefits of the product or advertising. On the next layer, they write down secondary benefits of the benefits mentioned, and so on. This allows consumers to express in their own words the benefits important to them and also shows the level of consciousness at which the benefits appear. "The carbon paper carries the answers through to the next level, so you're left with a chain of responses that shows you how people's thinking is interlinked," Feigin says. "You can find out how many people give you which particular benefits, at which levels of consciousness or depth of probing they occur, and how they are expressed in their own words."

In a study for Minute Rice, Grey developed a set of scaler ratings that measured women's attitudes toward cooking. It also used a Benefit Chain. It showed that the brand's traditional benefits, that it was quick and easy to prepare, were attributes desired by today's busy women, but the advertising (perfect rice every time) had been aimed at women who were insecure cooks, afraid of making mistakes. The research suggested that the brand phrase the attributes in a different way to fit the target market. "Women in this day and age were no longer frightened, insecure cooks, but busy, savvy, competent women who wanted Minute Rice to be a smart helper in their creative cooking," Feigin says. The resulting campaign emphasized how Minute Rice could fit the way smart, creative cooks live today.

## FOCUS GROUPS

Much of the early motivational research used one-on-one depth interviews. Highly trained interviewers queried a subject for hours and took copious notes, attempting to probe the depth of the subject's feelings. At some point, researchers began doing an abbreviated form of depth interviewing in a group situation, and the focus group was born. Dr. Joseph Smith, who along with Toby Oxtoby started the research firm Oxtoby-Smith in 1956, traces the origins of the focus group to two separate developments: the clinical group therapy work of Carl Rogers at the University of Chicago, and inquiries into intergroup relationships done by the military during World War II. These developments influenced George Lesley Smith at Rutgers to start doing group work in marketing in the late 1940s. "The reasons for clinical group therapy were not so intellectual," says Joseph Smith, a trained psychologist whose research resulted in NBC's peacock and the overhead luggage compartments on airplanes. "The therapists were running out of time. Turns out if you had eight or nine people in a room, you could attend a larger number of patients than if you did them an hour at a time. Moreover, it worked."

The same might be said for market researchers using focus groups today. Projective techniques are often administered in a group situation to get more input in less time. While the group environment is advantageous in that it produces a multiple of impressions in a single session, it also has potential drawbacks that can threaten the validity of the research. Sharon Livingston of Solutions Marketing Research advises that in order to ensure against other respondents being influenced by a group leader, all respondents should jot down their first impressions. These can be referred to later if bias becomes a problem. She also advises that groups be limited to six people so that the information collected is manageable and relationships between participants and the moderator are kept as intimate and nonthreatening as possible.

Another important factor in the success of projective techniques in a group setting is the skill and insight of the moderator. Participants must be made to feel comfortable revealing facets of themselves to the group, and this is often a function of the environment created by the moderator.

At this writing, the popularity of focus groups in marketing and advertising research is at an all-time high. And many research veterans fear that as more businesses turn to focus groups for insight, the validity of the research could become denigrated. "Conducting a group used to be regarded as it should—a highly skilled process," Smith says. "A trained group moderator would listen with a third ear, would watch the body language, and would pursue leads that lifted the corner of the blanket. Now I think there's a guide for moderators, and you can get a group moderator in any city including North Bend, Oregon. None of these people is especially trained. What it's become is a surrogate for interviewing—get a bunch of people in a room and ask them questions. What had been a fairly skilled art form is now a routinely performed research inquiry. But its subtlety and potential are demeaned."

One study by the Advertising Research Foundation's Qualitative Research Council found that the use of focus groups is increasing, especially among nonpackaged-goods companies. "Companies that didn't do any research in the past are more likely to jump in and do qualitative research because it's a lot less expensive," says council chairman Jay Faberman. "A lot of them are really prostituting its use."

Judith Langer, president of Langer Associates, suggests that businesses considering focus-group research take time to carefully review the credentials of the moderator and the qualifications of the focus-group facility, and to carefully check that recruits do indeed meet the demographic and usage qualifications desired. The success of the focus group process, she says, depends upon the design of the questioning, the skill and training of the moderator, the careful selection of the panelists, and the correct interpretation of the resulting conversations.

Sometimes the clients themselves can become so captivated by way-out techniques that they forget panelists must be treated as adults worthy of respect. Langer remembers one client who wanted her to start a focus group on pet food by asking the participants to get down on all fours and pretend they were their dogs at mealtime. "I told them absolutely not," Langer says. "I put myself in the position of the respondents, and I would definitely resent that."

The theory behind the use of projective techniques and group interviewing is that people need help revealing their true motivations, while direct questioning will produce only rationalizations. But Langer says you can also go too far in the other direction. "Sometimes it gets a little too touchy-feely," she says. "I think you can overburden the research with specific techniques to the exclusion of asking any direct questions at all. I happen to believe you should ask people how they feel about things and give them an opportunity to say it. Sometimes you can learn a lot that way."

## Ethnography

Sometimes the best way to understand motivations is to catch consumers in the act and then ask them why. This technique of direct observation is called ethnography and is a process borrowed from the field of anthropology. The use of ethnography goes back to the motivational research of the 1950s. In one pre-1957 study by the Color Research Institute of Chicago, women were observed in doctors' waiting rooms to discover their real preferences about decor. In the study, 84 percent of the women said they preferred a traditional decor, with period furniture, Oriental rugs, and luxurious wallpaper, as opposed to Swedish modern. But observation revealed that they had more confidence in a doctor with a modern image. They would only wait in the "preferred" room when there were no chairs left in the room with the Swedish modern furniture.

Observing people in the act of consuming or just living their daily lives goes straight to the truth. Actual behavior sometimes speaks volumes louder than the rational mind. Dr. Joseph Plummer, director of business development for DMB&B, reports that the use of ethnography by agencies is much more common today than it was in 1972, when he studied breakfast habits for Kellogg while at Leo Burnett. "I went into people's homes and did long interviews and took pictures and wrote scripts," Plummer says. "We found that the symbols and rituals of breakfast were changing."

Ethnography is not only useful for turning up insights into how cultural changes affect consumption, it is also the most effective way to measure actual purchases. When you ask people what they buy, often they'll tell you what they think sounds the best. "People will get embarrassed and say they only buy top-of-the-line brands," says Allison Cohen, a trained psychologist and director of account planning for Ally & Gargano. "But you can get a more honest answer if you catch them off guard." Cohen, who has used ethnography to help create advertising strategies for products as diverse as Tampax tampons and Swiss chocolates, routinely takes a video camera along on her field studies into people's homes. She chronicles her findings for agency creatives, who then use it as raw material for developing advertising strategies.

In a study for a chocolate manufacturer, Cohen found real "chocoholics" and went to their homes to see first-hand how chocolate fit into their lives. "We saw some aberrant behavior in otherwise sane people," she says. She found that they hid chocolate in lingerie drawers, in freezers, on top of china cabinets, and under sofas. They prioritized their chocolates by saving domestic brands like Snickers for everyday and hoarding Godiva chocolates to savor only on special occasions or after a particularly bad day. The ad concept "True Confessions of a Chocoholic" resulted when agency creatives watched video tapes of the chocoholics' behavior.

Cohen gets to do what most people secretly wish they could do when visiting somebody else's home—snoop. "I go through people's pantries and cupboards and their bathroom storage areas to get an idea of why they buy what they buy," Cohen says. "It's a lot of fun, actually. You get to see the role that various brands play in people's lives." Typically, she will go into consumers' homes, take notes on purchases, and interview the consumers on the spot. The ethnography may be only a small part of the entire research process, which could also include focus groups and quantitative studies.

She recently finished studying grocery shopping styles for a client that intends to launch a new household product. Cohen followed people around the supermarket aisles looking at how they approached the shopping experience and what they bought. The client will be targeting this new product at a group Cohen calls the "Strategic Shopper."

The strategic shopper is so controlled, she (most food shopping is still done by women) organizes her shopping list in the order that products are shelved in the supermarket. "They feel their time is at such a premium, and this shopping expedition takes so much time and effort and costs so much, that they want to do it in the most organized way they can," she says. "I'm a list maker myself, but even I wouldn't go this far. This is a very serious bunch of ladies." These shoppers also scrimp in areas that don't show, but indulge themselves when it counts. She has noted that these shoppers buy store-brand sugar, tomato sauce, or other items that will become part of other dishes, but splurge on Pepperidge Farm cookies or other brands where quality is perceived to be worth the extra price.

Some shoppers hate shopping, but others seem to relish the experience. Cohen tells of a mother and two grown daughters who drove 75 miles every Saturday morning to a special store to do their grocery shopping. They'd attack the aisles in an organized way, equipped with a huge box of alphabetically organized coupons. Then they'd eat out afterwards, turning a weekly chore into a pleasant family outing.

In one study, Cohen went into consumers' kitchens to see how they prepared their meals. A frozen-food manufacturer wanted insights into consumers' expectations for convenience foods. She found that there is a whole segment of consumers who "engineer" rather than cook their meals. One of the observees prepared a meal consisting of frozen fried chicken, frozen potatoes, frozen onion rings, and frozen pie. "This was home cooking to this family," Cohen says.

Ethnographic research helped Cohen get insights into one of the most delicate consumer areas—women's sanitary protection. A client, Tambrands, Inc., was putting together a video about the onset of menstruation, which was to be distributed to junior-high-school health classes. Cohen took her video camera to where the girls are during the summer—the beach, the mall—and had some 300 frank discussions about what they liked, disliked, and feared about having their periods and using tampons. The result was a film called "Kids to Kids," which demystifies puberty, but does it by showing real teens talking about their actual concerns. "We wanted to make a film that wouldn't make them cringe," says Cohen. Another offshoot of that research was new corporate positioning for Tambrands. Cohen held separate focus groups with mothers focusing on their concerns about their daughters using tampons. "One thing that came out of our research was that moms will say, 'She really talks to her older sister.'" The agency came up with a new positioning for the client as the company that knows more, cares more, and does more for women. "We're trying to position the brand as a friend who's just slightly more sophisticated, a little more knowledgeable, and can give you good advice," Cohen says.

Grey Advertising used ethnography in developing Crisco's "Recipe for Success" advertising strategy. Watching people making pie crust gave the agency's creative people exciting new insights into shortening. "I realized that baking a pie is much like knitting a sweater. I started to think of the dough in the baker's hands like clay in the potter's hands," creative director Jim Morrissey told *Newsweek*. The resulting commercial emphasizes the tactile involvement. "You see hands and pie crust, and the whole thing happens as a symphony before your eyes," Morrissey says.

Young & Rubicam used ethnography to tap into the relationship Americans have with their mail carriers. The client, the U.S. Postal Service, was especially interested in learning how it was meeting the needs of small-business people. Y&R researchers and cultural anthropologists spent days following mail carriers on their routes all around the country. "We found a kind of interesting paradox," says Margaret Mark, director of consumer insights. "We knew from the quantitative research that Americans in general can have an ambivalent attitude toward the Postal Service. It can feel institutional and impersonal, all the things you might expect from any government institution." The ethnographic research, which was later backed up quantitatively, showed that none of these ambivalent feelings applied to the carriers. "That guy was their friend, a member of the community, someone they knew on a first-name basis," Mark says. The agency synthesized this insight into the umbrella line "We Deliver," which was used on all postal services and products.

While ethnographic observation can provide valuable insights about how products, brands, and services fit into people's lives that might be unavailable from direct questioning, there is a fine line of privacy that researchers must respect. In 1989, a California couple filed suit against Nissan Motor Corporation, charging that a Japanese researcher they had invited into their home as part of an exchange program was actually spying on them for the company. Other critics charge that the findings from ethnography shouldn't be generalized, because the type of people who are comfortable with researchers snooping in their pantries may not be representative of the majority of consumers. It's clear that results gleaned from ethnographic technique, like other qualitative findings, should be viewed with a great deal of objectivity. Ethnography is most valuable when used as part of a wider research process that includes quantitative market surveys.

## Beyond Psychographics: Measuring Emotions

The study of emotional effects on consumption has been marked by the same obstacles that hampered early inquiries into consumer psychology: it has been difficult, if not impossible, to measure consumers' emotional responses to products and advertising. When psychographics emerged, it was hailed as a method for quantifying qualitative findings. It helped researchers measure and sort consumers in terms of their personality traits, attitudes, and lifestyles. Today, many market research operations are going one step beyond psychographics: they are developing methods of quantifying consumers' emotional responses.

The most high-tech methods have names like Emotional Lexicon™ and Emotional Sonar™. They use interactive computer programs to lead consumers through a semantic maze to identify the precise word or phrase representing how they feel. Several other research operations are also looking into ways to measure emotions using methods ranging from questionnaires to photo sorts. A new technique by BBDO involves a deck of photos showing actors depicting 26 categories of emotions. Consumers sort the deck to select the emotions that come closest to how they feel about using the brand or after viewing selected advertising. McCann-Erickson has a process, Emotional Bonding,™ that measures consumers' responses to brands, categories, and advertising concepts using a questionnaire that distinguishes among 36 emotions.

N.W. Ayer measures consumers' responses to various brands and advertising in a category in terms of 58 emotions. Consumers rate competing brands on a scale according to the emotions they elicit. They also rate the brand's advertising so researchers can identify inconsistencies between advertising and the brand's emotional impact. "We take all that information from questionnaires, do the simple tabulations, and then do much more sophisticated tabulations in terms of perceptual maps, which are actually a picture of the data without using any numbers," says Fred Posner, executive vice president. "What results is a quantitative approach to a qualitative understanding of the consumer."

All of these methods provide researchers with a quantitative aspect that projective techniques lack. While psychoanalytic tools can produce intriguing insights into consumers' preconscious motivations, they have been subject to perennial criticisms that their findings are too vague and inconsistent. The process is extremely dependent on interpretation. "Psychological research methods, like figure drawings and picture sorts, are not well quantified and remain subject to ambiguity and biased interpretation," says Dr. Tom Snyder, a neurobiologist and psychiatrist who developed Emotional

Sonar™, a patented interactive computer program designed to measure emotions. He developed the program while teaching a class at Wellesley on the psychobiology of human emotion. What was originally an academic tool for understanding emotion is now attracting attention from corporate America. Snyder's firm, Emotion Mining Company of Wellesley, Massachusetts has done and is in the process of doing studies for several major corporations, including Campbell Soup Company, Coca-Cola, Lever Brothers, and AT&T.

Leo Burnett USA uses its interactive computer program, Emotional Lexicon™, for major clients such as McDonald's. The Lexicon, which consists of 1,200 emotion words and phrases, was developed as a way to pinpoint emotions more precisely than can be done through words and interviewing alone. One of the greatest obstacles in measuring emotions is that they tend to be nonverbal and event-specific, while people talk about emotions in abstract mood language that describes a longer-lasting state of mind. When you ask someone, "How do you feel?" they will say, "Great!" or "I feel bad." They probably can't pinpoint what caused the mood to come on. "But if you probe further and give them alternatives, they're able to identify how they feel," says Josh McQueen, executive vice president, director of research for Leo Burnett. McQueen uses the analogy of the colorwheel, which enables one to identify the precise shade of green one prefers from 15 other shades. While the color can be readily identified visually, it's difficult to describe verbally. "The language we need to describe the color, or the emotion, is just not available to us," McQueen says. "So we started with the assumption that emotion could be recognized, as opposed to volunteered, by the consumer."

It took the agency more than two years and some 4,000 interviews to develop a lexicon of emotion words and phrases. The first six months were spent determining the nature of the beast—defining exactly what emotion is. Two people combed the literature and drew from the work of several psychologists to come up with the definition. They determined that emotion has three separate elements: it has valance, i.e., it is positive or negative; it has intensity; and third, emotion has referential direction. "Referential direction speaks to whether there is an implicit, explicit, or an interior or exterior sense of where the emotional event is originating," McQueen explains. "Frustration," and "terror" may be similar in valance and intensity, but "frustration" is an interior-directed emotion, while "terror" is externally directed.

Once the groundwork was laid with the definition, McQueen's researchers studied people's emotional responses to situations, showed them words and phrases, and determined how the words were related to each other. They devised a tree-like branching pattern of questioning directed by computer that leads subjects to the exact word representing a precise emotion. "Since we now know the relationships of all the different words to each other," McQueen says, "we show them, in essence, a thesaurus of individual words, and from that we get how people are feeling to a high degree of subtlety and idiosyncraticness."

Burnett has used the program in over 20 studies for clients, which have required 4,000 additional interviews. During the process, the respondent sits down at a computer and is asked to relive an experience, whether it be eating ice cream or eating at a fast-food restaurant, in great detail. They are asked a number of questions: What were you wearing? Who were you with? What time of day was it? What did you do while you were there? How did you feel about yourself as you walked out? Once they have recaptured the experience, they are asked to choose from a list of five words on the computer the one that gets closest to how they feel. Then they are given another list of five and another until they have gone through about 20 lists of five words. They indicate whether the words are getting closer to how they feel until the lists get shorter and the meanings get increasingly more precise. "It's like flipping through a thesaurus until you narrow down to the exact word that describes precisely how you feel," McQueen says.

The Emotional Sonar program of Emotion Mining Company contains all the emotion words in the English language. Its creator, Dr. Snyder, says it differs from Burnett's Lexicon in that it uses graphics to keep consumers under the surface of their awareness. Seated at a computer terminal, equipped with a mouse, heavy users of a brand and those of the competition are asked to relax and play. Before the process starts, they are told that there are no right and wrong answers; all they have to do is "express their complete, thoughtful emotional responses." They are then asked to draw a line that represents how they felt while using the product, watching the advertising, or listening to the concept. "Some people might draw a straight line, some people might draw an up-and-down line, some people might draw a squiggly line," Snyder says. "Then we tell the person, 'Retrace this line in your mind's eye and assign to successive segments emotion words that occur to you.' They'll type in five to eight emotion words, and we're off into the program."

Like projective techniques, the interactive computer programs get consumers to articulate the emotions and motivations that reside just below the surface, "where the trout swim." But neutral computers may have the advantage of reducing human biases. Snyder says that even older people, those who are skeptical about psychological research, and the computer phobic become so engaged using the program that they forget about trying to come up with the "correct" answers. "People get their feet wrapped around their chair, they refuse water during the two-hour session, they end up wanting to buy computers," Snyder says. "The tool has been honed to keep people under the surface of awareness, our typical overthinking, as much as possible."

These new methods have the advantage of measuring previously immeasurable emotions. For his part, Dr. Snyder sees this as a significant improvement for managers who want to maximize their marketing dollars. "We can point up to a slide that has clusters of emotions and say, this is where you should put your marketing dollars. Here are the new triggers, here are the resurrectible triggers, and here are the overused or wornout triggers," Snyder says. What's more, the program can be translated into different languages, to provide a method that gets around the cognitive barriers that have inhibited cross-cultural studies of emotions. "Our method allows clients to work closely, confidently, and deliberately with human nature in running their businesses," Snyder says. "The payoff is that their marketing dollars can work a lot harder for them in generating sales around the world."

McQueen is also enthusiastic about the future of tools like Emotional Lexicon™. The event-specific nature of emotion, he says, makes it especially important for advertisers. "The events that evoke emotional responses could well be what we show them in a commercial," McQueen says. "We've become very interested in how these emotions get transferred to the brand."

This is part of the mystery of persuasion. People are persuaded in a myriad of ways, and numerous factors can hinder or help the process along the way. One thing that computers still can't do is determine exactly how the process works. How are emotions transferred in the consumer's mind to a brand? "Frankly, that's still in the realm of art," says McQueen. "I can't tell you how that happens, but at least we now have a tool to tell us exactly what is being transferred."

Tools like these interactive computer programs offer an additional layer of insight into the complex process of persuasion, but that doesn't mean they should be used indiscriminately. "There are no magic wands or black boxes," says McQueen. Burnett uses the Lexicon as part of its Emotional Leverage Studies process, which looks at the totality of a brand—not just what people feel, but what they think about a brand. "We believe that the most stable, strongest emotions that you can build with a brand are those that flow from people's beliefs about the attributes of a brand."

Even given better insight into consumers' emotions, researchers still have their work cut out for them. Translating any research into effective advertising or a new product that hits its mark is still an art that is highly dependent on the ability of humans to make the right decisions. Not all advertising should be warm and fuzzy and emotional. Some must be cynical, some entertaining, some informational, some tongue-in-cheek. The important point, and the point that distinguishes today's advertising from that of the past, is that today's advertising is designed with the consumer in mind. One reason that more companies are searching for better research methods is because they want additional insurance against failure in an increasingly high-stakes industry. "It's not just a small cadre of wonderful people sitting around applying their brain power anymore," says Dr. Joseph Plummer of DMB&B. "These are ways to ensure that everybody gets a little bit smart and that decisions are based on consumer input, not just intuition." These days, the art of marketing and advertising must be rooted solidly in science.

# 8 | *Going Global: International Psychographics*

*I do not agree with some of my marketing colleagues who have decided that the world is getting global, and hence you have one single global way of doing business. My own view is that if you are going to globalize, you will find a segment that tends to be global. Yes, you do adopt a global strategy, but it is a global segmentation strategy.*

*— Professor Jagdish Sheth*
*University of California*

CORPORATIONS RUSHED to enter foreign markets in the 1980s, fueled by visions of global brands pulling in worldwide sales and profiting from huge economies of scale. The dream soon evaporated for all but the most universal products. Even high-powered strategists were forced to admit that globalization might not work for everyone. Still, with EC 1992, perestroika, and the dismantling of the Iron Curtain, the world has opened up to businesses. Global opportunities exist, but where are they? And how should a company marketing to the world for the first time approach this seemingly overwhelming task?

Unfortunately, marketers have most often responded to the incomprehensible complexity of this unfolding global marketplace by ignoring it. Until recently, most multinationals viewed whole regions of the globe as psychographically homogeneous. Not only is this approach misguided, it is potentially disastrous. Horror stories abound of companies that ignored market complexities and paid huge penalties for their global miscalculations. The greatest miscalculation is underestimating the effect that cultural differences can have on product demand.

Learning this lesson cost Campbell Soup more than $2 million in the early 1980s. In 1978, Campbell joined the Brazilian-owned meat producer, Swift-Armour S.A. Industria e Comercio to form SOPA (Sociedade Procutora de Alimentos Ltd.). An extensive marketing campaign was conducted prior to beginning soup production, but the canned product line failed. Too late, in-depth, in-home interviews revealed that Brazilian homemakers felt it was a duty to serve their families homemade soup and that anything less was the sign of laziness. The Brazilian cooks preferred the competing soup-starter products of Knorr and Maggi, which offered convenience but still allowed them to make their own creative mark on their soups. Campbell couldn't maintain sales after the first year.

Similar miscalculations will doubtless flourish in post-1992 Europe. The unified Europe is a market of more than 320 million people, a market larger and more complex than that of the United States. Consumer attitudes in the U.S. vary according to regions, ethnicity, life stage, and demographics, but a common history and governmental structure underlie American diversity. Outside the U.S., the marketer is faced with a vast range of distinct cultures, each with its own history, political awareness, and national identity.

While there are glaring differences between the U.S. and Brazil, or between the U.K. and France, there are also some commonalities. Every international marketer faces a classic dilemma: will it be more effective to capitalize on the differences or the similarities? Is it practical to create separate advertising strategies and alter products to fit variations in each country? Or is it possible to standardize products and marketing across diverse cultures and still see results? A standardized approach is attractive to many multinationals because it is less costly and easier to implement. But if it blurs or ignores local differences, it might be too general to be truly effective. Worse yet, a marketing effort that blankets diverse cultures and fails to consider local variations runs the risk of turning away or offending more people than it attracts. Recall that Chevrolet tried to market the Nova in Spanish-speaking countries, only to discover that "no va" means "doesn't go."

The most sophisticated international marketing efforts start the process of inquiry with psychographic research that identifies similar values, attitude, or lifestyle groups across cultures. From there, additional studies explore local differences and how they can be used to advantage in the execution of an advertising or marketing campaign.

Many of the most extensive international psychographic studies have been done by large multinational advertising agencies, which have the personnel and budget resources necessary to conduct the kind of cross-cultural survey that meets reliability criteria. This chapter will examine some of the best-known cross-cultural agency psychographic studies and look at the preliminary work surrounding SRI International's newly released Japanese version of the VALS Program.

## Culture Shock

Fascination with European consumer attitudes certainly did not begin with the European consolidation. Psychographic segmentations were done in Europe prior to the 1960s. In 1970, Dr. Joseph Plummer (now with DMB&B) started an international psychographic study for Leo Burnett & Company of Chicago. By 1976, Plummer had done studies in 19 countries, and the information had been used by clients such as Philip Morris, Hyatt, and Kellogg. There are reports of psychographics being used in Europe as far back as the 1940s. A British confectionary company evidently used personality traits to define targets for two separate products: one was a long-lasting candy that allowed slow, private sucking for the oral-narcissistic personality type; the other was a small, countable, and chewable candy for the anal-aggressive consumer type.

A major study, "A Survey of Europe today," was done by *Reader's Digest* in 1970. In the past 20 years, interest in international attitude surveys has steadily intensified as more businesses and advertising agencies become multinational. *Reader's Digest* conducted a followup study of European consumers in 1990.

Considerable debate has arisen recently about whether a grouping of disparate nations like Europe can be psychographically segmented at all with any degree of reliability. Is there a European consumer? Or are the countries too different to make the identification of similar attitude and lifestyle groups worthwhile?

Multinational companies such as Coca-Cola and PepsiCo, which sell one product all over the world, have commonly standardized all or part of their international marketing operations. They believe that standardization is necessary, at least to some degree, because of cost and brand-image considerations. Maintaining a single identity and a consistent brand image the world over has been a central element of the international marketing efforts of such packaged-goods giants. Other key elements of PepsiCo's approach to international marketing were published in the *Journal of Advertising Research*:

- PepsiCo is one international company.

- Our brand image is an essential part of the product Pepsi-Cola, and the success of Pepsi-Cola flows from the advertising that created that image in the first place.

- We do not believe that each country requires an individual advertising and product approach.

- In developing our international marketing strategy, we believe in the basic psychological truth that there are greater differences within groups than between groups.

- It is the sameness in all human beings on which we believe we must base our selling appeals.

Is it always advisable to take a mass-market approach in multinational marketing? The answer revolves around whether there is a sameness in all human beings to which one can appeal. PepsiCo is not the only company to believe that a universal product can be sold on a universal appeal that touches some fundamental emotion in people. Other multinationals have adopted the hypothesis that there is a global consumer and have set out to identify these elusive archetypal buyers.

There is also a compromise position: i.e., forming a standardized marketing philosophy and brand image that extends across diverse cultures while subtly adapting the message or delivery to local audiences. Many of the most sophisticated international advertising and marketing firms are now doing this, but before embarking on this course, the marketer needs a fundamental understanding of how the cultural differences can affect product demand. That understanding often begins with a psychographic breakdown of attitude and lifestyle groups.

Psychographic research becomes even more complicated when administered across diverse cultures. The following study, published by Alfred S. Boote several years ago, is a good example of how an international survey is administered and analyzed. It is also valuable because its findings are open to scrutiny, something that is rare with the proprietary psychographic studies of advertising agencies.

Boote studied the comparative values structures of women in Germany, the United Kingdom, and France, and found several crucial differences. A sample of 500 women was randomly selected in each country; each sample had been prescreened for ownership of several household appliances. During in-home interviews, respondents were asked to rate 29 value items considered instrumental in the formation of attitudes toward specific products. For example, they rated phrases such as "having expensive-looking possessions," "devoting most of your time to home," or "saving money whenever possible," on a five-point scale from "very important" to "not important at all."

When ranked in order of importance, several of the 29 items revealed a great variety among countries. For Germans, "having a familiar routine" ranked number one, while it ranked 10th for British women and 23rd among the French. "having beautiful things in your home" and "being with people with up-to-date ideas" were also more important to the Germans than to the British or French. At the same time, "having something to keep busy at" was ranked 6th by the French and British, but only 21st among the Germans.

Further analysis seemed to uncover greater similarities across the three countries. Two segments were found among the Germans: one methodical, frugal and home-oriented; the other more impulsive, fashion-oriented, and progressive. Three distinct groups were found in Britain and France. While each country had segments that could be called traditional and modern, the French and British segments differed in key respects with each other as well as with the corresponding German group. For instance, there was an aesthetic element in the French modern group not present in the other two countries, while the German traditional segment was much more home-centered than the corresponding French group.

Boote manipulated the data in two ways to find out whether a standardized advertising campaign would work in these countries. First, he combined data from all three countries to form one values segmentation. Three groups emerged—the home-centered woman, the contemporary homemakers, and women with outside interests. On the surface, these groups seemed to reconcile the differences that had been previously seen in the individual countries.

But then Boote cross-tabulated the factor analysis another way and came up with a four-group solution. The four segments were Traditional Homemaker, Spontaneous, Contemporary Homemaker, and Appearance Conscious.

*Figure 8-1  Boote's Value Segments for European Women*

| Countries | Traditional Homemaker | Spontaneous | Contemporary Homemaker | Appearance Conscious |
|---|---|---|---|---|
| U. K. | 37% | 29% | 53% | 16% |
| France | 36 | 66 | 23 | 3 |
| Germany | 27 | 5 | 24 | 81 |

*Source: Alfred S. Boote,* Journal of Advertising Research, *1983*

Looking at the data this way, it became apparent that the earlier combined segmentation had concealed important differences between the countries. The composition of the groups was uneven across countries, with some groups composed almost entirely of people from one country. For instance, the Appearance Conscious group was made up almost entirely of Germans, while the Spontaneous group was mostly French.

Boote concluded that "data from several countries should not be combined into a common base for a segmentation analysis. While the resulting output may be interpretable, it is likely to conceal country differences which should be considered when developing advertising themes."

This example illustrates the potential dangers inherent in a cross-cultural psychographic segmentation. It is a good research tool to start with, because it illuminates the important similarities and common groups across cultures. But because it is by nature a generalization, it should not be viewed in isolation. There are bound to be important cultural differences within the groups that get lost in a broad segmentation. This problem can be minimized if psychographics is made part of a multilayered research plan, and if local differences are emphasized during the execution phase of the marketing or advertising effort.

## BSB's Global Scan

Backer Spielvogel & Bates Worldwide (BSB) fielded the first U.S. Global Scan study in 1985. Since then, the agency has invested more than $2 million, and surveys have been done or are in progress, in 18 different countries,* according to agency executives. Global Scan requires a tremendous investment in time and personnel from the agency. Why has the agency made the strategic decision to devote such extensive resources to Global Scan?

The agency publicizes Global Scan as the largest such study ever conducted in the advertising industry, saying "no other agency in the world is conducting a survey of this size, in this depth, and with this power." It might be worth the investment just to be able to make that claim. Another explanation lies in the words of Chairman Carl Spielvogel, "In essence, [Global Scan] gives voice to a modern-day Everyman—the global consumer." International corporations want to market to the sameness in humans, and Global Scan is a high-profile window on the world designed to find those crucial similarities.

Not only is Global Scan glitzy and topical, however, it is also an effective business tool. "Because Global Scan is already in place and so broad, it helps us get a running start on a new client in a new business situation," says Jacqueline Silver, BSB's director of research services and strategic planning. "Obviously, no major advertiser is going to sign on just because we have a research study. But it shows we have a real sensitivity to people and that we can execute creative and marketing communications against it."

Global Scan measures a wide variety of attitudes and consumer values, as well as media use, viewing habits, product use, and buying patterns. In designing the study, emphasis was placed on coming up with a model that accurately predicted consumer behavior, to avoid the applicability problems that plagued the original VALS. Respondents are questioned on their use of more than 1,000 products and brands, and these data are analyzed against 250 items on attitudes, values, lifestyles, and media use. This helps the system better identify the attitudes that affect purchase behavior for various product categories. This is also why the BSB researchers decided not to base the segmentation on cluster analysis. "We tried it in our experimentation, and it did not reflect the product usage," Silver says. "It also delivered artificially equal size segments which did not reflect the true population. That concerned us a lot."

During a two-year testing and pre-testing process, BSB researchers looked for attitude items that would be the best discriminators of behavior. Eventually, they settled on a multi-stage segmentation, the validity of which is tested again every two or three years to make sure the model is still reflective of the population.

* *Australia, Belgium, Canada, Denmark, Finland, France, Germany, Holland, Hong Kong, Italy, Japan, Mexico, Norway, Spain, Sweden, United Kingdom, United States, and Venezuela.*

BSB won't release the questionnaire or reveal much about how the data are analyzed to form the five global values groups. Representatives only speak in general terms about the content of the survey. Global Scan annually surveys about 1,000 people in each country, except in the United States, where 3,500 are surveyed. The questionnaire uses a five-point scale to measure 250 attitudes—130 are specific to the country and 120 are global attitudes running across cultures. Subjects rate their degree of agreement or disagreement with statements like, "The harder you push, the further you get" and "I never have enough time or energy."

The 120 Global Attributes include high-order values (self-sufficiency, self-esteem), personality characteristics ("I like to talk about my adventures and experiences"), lifestyle attitudes ("I'd rather spend a quiet evening at home"), and more pragmatic product attitudes such as how they feel about convenience or buying on impulse. It also includes attitudes on specific categories such as diet, nutrition, and eating habits: "I often decide what to serve for dinner at the last minute" and "I try to avoid fat in my diet." Attitudes on dozens of other categories are also included, such as financial services ("I wish I could get better financial advice") and automobiles ("Imports are better cars than American cars").

Global Scan also takes a reading on a range of political questions that vary according to the country being surveyed. For instance, U.S. respondents might be asked to agree or disagree with the statement, "President Bush is doing a good job," while the Japanese would be asked to rate their own leader. Some attitudes about social issues are measured in every country; these include items such as "I believe people with AIDS should be quarantined," "people should live together before marriage," and "the government should monitor corporations."

Some parts of the questionnaire had to be adapted to local realities. In densely populated Hong Kong, Western items relating to dining out had to be eliminated. "Eating out of the home works backwards for them," Silver says. "The affluent people eat in the home because they are the ones who can afford to have kitchens. Everyone else eats out." In Japan, the subject of drug use was taboo.

Methods of data collection also vary by country. In the U.S., the survey is mailed, a method that won't work in many European countries because of fears of terrorism and letter bombs. Nor will mail surveys work in less developed countries, where mail delivery is unreliable and literacy rates are low. In these countries, interviews have to be delivered personally or administered by a trained interviewer. "We try to be sensitive," Silver says, "and adjust our techniques to fit the country."

## WHO IS THE WORLD?

Global Scan's fusion of attitudes with purchasing data has created a segmentation the agency calls TARGET SCAN, derived by combining data from all of the countries. The agency calls the scheme a "high-definition picture of consumer segments, based not just on what people believe, but on what they buy." According to TARGET SCAN, there are five global psychographic types representing 95 percent of the combined populations of all the countries surveyed (the remaining 5 percent of the sample could not be assigned to any of the segments):

*Figure 8-2 Global Scan Segments in Three Countries*

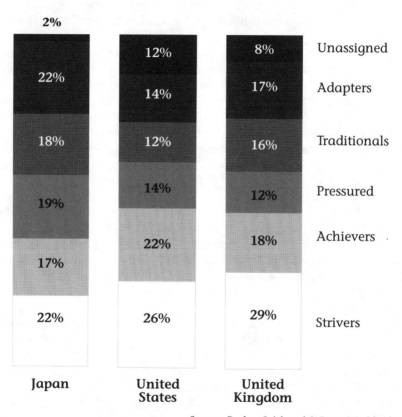

*Source: Backer, Spielvogel & Bates Worldwide*

**Strivers** (26 percent) They are young people (median age 31) living hectic, time-pressured lives. They push hard to achieve success, but because they set their goals too high, sometimes they fail to meet them. Short on time, money, and energy, they are concentrated in the peak consumption years. They're materialistic, seek pleasure, and demand instant gratification. Convenience is a big selling point with them.

**Achievers** (22 percent) are slightly older and have achieved some of the success the Strivers covet. They are affluent, assertive, and upward bound. They are the opinion leaders and style setters who shape mainstream values. Extremely status conscious, Achievers buy for quality. Together with the Strivers, they created the youth-oriented values that shape U.S. society today. They were responsible for the fitness craze, and their demands still influence what people eat, drink, and wear today.

**Pressured** (13 percent) This group runs across all age groups and is largely composed of women who face constant financial and familial pressure. Managing all of life's problems is so difficult for this group that they have little physical or emotional resources left over with which to enjoy life. They feel overtaxed and downtrodden.

**Adapters** (18 percent) are older people who are content with themselves and their lives, but manage to live comfortably in a changing world. They maintain their own time-honored values, but keep an open mind. They aren't shocked by the new, but often take up whatever new ideas or activities they see as enriching their golden years.

**Traditionals** (16 percent) hold fast to the oldest values of their countries and cultures. They resist change and prefer comfortable routines and familiar products. They are conservative, rooted to the heartland, and tied to the past. Their habits reflect their preference for established ways of thinking, eating, and living their lives.

The five general groups are found in varying proportions in each of the 18 countries measured. More than one-third of the French and the Americans are Strivers. In Germany, the older, staid Traditional and Adapter segments dominate, making up 54 percent of the population. In the booming new economy of Spain, six out of ten people are either Achievers or Strivers.

## WHAT'S THE DIFFERENCE?

Global Scan is commonly used to illuminate the similarities between consumers across diverse cultures, but because the nature of the groups varies slightly from country to country, it also uncovers crucial local differences that may have implications for advertisers. "It helps us and our clients understand the commonalities of message and areas where they have to change to be locally sensitive," Silver says. For example, in the U.S., Strivers and Achievers are mostly baby boomers and account for more than half the population. In Germany, which had a much smaller baby boom, Strivers are older and make up only 16 percent of the population.

No study, no matter how valid or accurate, can really reflect all the infinite attitudinal variations found in all the countries of the world. But Global Scan offers a kind of yardstick with which researchers can measure a series of consumer attitudes. Some interesting variations have been discovered in the countries studied.

## CANADA

Some people might think of Canada as simply a smaller version of the United States.

But Global Scan finds acute attitudinal differences between the two countries, as well as between the English- and French-speaking populations of Canada.

In general, Canadians are found to be concerned with physical fitness, worried about the environment, and skeptical about the benefits of free trade. In addition, Canadian workers are more satisfied with their jobs than workers in any of the other countries surveyed.

Canadian Strivers are much more open-minded and liberal than their U.S. counterparts, but they are also more materialistic, ambitious, optimistic, and risk-taking:

- 72 percent of Canadian Strivers believe it is important to make a great deal of money, compared with 54 percent of U.S. Strivers.

- 86 percent push hard for success, compared with 67 percent in the U.S.

- 79 percent think their greatest achievements still lie ahead, versus 67 percent.

- 47 percent enjoy taking risks, compared with 32 percent.

- 73 percent are more satisfied with their jobs, versus 53 percent in the U.S.

The study also found that Canadian Achievers, the affluent opinion leader segment, enjoy one of the highest-quality lifestyles of any country surveyed. They also have stronger marriages and more satisfying careers. The Pressured segment, those women with familial and financial worries, are found in greater proportions in Quebec than in any other Canadian province.

Within Canada, it's no news that attitudes of the English-speaking and French-speaking populations vary widely. Global Scan, however, lists specific differences for businesses that might have been content to treat Canada as one giant consumer market. French-speaking Canadians seem to be more pressed for time when it comes to diet. Fully 55 percent of them say they find it difficult to control what they eat, versus 31 percent of the English speakers. More of the French- than English-speaking Canadians also say they decide on their dinner menu at the last minute and think dinner preparation should take as little time as possible. French Canadians also reveal more worries about unemployment; 73 percent say they worry about it, compared with 55 percent of English-speaking Canadians.

## JAPAN
Japanese society is often viewed in stereotypes—the geisha girl, the achievement-driven teams of businessmen, the efficient automaton workers willing to live and die for the corporate good. Stereotypes of the Japanese always focus on a lack of individuality. A bit of scrutiny, however, reveals that affluence and Western influences are having profound affects on attitudes in Japan, especially among the young. New views are challenging long-established traditions, and the long-term result of this confrontation may be societal changes similar to the attitudinal shifts that rocked American society during the 1960s.

*Figure 8-3  The Man is Boss in Japan*

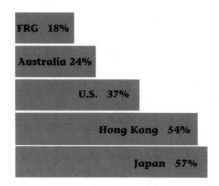

**The Man is Boss In Japan**

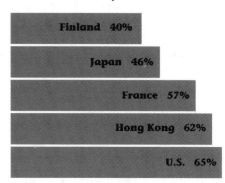

**Americans Believe Women
Should Put Family First**

*Source: Global Scan, BSB*

Global Scan finds that the two youngest segments, the Achievers and Strivers, are the forces behind change in Japanese society today. These consumers are highly materialistic, value premium goods and luxurious lifestyles, and are very optimistic about their financial futures. It is within these groups, too, that attitudes about gender are shifting most.

While the vast majority of Japanese still hold the belief that the man is lord of the household, many women, influenced by the advances of Western women, are questioning women's traditional family-oriented role in the Japanese home. Global Scan found that 65 percent of Japanese men think the man should be boss, while only 35 percent of Japanese women are ready to put family before career. In addition, 53 percent of Japanese women believe their husbands should share equally in the housework, while other research shows that Japanese men spend much less time then men in other developed countries helping around the house.

Other conflicts and pressures lurk beneath the surface of Japanese prosperity and industrial success. Many Japanese feel under increasing personal pressure. Most Strivers are time pressured and believe they have to live up to very difficult personal goals. Another measure of pressure is seen in the greater tendency of the Japanese to consume alcoholic beverages. Japan ranked first among all the countries surveyed in the number of people, both men and women, who take a drink to unwind.

Despite these pressures, however, Japanese Strivers are the most financially optimistic group of all countries studied. Only 10 percent of the Japanese Strivers feel they can't get ahead personally, compared with fully 71 percent of U.S. Strivers.

In the U.S., Strivers are under both time and money pressure, while in Japan, Strivers are under time pressure but have enough money. "The average young person in Japan gets married with $25,000 in the bank, while in the U.S. they're at least $5,000 in debt," Silver says. What the Japanese don't have is space.

Understanding the different kinds of pressures experienced in different cultures can translate directly into market opportunities. For example, U.S. Strivers want cars that are fun, stylish, fast, and a good value. Japanese Strivers, on the other hand, consider their car an extra room and will spend extra money to add lace curtains or expensive stereo systems to them. A value appeal that might work on a U.S. Striver would be lost on a Japanese Striver, who likes extra features. "It brings up a whole new dimension of the meaning of home and privacy in Japan," says Silver. "We worked very closely with the Japanese to understand these local differences."

## VALS Japan

Global Scan is not the only psychographic study that has been done in Japan. SRI International is setting up a Japanese version of its Values and Lifestyles Program (see Chapter 5). Japan VALS, which was completed in 1991, attempts to determine the effect of changing values and social behaviors on the future evolution of Japan.

After World War II, the Japanese wanted to catch up with Americans. Many of the society's elite aspired to the lifestyle they saw in Western movies and TV programs. Forty years later, they have caught up, and in certain ways, surpassed the West. Now the question arises, What comes next? "Our client wanted to be able to say, 'Aha, here's what's coming next,'" says Bruce MacEvoy, project director. "So our strategy was to find out where the trend leaders were and then to ask them what values and lifestyle issues are important to them."

Like the new VALS 2 program in the U.S., the Japan VALS typologies are based on product usage and behavior as well as attitudes. Following a pretest of 500 people, SRI fielded a survey of 3,100 Japanese consumers in four regions of Japan (Tokyo, Osaka-Kyoto, and the rural cities of Okayama and Morioka). The survey asked them to rate 187 attitudinal items and queried them on more than 300 product choice, media, and activity items, as well as demographics.

After the development survey, SRI conducted a validation survey that offered more than 600 product choice, media, and activities items to 5,600 respondents all over Japan. This survey verified that Japan VALS retained 93 percent of its predictive power in the new sample and confirmed the characteristics of the ten Japan VALS segments in the national population. The validation survey also added more detailed information to the Japan VALS database on shopping habits, food and cooking, clothing and fashion, automotive, media, travel, sports and leisure activities, social values, and life history.

This rich database can be tapped by Japan VALS subscribers for further research into consumer motivations.

*Figure 8-4 Japan VALS Innovators, Adapters, Followers, and Laggards*

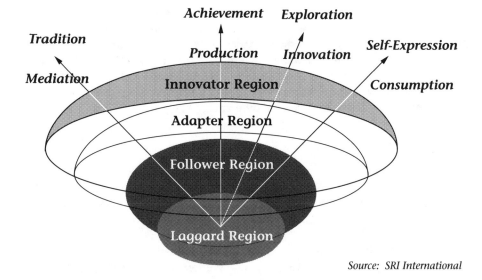

Source: SRI International

The Japan VALS, which MacEvoy says is not based on cluster analysis, identifies leaders of change and their relationship to emerging social trends. Attitudinal differences between groups are examined, but product usage and activities are the standard for comparing groups. By measuring leadership, media usage, travel, social and professional activity, Japan VALS identified four change-leader groups in the Japanese population: Innovators, Adapters, Followers, and Laggards.

Central to the Japan VALS structure is a measure called Exploration. Exploration—an individual's active involvement in life and motivation to master new challenges—is the key contrasting element across the groups. The exploratory behavior of change leaders is the catalyst for social change within the country.

Japan VALS also identifies three *life orientation* dimensions that motivate exploratory behavior. These are made up of different goals and types of knowledge:

•Self-Expression—independence, stimulation, fashion, and recreation

•Achievement—career, status, leadership, and culture

•Tradition—stability, order, community, and traditional beliefs

The exploration and life orientation dimensions are statistically designed to predict human activity within four basic categories of social function: innovation, consumption, production, and mediation (social control). This is the step that links individual values to social processes and identifies the underlying themes of social tension and cultural change.

Crucial to understanding change is understanding the four change-leader groups, those that measure highest in each of the life orientations: Integrators are on the high end of the Exploration measure. Self-Innovators rate highest in Self-Expression. Ryoshiki (a Japanese term meaning "social intelligence") Innovators are high in Achievement. And Tradition Innovators are the leaders in the traditional life dimension. In all, there are ten standard Japan VALS groups:

## EXPLORATION
**Integrators** are well-educated, very affluent, sociable, adventurous, and stylish. Their values are modern with some traditional ideas. They enjoy the new and risky, and rank highest on a variety of consumer indicators. Integrators travel and read widely, and are attracted to high-quality, prestigious products.

**Sustainers** are at the low end of the Exploration dimension. They are resistant to change and lead lives of calm simplicity and traditional routine.

## SELF EXPRESSION
**Self-Innovators** are young, active, sociable, and very interested in fashion and leisure sports. They spend more on themselves in proportion to their income and are able to do so because many live with parents or friends.

**Self-Adopters** pattern their activities and product choices after the Self-Innovator group but are somewhat older and less active. They have below-average incomes and are less educated. They are shy, unassertive, and sensitive to others' opinions. They enjoy sports, tend to be impulsive shoppers, and read comics and fashion and lifestyle magazines.

## ACHIEVEMENT
**Ryoshiki Innovators** are committed to career and the social status quo. They have high education but average income, and many are middle-aged specialists or teachers. Their tastes tend toward cultural pursuits, fashion, exercise, socializing with spouses, and continuing education for self-betterment.

**Ryoshiki Adapters** have higher incomes than the Ryoshiki Innovators. They are less assertive, less stressed, and more down-to earth, well adjusted, and active. They have a moderate, modern outlook on life. Many own European furniture, expensive artwork, and home computers, and play golf. They read the business newspaper *Nikkei* and business magazines.

## TRADITION

**Tradition Innovators** are mostly middle-aged homeowners with jobs in middle management and primary industries who are active in community affairs. They are successful but avoid risks. They are highest in use of organic foods, health magazines, home repair, carpentry, local newspapers, and large luxury cars.

**Tradition Adapters** are high but not extreme in the traditional orientation, and have adapted the Traditional Innovator lifestyle. They are younger and better-educated than Traditional Innovators and are the second most affluent of all the groups. Many are managers, entrepreneurs, farmers, or work in primary industries. They travel frequently on business, read health magazines, and like to do home repair, go fishing, and golf. They put their money into real estate and postal insurance funds.

Two other groups don't show a strong tendency on any of the dimensions. They are called the Realist orientation:

## REALISTS

**High Pragmatic** are middle-aged, above-average in income and education but average in consumption. The group least likely to agree with any attitude statement, they seem withdrawn and suspicious. They are unconcerned about self improvement, fashion, leading others, or preserving traditional customs. They appear to follow a flexible, even reactive orientation to life with few fixed beliefs.

**Low Pragmatic** are attitudinally negative and show no strong psychological tendency, except a slightly more positive stance toward traditional customs. This group includes married women who take care of children at home and men who work as laborers, farmers, and fishermen. Their housing is modest, and many commute by bicycle. They are below-average consumers and prefer inexpensive goods and established brands.

There are ten standard groups, but the Japan VALS database is different from former VALS systems in that it's intended to be highly flexible. MacEvoy describes it as a network of interconnected links between different kinds of products run by high-graphic-loading, user-friendly software. "If you think that there is a new segment in the population possibly emerging that lives in the city, rents an apartment, is single, wears trendy clothes, rides motor scooters, reads the *New Yorker*, and flies to Europe every summer, you can put all those indicators in the database, select the top 5 percent of the population on those products and look at them, then find out how they think," MacEvoy says.

In addition to the standard segmentation, Japan VALS defines three other levels of analysis that allow subscribers to focus on specific industry markets, niche segments for

*Figure 8-5 Japan VALS Change Leader, Adapter, Follower, Resister Segments*

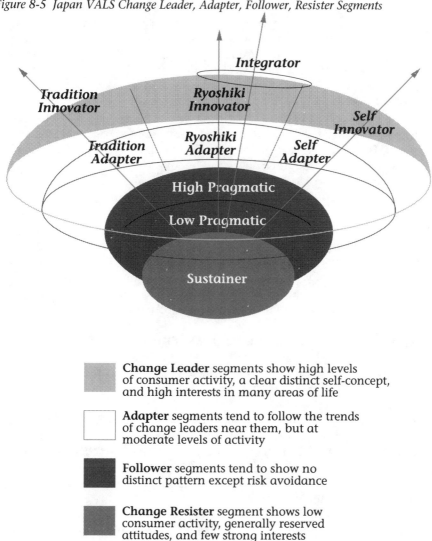

**Change Leader** segments show high levels of consumer activity, a clear distinct self-concept, and high interests in many areas of life

**Adapter** segments tend to follow the trends of change leaders near them, but at moderate levels of activity

**Follower** segments tend to show no distinct pattern except risk avoidance

**Change Resister** segment shows low consumer activity, generally reserved attitudes, and few strong interests

*Source: SRI International*

specific products or market opportunities, and international comparisons. MacEvoy calls the international comparison aspect one of the most exciting features of Japan VALS and says the method allows researchers to compare, for example, the prestige and trendiness of consumers in the Japan and United States.

MacEvoy, however, resists the notion that one segmentation system can be applied across cultures. The Japan VALS, he says, is an entirely new system, not merely the U.S. VALS questionnaire applied to the Japanese culture. "There's something kind of glib about taking the same number of groups across a lot of different cultures, and then saying that because the theme of the questions and the methodology is the same, the groups have comparable meaning," MacEvoy says.

## THE NEW JAPAN

In the process of collecting the Japanese data, some interesting insights emerged about Japanese attitudes. MacEvoy says that the stereotyped image of happy, impersonal Japanese workers is groundless. The initial survey found that 60 percent of the Japanese don't like their jobs, and about 93 percent say that the most important aspect of work is relationships with coworkers. It is true, however, that individual uniqueness is less a factor in consumer behavior in Japan than it is in the United States.

Attitude measures, such as persistent effort (gambaru) and desire for harmony (wa), showed no appreciable effect on behavior. At the same time, however, many of the psychological motives for consumption (status, stimulation) were similar across the two cultures. For example, leadership was found to be related even more closely with fashion-consciousness in Japan than in the United States.

Japan VALS shows, as common wisdom holds, that young people in Japan show significant differences from older people in attitudes about work, leisure, and self-expression. However, in attitudes about social responsibility to others and respect for elders, young and old share nearly identical beliefs.

The Integrator group seems to offer the most promising insights about influences that underlie the social changes occurring in Japan. Integrators are the greatest users of international travel and print media, and they have developed lifestyles that are a harmonious blend of the modern with the traditional. This seems to suggest that wider experience and information are key factors of cultural change in Japan, as they have been in other parts of the world.

The VALS work has also revealed a growing dissatisfaction among Japanese women that has translated into more political action among former housewives, increasing concern about quality-of-life issues such as environmental pollution, more interest among urban dwellers in returning to their home towns, an increasing emphasis on the companionship of marriage, and more interest among workers in joining networking clubs that offer a forum for socializing after work.

VALS expects the primary users of the new system to be mid-sized, independent Japanese manufacturers and media and service companies that lack in-house market research departments. Due to Japan's rigid trade barriers, MacEvoy doesn't expect the system to elicit much interest from American companies, at least in the short term. Initial market research, however, suggests that smaller Japanese companies would be interested in a psychographic tool that is specific enough and sells for a reasonable price. "I think market specificity is the key," says MacEvoy. "The more focused you make the market information, the larger the potential market. There are thousands and thousands of companies each marketing to a slightly different niche. That creates a tremendous opportunity for a standardized product that can be made flexible enough to respond to the needs of each of those different companies."

SRI also intends to enter the search for the Euroconsumer and explore the opportunities for psychographic research opening up in Europe. SRI has signed a contract to do a Germany VALS and is negotiating to do a Norway VALS. Studies in France and Italy are also possibilities. "This is a strategic goal for us," MacEvoy says. "We're an international consulting company with offices around the world; it's only natural we should take advantage of that to build a global database."

## Search for the Euroconsumer

As U.S. corporations continue to slash research budgets, the largest research firms are increasingly looking overseas for growth. Consequently, more international advertising agencies and marketing research firms are searching for the Euroconsumer.

A D'arcy Massius Benton & Bowles research team drawn from agency offices in 15 different countries fielded the study "The Euroconsumer: Marketing Myth or Cultural Certainty?" The study found similar classes of consumers in countries as diverse as Norway and Spain. It also identified four lifestyle groups common across Western Europe and one prevalent only in Southern Europe. The four European groups, in order of descending affluence, start with the Successful Idealists and the the Affluent Materialists, who together comprise the elite of European society. Then come the Comfortable Belongers and the Disaffected Survivors, who make up the European mainstream. Optimistic Strivers are prevalent in Southern Europe and represent younger people who have moved from country to town, or those who are trying to move up out of the Disaffected Survivor group.

**Successful Idealists:** They have attained professional prestige and material success, but remain firmly committed to the larger issues in life, such as art, personal freedom, and the destruction of the planet. They have money, position, and education, but their lives revolve around more abstract, esoteric, or socially responsible ideals. Or they may use their greater awareness closer to home in pursuit of longer life through better nutrition and exercise. Either way, this group, which ranges from 5 to 20 percent of a given national population, is an intelligent and sophisticated bunch who are especially prevalent in Germany and Scandinavia.

**Affluent Materialists:** They haven't made it to the top yet, but they are enjoying all the trappings of success they can charge on the way up. They are status-driven and view their possessions as signs that tell the outside world they can afford the good life. Their mindset is linked to the American Business ethic, "Success is all. If you've made it, show it." The majority of them are members of the new merchant class of business professionals. This group, however, faces a dilemma. As they display more perks of their positions, it becomes harder to stand out from their peers. It is expected that this group will begin embracing less materialistic icons during the 1990s—better diet, world peace—and eventually, the posture may become reality as many move from this group to the Successful Idealist group.

**Comfortable Belongers:** This group, the backbone of a country's traditional society, lives in strict accordance with accepted everyday mores. They can make up anywhere from 25 to 50 percent of a population. They are conservative and seek to maintain the modest level of prosperity and self-sufficiency they have achieved. However, they can be quite open to change in their everyday behavior, adopting labor-saving devices after they have proven reliable. Mostly, this group wants to belong and lives within a comfortable microcosm composed of family, a small circle of friends, and their community. They seldom venture from the safety of the familiar. It is expected that the size and buying power of this group will remain constant but that their comfort will start to be tinged with fear. This may lead them to demand even more of the familiar—products linked with their own culture or established brands.

**Optimistic Strivers:** This group of people with relatively low economic status and shaky roots is proportionally greater in Southern Europe. They are often in transition—moving from country to city living, or making their way up from the Disaffected Striver to the Comfortable Belonger group. They have a way to go before completing their transition, but they have the ambition and skills necessary to accomplish it eventually. They are significant from a marketing standpoint because of their dynamism and increasing affluence. They like to demonstrate their rising economic status with new purchases. Their tastes, however, tend to be parochial, leaning toward those of the Comfortable Belongers.

**Disaffected Survivors:** At the bottom of the pile in terms of affluence and power, the members of this group are either resentful or resigned. They have little sense of belonging and little hope of rising in the social hierarchy. This group is most prevalent in the United Kingdom, where they account for 20 to 30 percent of the population. Here, they become similar to residents of the U.S. inner cities. Because of their circumstances, they are forced to live in high-crime areas, in daily contact with the failures of the social system. They are expected to be significant to marketers because their attitudes affect the rest of society and because they buy "badge" brands.

# Y&R's Four Cs

Young & Rubicam has an international segmentation scheme called Cross Cultural Consumer Characterizations™ (4 Cs) that is similar to the original VALS (see Chapter 3) in that it is an a priori, theory-based, segmentation tool. Like VALS, it is a typology that segments populations into groups according to their shared values. "We believe that a theory-based segmentation allows for richer, more meaningful interpretation of the segments than an ad hoc, empirically driven segmentation, because it has been developed based on well-researched, generally accepted theory about human motivations," says Margaret Mark, director of consumer insights.

Four Cs identifies seven consumer segments believed to exist in developed cultures. It differs from other typologies in that it focuses on the elements that make up *choice* in human behavior. Rather than describing lifestyles and demographics, the 4Cs model attempts to discern goals, motivations, and values. This makes it more predictive of behavior, the agency says, because together, goals, motivations, and values determine the choices consumers make.

"Choice can be thought of as the link between the internal factors of goals, motivations, and values on one side, and the external (observable) factors of lifestyle, work, and purchase patterns on the other side," the agency states. For example, an individual might choose to buy an expensive automobile because he is motivated by envy and values social status. Conversely, a person motivated by social consciousness, who values social altruism, might choose a car that gets high gas mileage.

The agency has worked with the theory in 20 countries and has fielded quantitative studies to develop a research instrument for classifying people into 4Cs segments in 12 of those countries. The sample size of the surveys ranges from 2,500 in the U.S. to 1,000 or less in smaller countries. People are classified into 4Cs segments according to their responses to a battery of questions designed to measure motivations, values, psychological attributes, and demographic characteristics. A five- or seven-point scale rates the extent to which they agree or disagree with items such as "I like things to be certain and predictable" or "I like other people to think I'm a financial success." Some items are weighted to take country-by-country differences into account.

Choices can depend on external factors such as the nature of governmental structures (democracy as opposed to a totalitarian regime) and societal factors such as affluence and education. But the 4Cs takes the perspective that there are underlying psychological processes involved in human behavior that are culture-free and so basic that they can be found all over the globe. The fundamental psychology of certain groups of individuals leads them to make similar choices in the marketplace. Upon this premise, 4Cs has identified seven groups of consumers characterized by their similar goals, motivations, and values.

*Figure 8-6  The Seven 4Cs Consumer Groups*

| TYPE | GOAL | MOTIVATION | VALUE |
|------|------|------------|-------|
| **Constrained** | | | |
| • Resigned Poor | Survival | Given up | Subsistence |
| • Struggling Poor | Improvement | Escape from hardship | Hope and luck |
| | | | |
| **Middle Majority** | | | |
| • Mainstreamers | Security | Conformity, Family responsibility | Social acceptance |
| • Aspirers | Seen as successful | Envy | Status |
| • Succeeders | Control, "Material success" | Achievement | Recognition |
| | | | |
| **Innovators** | | | |
| • Transitionals | Self-identity | Rebellion Self-confidence | Self-satisfaction |
| • Reformers | Social betterment | Social conscience Moral certitude | Self-esteem Social altruism |

*Source:  Young & Rubicam*

Constrained, Middle Majority, and Innovators are three larger groupings that represent the position of the types in the larger society. Constrained types have lower incomes and spend much of their energies trying to subsist. The Middle Majority reflect the status quo in any culture. They spend their lives trying to remain comfortable and seeking security, status, or recognition. The Innovators are the movers and shakers of society and try to effect change in various ways.

Part of the 4Cs theory originates in Maslow's theory of a human-needs hierarchy that starts with basic needs such as survival, which once satisfied, progress to higher intellectual needs such as self-actualization. Another facet of the 4Cs work includes Roger's theory of the diffusion of innovations—that there are innovative groups in any culture that adopt change first and spread it to the rest of the population. "We believe that these assumptions are so fundamental to people that they don't change a great deal geographically, and they don't change over time," says Mark. "The expression changes geographically and over time, but not the fundamental values." The 4Cs theory further provides common attitudes, occupations, lifestyle activities, and purchase behaviors of the groups.

Once the 4Cs instrument has been developed in a country, Y&R researchers can link the segments to syndicated data from consumer panels to predict likely product and category consumption for the various segments.

*Figure 8-7  The 4Cs Groups: How They Live and What They Do*

## Resigned Poor

| ATTITUDES | WORK | LIFESTYLE ACTIVITIES | PURCHASE BEHAVIOR |
|---|---|---|---|
| Unhappy | Sporadic | Shut-in | Staples |
| Isolated | Labor | Television | Price |
| Insecure | Domestic | | Seek reassurance |
| Distrustful | Unskilled | | (brands, guarantees) |
| Longs for family | | | Resourceful |
| and Past | | | Used goods |

## Struggling Poor

| ATTITUDES | WORK | LIFESTYLE ACTIVITIES | PURCHASE BEHAVIOR |
|---|---|---|---|
| Unhappy | Labor | Sports | Price |
| Suspicious | Factory | Music | Time payments |
| Rebelling | Craftsmen | Television | Instant gratification |
| Dissatisfied | Domestic | | Resourceful |
| Left out | Minimally skilled | | Discount stores |
| Status | Temporaries | | |

## Mainstreamers

| ATTITUDES | WORK | LIFESTYLE ACTIVITIES | PURCHASE BEHAVIOR |
|---|---|---|---|
| Happy | Craftsmen | Family | Habit |
| Family-centered | Union skilled | Letter, cards | Brand loyal |
| Belong | Clerical | Gardening | Seek reassurance |
| Save | Gray-collar | Spectator sports | (brand names) |
| Cautious | Bureaucratic | Television | Approved stores |
| Conventional | Teaching | | Made from scratch |
| Patriotic | Personal service | | No credit |
| Trusting | Health practitioners | | |

## Aspirers

| ATTITUDES | WORK | LIFESTYLE ACTIVITIES | PURCHASE BEHAVIOR |
|---|---|---|---|
| Unhappy | Sales | Trendy sports | Conspicuous |
| Dissatisfied | Clerical | Fashion | consumption |
| Suspicious | Entry-level | magazines | Fads |
| Ambitious | White-collar | | Impulse |
| Display | Nonmanufacturing | | Credit |
| Little confidence | Personal care | | |

## Succeeders

| ATTITUDES | WORK | LIFESTYLE ACTIVITIES | PURCHASE BEHAVIOR |
|---|---|---|---|
| Happy | Managerial | Travel | Luxury |
| Confident | Professional | Competitive | Top of line |
| Satisfied | Owner | Sports | Quality |
| Industrious | Entrepreneur | Sailing | Convenience |
| Family is priority | Government | Dining out | Status |
| Competitive | White-collar | Dinner parties | |
| Establishment | Leadership positions | | |
| Search for progress | | | |

## Transitionals

| ATTITUDES | WORK | LIFESTYLE ACTIVITIES | PURCHASE BEHAVIOR |
|---|---|---|---|
| Rebellious | Student | Unconventional | Impulse |
| Experimental | Unconventional | Music fields | Unique products |
| Self-expressive | Health, helping | Movies | Travel |
| Process important | fields | Arts/crafts/cooking | |
| Intuitive | Nonmanufacturing | (making, doing) | |
| Self-indulgence | | Special-interest | |
| Seek change | | magazines | |
| Liberal | | | |
| Unambitious | | | |

## Reformers

| ATTITUDES | WORK | LIFESTYLE ACTIVITIES | PURCHASE BEHAVIOR |
|---|---|---|---|
| Inner growth | Professional | Reading | Ecology |
| Simplicity | Entrepreneur | Cultural events | Conservation |
| Involved | Academic | Intelligent games | Authenticity |
| Self-confident | Health, social | Civics, politics | Aesthetics |
| Broad interest | fields | Educational TV | Voluntary |
| Natural, health | | | Eclectic tastes |
| Improve world | | | Homemade/grown |
| Issue-oriented | | | |

*Source: Young & Rubicam*

The crucial function of the 4Cs is to identify similarities across cultures. Y&R states that multinational marketing starts with the question, "Is there a segment of consumers in population A that is similar to a segment of consumers in population B, both of which are viable targets for a marketing effort?" The 4Cs approach suggests that there is more similarity between a consumer type in one culture and its counterpart in another than between different types within the same culture. The needs and behavior patterns of an American farmer, for example, might be more similar to those of a Soviet farmer than to an American investment banker who lives in Manhattan.

The 4Cs is most valuable when used in combination with other types of data that allow analysts to gain insights into consumer motivations. "No research tool should be considered the panacea," Mark cautions. "When we have a specific marketing or communications issue to deal with, we use this segmentation as a framework for thinking about targeting and about how we might tailor our marketing activities and communications plans." The 4Cs, then, often serves as a base of understanding for further research, such as focus groups, family life cycle, and other tools, to help establish core-brand essences consistent across cultures for Y&R clients. "That's not to say that you develop one strategy and one commercial and force feed it to different cultures, "Mark says. "As you get closer to the executional level, you need to be acutely sensitive to cultural differences. But at the origin, it's of enormous benefit to be able to think about people who share common values across cultures."

## What Good Is Global Psychographics?

Over-generalization has been a continuing concern surrounding large-scale psychographic segmentations, especially when they are attempted on a global scale. Whenever a large population is segmented into smaller groups defined by shared characteristics, something of the inherent diversity and richness of the larger group is lost in the translation. Regardless of whether they are defined by purchasing patterns or common values, 5, 8, or 10 groups can't really do the larger group justice. On the other hand, creating 30 groups that more closely reflect the complicated attitudinal reality of the population won't do anybody any good, because such a segmentation is too complicated to understand and use.

The question of validity becomes more of an issue when such systems are compared across diverse cultures. Serious consideration needs to be given to language and cultural obstacles. A user of such data should ask certain questions: Have pains been taken to assure that the original meaning of the attitudinal items has been translated accurately? Have customs or cultural differences that would prevent candor been taken into account? Has the survey been done by professionals dedicated to accuracy? If the questionnaire was designed for one country, has it been altered so it is applicable to others?

No critical assumptions have been made about the above global psychographic studies. The proprietary nature of the studies made it impossible to get enough specific information to make any determination one way or another about validity or reliability. Nor was it possible to gain access to any case study information that would better illustrate how the systems have been used for clients.

Each agency says that its global psychographic research is one of the first tools it uses when taking on a new international client. The best use of psychographics in the international sphere seems to be in forming a first impression of a potential target. Once the first cut has been made and the focus of the project has been narrowed sufficiently, then it's time to do more a detailed study to reveal the attitudes of specific people in specific countries about specific products. One of the most universal global marketing maxims appears to be, "Market to the similarities, but never forget the differences."

# 9 | *Going Local: Broadcast Markets*

*"It wasn't rocket science that told me we needed to do separate psychographic segmentations for each local market. We know that no two markets are the same, that you can't employ the same strategy in one market and have it work in another."*

— *Leigh Stowell*

**W**HILE SOME are exploring ways to measure attitudes and values of consumers on an international level, other firms are taking a micro approach to psychographics. At the micro level, the American marketplace is a complex tapestry of hundreds of thousands of local markets. Each local area, be it a city, county, or broadcast market, has a unique demographic and psychographic character that influences the types of products and services demanded in that market.

Up until recently, national advertisers had no way of knowing how San Franciscans differed from Atlantans in terms of attitudes, values, and lifestyles, aside from surveying each individual market—a cost-prohibitive task even for the largest manufacturers. Smaller regional companies, if they were interested in the preponderant attitudes in their local markets at all, usually relied on intuition and observation to tell them what their customers thought or how they lived.

About a decade ago, however, some firms started to do customized surveys of local markets. One industry with a growing demand for local market information is broadcasting. As the nation dipped into recession in the early 1980s, local radio and television stations saw growth slow to disappointing single-digit levels. For the first time, growth wasn't effortless, and competition for advertising dollars was coming from new areas such as barter syndication and cable channels. Traditional competitors such as newspapers were getting tougher, offering more color and special sections to help local advertisers home in on customer segments. At the same time, the total pie was shrinking as companies shifted more of their advertising budgets from media to promotions and direct-mail campaigns.

Advertisers also started to put more pressure on media to prove that broadcast advertising got results. Broadcasters, however, had little proof to offer beyond broad-brush demographics in the form of age and sex breakdowns from standard Nielsen and Arbitron ratings. Faced with the task of convincing advertisers that TV and radio ads were reaching the customers they wanted to reach in the most cost-effective way, station owners began to realize they needed more specific information about their audiences. They needed answers to questions like: Who was watching or listening to their stations? When did they watch or listen, and what programs or formats did they prefer? What did they spend their money on? What did they think and feel? Custom research firms, like Leigh Stowell & Company of Seattle and Marshall Marketing & Communications Inc. of Pittsburgh that specialize in broadcast markets, saw their client lists swell during the last decade, thanks to this new thirst for information.

## Taking Account

Stowell and Marshall are now in 60 to 70 broadcast markets nationwide. Contracted by one station in each local market, these firms survey residents and create a single-source database with specific demographic, psychographic, media preference, and product-use information for the local market. In many markets, they are hired by competing stations, which then use the information as a selling tool to show advertisers precisely where to run their ads to reach their target audiences most efficiently. Using local psychographic information, stations can also help advertisers tailor their ads using images and keywords specifically directed at targeted attitude groups. Marshall uses SRI's VALS2 program to analyze local market psychographics, while Stowell creates unique attitude segmentations for each market.

It works like this: armed with the information from the survey, a sales representative from KNSD-TV in San Diego, for example, can go into a local Mazda dealership and tell the manager all about the people who said they were considering buying a Mazda in the next year. They can determine that these people are mostly Achievers and Fulfilleds who watch "Murphy Brown" and the local 6:00 news. Then their advertising agency can create ads using words like "intelligent" and "prestige," showing intimate circles of friends in comfortable upscale or cultural settings. "Not only can we tell car dealers what images will appeal to Mazda buyers," says Lorraine Harris, KNSD's marketing research manager, "but we can teach their salespeople to use that information, too."

Ironically, both firms originated in Seattle at the start of the 1980s, brainchildren of researchers working for competing stations that were literally across the street from one another. GMA Research developed a survey for KOMO, and shortly afterwards, competitor station KYRO-TV signed on as the first client of Leigh Stowell, a former KYRO general manager. GMA Research's program, Target Dollars, was acquired in 1985 by Craig Marshall, who had been a sales manager at Pittsburgh's WTAE. After using Target Dollars, Marshall says he realized that better information about local markets would be the strategic selling tool of the most successful stations in the future. "The time when broadcasters could just sit back and let the money come to them is gone. It is a dinosaur, as dead as the steeltown glory days in Pittsburgh, " says Marshall. "Broadcasters of today have to be marketers. They have to get out there and get more of the pie."

The growth of both Marshall and Stowell's companies suggests that more broadcasters are turning to market-specific information as a strategic selling tool. Having access to such precise information changes the relationship between station and advertiser from the standard buyer-seller relationship to a marketing partnership, says Leigh Stowell. "Both advertisers and broadcasters are realizing that their common goal is to move each other's product," Stowell says. In the past, the emphasis was on getting the lowest "cost per thousand" and reaching the greatest number of people within a broad demographic group (such as men age 18 to 49) for the least amount of money. "More accountability is now being demanded on both sides," Stowell adds. "Broadcasters need to be able to come into an agency or an account with a success story, to say, 'See, the campaign worked, it reached your target and sold more product.'"

The demand for accountability has sparked more interest in psychographics, even at the local market level. Marshall first added the VALS psychographics questions to its surveys in 1987, says Kay Marikos, Marshall's director of client services. When Marikos first talked to clients about psychographics, hardly anybody knew what she meant. Local advertisers and station reps are more sophisticated now, she says. "Now, when I say VALS or psychographics, people nod their heads. They know what I'm talking about, so I don't have to go through quite so much explanation."

## Single Source

As noted in the beginning chapters of this book, psychographic information becomes much more actionable when it is tied to information on purchasing, media habits, and demographics. Demographics reveal who the consumer is; psychographics shows their attitudes, interests, and opinions; purchase data tell what they buy; and media data say how to reach them—whether they prefer print, radio, or television, and when they are likely to be reading, watching, or listening. Both Stowell's Consumer Market Profile and Marshall's Target Dollar$ cover all four areas.

Marshall and Stowell conduct an initial series of meetings with client stations or representatives and their major advertisers to identify any sales problems and to establish the questions that will be asked about purchasing habits in the market. In telephone interviews lasting less than 30 minutes, respondents answer more than 100 questions. The size of the sample ranges between 750 and 2,500 people, depending on the size of the market and the number of advertiser-specific questions. People are asked about 20 demographic questions—age, education, marital status, race, presence of children, income, etc.

The purchase questions on Stowell and Marshall surveys vary widely depending on the major advertisers in a market. Some standard categories include grocery, automobiles, furniture, home electronics, major appliances, eyewear, shoes, and fast food. For instance, respondents may be asked whether they are the primary shopper for their household, where they do most of their shopping, and how much they spend in an average week. Habits, such as the tendency to buy on impulse, clip coupons, or to look for the lowest prices, are also measured.

The media preference questions vary depending upon whether the client broadcaster is a radio or television station, although the basic media information includes whether people read newspapers, when, what sections, what radio station they listened to yesterday and when, what television stations they watched, and whether they watched any of a list of about 30 specific programs. Stowell's survey differs from Marshall's in that Stowell only asks about viewership of client stations, while Marshall gathers data on viewership of all stations in the market. Both surveys have also included questions on exposure to cable, promotions, and direct-mail advertising.

The power of a single-source database is its convenience, says Anthony Schlee, Stowell's director of psychographics and technical services. It's like one-stop shopping for all the information you need to understand a local market. Not only does the database show Safeway customers who spend more than $100 a week, it also reveals what else they buy frequently, whether they buy on credit or clip coupons, and shows a whole range of psychological characteristics. Do they have high self-esteem, or do they need flashy material possessions to reaffirm their status? Once advertisers understand more about how their customers think, says Schlee, they can write ad copy that strikes a responsive chord with those customers. "We can even go one step beyond that and show them exactly where to place their ads so they can reach perhaps 70 percent of that very specific segment," says Schlee.

Through these local surveys, psychographics is taken down to the one-on-one level where it has, perhaps, the greatest likelihood of affecting the way broadcasters and merchants serve their communities.

## Psychographic Specifics

The psychographic component is what really separates the Stowell and Marshall surveys from scores of other market research firms. Marshall is the only company in the country licensed by SRI to administer the VALS2 questionnaire for broadcasters. Stowell's unique psychographic program was developed in-house especially for use in segmenting local broadcast markets.

The rest of this chapter will first examine Stowell's psychographic segmentation system, including a comparison of schemes in two different markets. Then we'll see how Marshall has adapted the VALS 2 system to local market use. We'll compare the two systems in one market, and finally, examine case studies from client stations to address the question of how to apply psychographic information at the local level.

## The Stowell Approach

In developing Stowell's segmentation scheme in 1981, Dr. Anthony Schlee, a social psychologist, started with 150 questions that measure different psychological attributes. Respondents rate the extent to which they agree or disagree with statements such as, "I like to buy things on impulse." The questionnaire also goes into detail about leisure activities, as well as interests and opinions. The battery was honed down to 48 and then 40 questions, as testing determined the attributes that really discriminated among different types of consumer behavior. The resulting model is unweighted, which produces better replication of results over time, according to Schlee.

Schlee points out that economic downturns or major news events can cause fairly significant, albeit short-term, fluctuations in attitudes such as self-esteem and cynicism in local areas. In 1987, for example, oil prices fell below $15 a barrel, and within four months, Houston lost more than 122,000 jobs. Many unemployed residents defaulted on their mortgages and lost their homes. In the ensuing year, 150,000 people left Houston in search of work elsewhere. This had a major effect not only on the demographics of the area, says Schlee, but also on the way Houstonians felt about themselves and their city. "Had I weighted certain things," Schlee says, "I would have ended up with a very skewed sample of psychographic groupings. With the unweighted model, we got a fairly stable resolution."

The most unique thing about the Stowell system is that psychographic groups are created for each market. "It was not rocket science that told me we needed to do this," Leigh Stowell says. "We know that no two markets are the same, that you can't employ the same strategy in one market and have it work in another." This approach does limit the applicability of the Stowell system for larger national advertisers, but Stowell says this isn't a problem, because there is no intention of turning the system into a national database or competing with VALS on a national basis.

Some national advertisers have asked for psychographic data so they can cluster regional markets, but Stowell says even that application goes against the firm's charter. "We have clients in Seattle and Tacoma, Dallas and Fort Worth, and they're all different marketplaces," Stowell says. "We're not going to collapse them and say, psychographically, they can be appealed to with these common variables. They're just too different."

## COMPARING TWO MARKETS

The best way to understand why Stowell thinks this way is to take a look at what surveys revealed about two very disparate local markets. What could be more different than New York City and Fort Wayne, Indiana? New York is a volatile mix of people from diverse ethnic, racial, and economic backgrounds, forced to compete for scarce resources like housing and to interact in a finite space made more stressful by the pressure-cooker atmosphere of the declining international city. Fort Wayne, on the other hand, is nestled amid the wide-open spaces of the industrial heartland. While it has faced some economic setbacks with the decline of heavy industry, it has a more homogenous population than New York, a lower crime rate, lower taxes, and cheaper housing.

These are just the surface differences apparent even to observers lacking the ability to see the cities' psychographic hearts. Peel away the layers of demographics, and Stowell's Consumer Market Profile found nine predominant attitudinal groups in the New York market based on a survey sample of 2,500:

### NEW YORK, NY

Stowell's survey found that the largest portion (22 percent) of the New York population is made up of Group VIII—mostly older retirees living on fixed incomes who have to struggle to make ends meet and often reflect on the less complicated days of their youths. The next largest groups are Group IV (13 percent of the population), the optimists who enjoy living life and having a good time, and Group V (12 percent of population), whose members are focused on home and family and consider themselves ordinary people.

GROUP I (10 percent of the population) This is an affluent, well-educated bunch that manages to balance satisfying professions with political action. They are in control of their lives, confident, and comfortable with taking risks and being innovative. They are liberal and compassionate. They see themselves as leaders who owe it to themselves and those more powerless to try to change for the better the inequities they see in the governmental and community institutions around them.

*Demographics*: They are white (91 percent), slightly more female (53 percent), have incomes above $95,000 and a median age of 44. They are frugal and buy from discount stores.

GROUP II (11 percent) They are the most affluent, satisfied, and stable group in the market. Politically conservative, they truly enjoy the business world and their careers close to the hub of U.S. commerce, and have faith in their own abilities to find solutions to business and management problems. They will consider taking business risks, but are far less likely to take personal or political risks. After work, they commute to gracious homes outside the city, where they enjoy a warm, stable family life with all the amenities of suburban living. They tend to believe that women should follow traditional paths and that government should stay out of the way of business. They buy for quality and style, and time-saving service is important.

*Demographics*: They are more likely to be male (66 percent), college-educated (46 percent), have average incomes of $97,000 and an average age of 43. Ninety percent are white, and 65 percent are married.

**GROUP III** (8 percent) This group has the highest proportion of dual-paycheck households of any group and the third highest income. They are happy with where they are at this stage of their lives, but see themselves as still on the way up. They are likely to play it safe where business or personal risks are concerned. Many are in sales and want to move up into management positions. They are apolitical and cynical, believing that politicians aren't responsive to anyone outside the power structure and that big business holds the real power. The married IIIs are just starting their families, while the singles are likely to spend their money on clubs, restaurants, and other indulgences. As consumers, they watch for sales, but still appreciate quality.

*Demographics*: Their average age is 39, and they are slightly more female (53 percent) than male (47 percent). Average household income is $98,000, and 64 percent live in dual-earner households. Fully 64 percent are married. Most are white (81 percent), but 13 percent are black and 7 percent are Hispanic.

**GROUP IV** (13 percent) These are optimists who enjoy living life and having a good time. Their career aspirations are modest, as are their incomes, and they seek fulfillment through satisfying personal relationships. They have high self-esteem and are natural leaders among their peers because of it. These dyed-in-the-wool New Yorkers thrive on the rich diversity of the city. Politically, they tend to be liberal, but are not likely to act on their beliefs. Since they work regular 40-hour weeks, they have time to enjoy a wide variety of leisure activities, from partying with friends and eating out, to taking in cultural and artistic events. They love to shop and, though attracted to sales, find ways to justify buying expensive items they really want.

*Demographics*: Women make up 53 percent of this group. Average household income is $60,000, and 57 percent live in dual-income homes. Most have finished high school (73 percent) and are employed as clerks or in lower-level managerial, service, or skilled blue-collar jobs. Whites make up 83 percent, blacks 13 percent, and Hispanics 5 percent.

**GROUP V** (12 percent) Focused on home and family, they consider themselves the ordinary people. They are optimistic about the future, feel their incomes are adequate, and see their jobs simply as a means of making a living. While not always actively religious, many strongly believe in the teachings of the Bible. This conservative group feels that womens' rights get too much attention and women are best off tending to their families. They prefer spending time with their families to going out, but when they do, it's likely to be a family activity. They see themselves as leaders among their peers. As consumers, they buy practical, durable items, appreciate value, and think quality is more important than price.

*Demographics*: Men make up 56 percent. Average household income is $47,000, with 53 percent coming from two or more wage earners. The average age is 47. More than three-quarters (76 percent) are high school graduates, and most are employed as clerks, blue-collar workers, mid- or lower-level managers, or service workers. Whites make up 87 percent, blacks 8 percent, and Hispanics 8 percent.

**GROUP VI** (11 percent) They are dissatisfied with life and feel that, though they work hard, they get nowhere. They feel life hasn't been fair to them, their incomes are not adequate, and they hold no hope that the future will be any better. They feel uncomfortable with the way things around them are changing, avoid risks, and prefer regular schedules. Hardly social butterflies, this group prefers quiet family evenings to social gatherings even if they feel they have the money to go out. Politically alienated, this group feels its opinions aren't taken seriously and politicians only listen to big-money campaign contributors. They hold non-traditional values, believing women should be compensated for equal work and household chores should be shared equally. As consumers, they are careful, planning shopping trips and clipping coupons. They like practicality and affordability, and are price driven.

*Demographics*: Females make up 58 percent of this group. They have average incomes of $43,000, and their average age is 39. Eighty percent are high school graduates. Most are white (73 percent), while 23 percent are black, and 14 percent are Hispanic.

**GROUP VII** (7 percent) This group is the least affluent, and has the lowest educational levels and highest proportion of minorities. They are frustrated with their lot in life and pessimistic about their ability to change it. They tend to dream of doing something different, but are trapped in set routines and unwilling or unable to take risks. They don't see themselves as leaders even among their peers and get a good deal of their entertainment from television. They stay home or get together with small groups of friends. They are politically alienated, and say that big corporations hold all the power and political officials are their pawns. They are ambivalent about women's issues, and although not deeply religious, they hold to a literal interpretation of the Bible. As consumers, they are very price sensitive, but occasionally they will buy a small item on impulse just to make themselves feel better.

*Demographics*: Women make up 60 percent, and average annual household income is $22,000. The average age is 48 years, and 29 percent have not finished high school. Only

43 percent have full-time jobs. Whites make up 73 percent, blacks 20 percent, and Hispanics 16 percent.

**GROUP VIII** (22 percent) This is the oldest group in the market, made up mostly of retirees living on fixed incomes. They have to struggle to make ends meet, but don't dwell too much on money problems. Surrounded by rapid changes, they take comfort in the familiar and often reflect on the less complicated days of their youths. They stay home and get most of their entertainment from television because they don't feel safe going out. They don't pay much attention to politics, but they do support women's rights. Many are deeply religious, attend church regularly, hold to strict moral standards, and believe in a literal interpretation of the Bible. As consumers, they plan shopping trips, use coupons, and look for sales to stretch their limited funds. Price and quality are important, and they are likely to be loyal to familiar brands.

*Demographics*: Women make up 66 percent, and average income is $25,500. The majority are high school graduates (78 percent), and 19 percent did not complete high school. Average age is 48. Whites make up the majority (79 percent), while 15 percent are black, and 13 percent are Hispanic.

**GROUP IX** (5 percent) This group is mostly young and unattached. Their incomes are low, but because they have no dependents and few commitments, they feel their incomes are adequate to their needs. They are open to new experiences and may enjoy taking risks, but also like their days regulated by set schedules. They are optimistic about the future, but are not highly ambitious. They are very social and prefer going out with friends to spending time with family. They have little interest in politics and hold no strong political views. They tend not to support women's rights or nontraditional sex roles. As consumers, they look for good value and think that quality and convenience are more important than price. They often buy clothing to attract the opposite sex.

*Demographics*: Males are 52 percent of this group. Average income is $29,000, and average age is 40, although 44 percent are under age 30, and 23 percent are 60 or older. The majority are high school graduates (76 percent), and about 12 percent have completed college. Nearly 70 percent are employed either as clerks, service workers, or skilled blue-collar workers. While 29 percent are married, nearly half (48 percent) have never married. The majority are white (81 percent), 15 percent are black, and 11 percent are Hispanic.

### FORT WAYNE, IN
The Consumer Market Profile found four groups in the Fort Wayne market, each approximately one-fourth of the population. The largest groups are Group III at 28 percent, and Group IV at 27 percent. Group III is traditional, focused on home, family, and children. Group IV is the dispirited older, retired, and predominantly female group.

**GROUP I** (23 percent of the population) Young, well-educated and affluent, this group is content with their lives both personally and professionally. They entertain and go out often, frequently with business associates. They like to be considered trendsetters and leaders among their peers. Often sports-oriented, they spend leisure time swimming or playing golf, racquet sports, or team sports. They are career-oriented and don't mind working long hours. They are also well-educated and well-informed and make a special effort to keep up with latest developments, both in the world and in their fields. Change doesn't threaten them; rather, they see it as an opportunity to broaden their experiences. They are politically liberal and believe in nontraditional sex roles. As consumers, they go for style and quality and buy clothing that projects a successful image. They use coupons on occasion and like to try new products.

*Demographics*: Men make up 53 percent of this group. The average age is 36, and average income is $49,000—69 percent coming from dual-income households. Fully 53 percent are college graduates, and 91 percent are white.

**GROUP II** (22 percent) This is the most affluent group in Fort Wayne. They place more emphasis on family life than on pursuing their careers. They enjoy spending time with their families and often participate in social activities with their families. They are content with their positions in life. This group is more politically involved than other groups in the market and tends to be conservative and patriotic. They are conservative in their personal values as well, feeling that the Bible should be interpreted literally and women should get no special considerations in the workplace. They are often angered by sex and violence in the media. As consumers, they want high quality and become loyal to brands that serve them well.

*Demographics*: Men make up 56 percent of this group. The average income is $49,5000, the average age is 43, and 92 percent are white. Most (60 percent) are high school graduates, but college graduates make up 38 percent.

**GROUP III** (28 percent) They see themselves as average Americans. Home, family, and children are their primary focus. While they enjoy spending time with their families, they also like socializing with others, whether it be going out for a beer with the guys after work, going out to a family-style restaurant, or having friends over for dinner. These people are satisfied with their jobs, but not extremely ambitious. They work their shift, but relish evenings and weekends when they can do as they please. Many see themselves as leaders among their peers and take pride in knowing their opinions are important to others. This group is not particularly active, but holds strong political views. Their personal values are traditional—literal interpretation of the Bible, concern about looser sexual mores, and discomfort with alternative sexual lifestyles. As consumers, they tend to shop for quality, but they also clip coupons and look for sales to stretch their paychecks.

*Demographics*: Women make up 57 percent of this group. Their average age is 44, and more than three-quarters (78 percent) have a high school diploma. The average household income is $23,000, and most are employed as laborers, clerks, service workers, or skilled blue-collar workers. Fully 94 percent are white, and 3 percent are black.

GROUP IV: (27 percent) Members of this group tend to be older, retired, and predominantly female. Most aren't happy with their lives, but feel there's little hope that things will improve. Those who do work are stuck in dead-end jobs, but prefer to avoid risks and stay with what is familiar and comfortable. Their circle of friends is very small, and a quiet night of television or a card game is often their only entertainment. Most like to reminisce about bygone, simpler days. They see themselves as followers and feel their opinions aren't taken seriously by others. They hold both politically conservative and liberal views and are, on the whole, deeply religious. They go to church, take the Bible literally, and feel that alternative lifestyles will lead to a breakdown of our society. As consumers, they are very price conscious and routinely clip coupons and scan newspapers for sales and specials. Although they'd like to buy quality, they are usually forced to buy whatever is least expensive.

*Demographics*: Women make up 59 percent of this group. Their average age is 47, and their average annual income is $20,000, with 24 percent reporting no wage earners. Most have a high school diploma (70 percent), while 29 percent did not complete high school. This group has the highest proportion of minority members—7 percent are black.

## Marshall's VALS 2 Approach

While Stowell creates separate groups for each market, Marshall applies a standard national model, the VALS 2 model, to every market. There are pros and cons to both approaches: some say that fitting a local market to a national model is like forcing clay through molds—you always produce the same shapes in the end. The Stowell people claim that their system identifies local nuances in a way that a standard system like VALS 2 does not.

The uniformity of the VALS 2 groups, however, brings an added dimension to local psychographics. VALS 2 tells us that Actualizers, Fulfilleds, Achievers, Strivers, Experiencers, Makers, Believers, and Strugglers will always be the same whether they live in Kalamazoo or Los Angeles. With VALS 2, comparing groups across markets is easier—comparing apples with apples instead of trying to find similarities between apples and oranges. Marshall's clients can compare the psychographic breakdowns of their populations with other markets as well as with the national average.

Marshall data from the 61 markets surveyed in 1990 hold some interesting insights. Where do the cream of the VALS 2 crop, the Actualizers, live? This independent, affluent, intelligent, and sophisticated group is a significant proportion of the populations of San Francisco (21 percent) and Washington, D.C. (19 percent). Both shares are more than double the national average of 8 percent. Fort Smith, Arkansas, and Cedar Rapids, Iowa, have the fewest Actualizers. Washington, D.C., also has the highest proportion of upscale Achievers, 22 percent, well over the national average of 13 percent.

Where do the largest proportions of regular, work-a-day, middle-class, mainstream Americans live? Not in San Francisco or Washington; the traditional, family-oriented Believers were scarcest in these cities. Greenville, Fort Myers, Detroit, and Tampa topped the list of cities for share of Believers. Makers, a self-sufficient, do-it-yourself, blue-collar bunch, don't care much for Washington, either. They are found in greatest proportions in Johnstown, Pennsylvania; Cedar Rapids, Iowa; Little Rock, Arkansas; Davenport, Iowa; and Fort Smith, Arkansas.

Where do the Strugglers live? This group, composed largely of inactive elderly people squeaking by on fixed incomes and longing for a simpler, happier past, is most populous in Fort Smith, Arkansas; Savannah, Georgia; Jacksonville, Florida; Johnstown, Pennsylvania; and Tulsa, Oklahoma. Washington, Austin, San Francisco, and Miami have the fewest of this group.

There is something fundamentally attractive about the VALS 2 groups. Even those who don't believe all Americans fit into the eight VALS 2 types have to admit an interest in seeing how individual cities rate on their share of Actualizers versus Believers, or Achievers versus Strugglers. VALS 2 provides a common framework through which marketers can get a sense of how the flavor of Austin differs from that of Savannah, and what approaches and products might work in Jacksonville, but bomb in Miami.

## TARGET DOLLAR$

The actual Target Dollar$ program consists of two parts: the first is Marshall's annual basic marketing study, which gathers purchase, media, and demographic information for an area. The second part is the VALS 2 study. The VALS 2 questionnaire includes 42 items like, "It wouldn't bother me to put a worm on a hook" and "I am a talkative person," with which the subject agrees or disagrees. As discussed in detail in Chapter 5, the VALS 2 system measures two dimensions of consumers—self-orientation and resources. Self-orientation refers to whether people are motivated by principle, status, or action. The resources dimension includes any material or psychological means (income, intelligence, health, energy, education) that affects consumers' ability or desire to buy.

The interviewing goes on for three to four weeks and includes up to 2,500 people, depending on the market size. Marshall processes the results of the marketing study, while the VALS 2 data are sent to SRI International for processing. Marshall trains station personnel in understanding the VALS 2 consumer groups. Once the results are in, Marshall presents its findings about the psychographic makeup of the market to stations, advertisers, a national representative, and news media. One such meeting in Jacksonville produced a rash of local articles, including a three-part series in a local paper announcing, "Jacksonville's population has high number of 'Strugglers,' market research discovers." (Another attribute of VALS 2 is that the group names are clever enough to grab headlines.)

## BOSTON VS. FORT WAYNE

The fairest way to understand how Marshall applies psychographics to local markets is to compare the findings for two broadcast markets. Because Marshall hasn't surveyed the New York metropolitan market, we've chosen another eastern city, Boston, to compare with the Fort Wayne, Indiana market. Since the VALS 2 groups are explained in Chapter 5, we'll merely look at how the two cities compare.

| Category | National | Boston | Fort Wayne |
|---|---|---|---|
| Actualizers | 8.0% | 16.0% | 8.5% |
| Fulfilleds | 11.0 | 16.1 | 11.2 |
| Believers | 16.0 | 11.0 | 12.5 |
| Achievers | 13.9 | 17.2 | 12.1 |
| Strivers | 13.0 | 9.6 | 14.8 |
| Experiencers | 12.0 | 16.3 | 17.8 |
| Makers | 13.0 | 8.1 | 13.1 |
| Strugglers | 14.0 | 5.7 | 10.1 |

Boston is above the national average in its proportion of Achievers, Experiencers, Fulfilleds, and Actualizers. Fort Wayne is above the national average in Experiencers, Strivers, Makers, and Actualizers.

# Marshall's Fort Wayne vs. Stowell's Fort Wayne

Depending on who is surveyed, how the research is done, and how the data are processed, Fort Wayne can look quite different. The differences in the surveys point out the differences in the psychographic systems.

Stowell found four groups that each represented close to one-fourth of the population. The largest group, at 28 percent of the population, was the traditional one whose members see themselves as average Americans and focus on home, family, and children. Next was the dispirited older, retired, and predominantly female group whose members rarely go out and who like to reminisce about bygone, simpler days. In some respects, these groups seem similar to VALS 2 Believers and Strugglers.

The VALS 2 survey found that Fort Wayne had a high proportion of Experiencers and relatively few Strugglers. Believers were present, but at levels much below the national average. The two views of Fort Wayne are very different, and it is beyond the scope of this discussion to rate one approach over another. Suffice it to note that the Stowell system, while attempting to point out local nuances, generalizes the Fort Wayne market into four larger segments.

Because Marshall was using VALS 2, it had essentially predetermined that eight groups existed in the Fort Wayne population and consequently found eight groups in the population. But rather than thinking of eight groups, think of the measurement as eight personality attributes. VALS 2 measures the extent to which these eight personality and resource combinations are found in a given population. The power of this approach comes from the ability it provides to make comparisons with other areas.

## Keywords and Images

The group summaries for the New York and Fort Wayne markets provide nutshell descriptions of the shared characteristics and attitudes of the people who make up the groups. But advertisers and stations need more information to use the psychographic dimension in marketing. Both the Marshall VALS 2 system and Stowell Consumer Market Profile include archetypes that paint a more detailed portrait of customers in the groups. Stowell's archetype is a first-person narrative by a composite member of each group.

For example, the archetype for Stowell's Group I in the New York market is a 37-year-old attorney with a major law firm. We'll call him Joe. "Strategy is extremely important," Joe says. "Whenever you're doing something that's not routine, there's always the chance of failure, and the agony of defeat is great. Nevertheless, I'm an optimist, so even if I lose a case, I'm always looking forward to the next time. And the next time is usually a win." His wife is a busy interior decorator, and both of them routinely put in 60- or 70-hour weeks. "She doesn't put in nearly the hours I do," Joe adds, "but that's a good thing. One of us needs to have more time to go grocery shopping and take care of the household errands. We have a maid come and clean our place once a week, but there are still plenty of things that need to get done."

The Consumer Market Profile also lists the images and key words that appeal to members of various groups. Stowell's literature states that "as a general principle, the more that images depicted in an ad resemble the group members' lives or their dreams of the type of life they would like to lead, the more likely these people are to view the ad and what is advertised in a positive light."

There are two points that should be made here for the sake of perspective. One is that not all advertising researchers agree that the best way to sell a product in an ad is to mirror the target's lifestyle or attitudes. Some think that ads have overused the technique to such an extent that it no longer works. The other point is that these keywords and images are not carved in stone; that is, there is an arbitrary nature to them. For example, researchers infer that Group I will respond to images of speed and the word "speed," because they are time-pressed and view their time as a valuable commodity.

These are the images and keywords that the Consumer Market Profile suggests using when targeting Group I in the New York market:

*Figure 9-1  Stowell's Group I in New York*

| **Images that Attract** | **Images that Alienate** |
|---|---|
| •Strategic meetings, creative solutions | •Simplistic explanations |
| •Images of speed | •Inarticulate people |
| •Technology, science | •Slapstick, crass humor |
| •Cultural events, arts, classical music | •Unsophisticated settings |
| •Exotic vacation places | •Overly religious people |
| •Sophisticated luxury, upscale resorts, gourmet food | •People living traditional lives |
| •Intelligent, articulate, witty people | •Red-neck conservatives |
| | •Bargain basement |

**KEYWORDS**

| | |
|---|---|
| innovative | uncompromising |
| discover | unique |
| science | elegant |
| excellence | custom |
| responsive | imported |
| speed | natural |

*Source:  Leigh Stowell & Co.*

It's interesting to note that Group I in New York is not that much different from Group I in Fort Wayne. The Fort Wayne Group I archetype is also a successful, career-oriented lawyer who works for a private law firm, but his wife is a personnel officer. About the only point of difference is that in Fort Wayne, members of Group I are expected to respond more favorably to images of fast, competitive sports and spectacular scenes of nature. To get more of a sense of contrast, let's look at two demographically similar groups from each market that have more pronounced attitudinal differences.

Diane is a member of New York's Group VI. She's married to a delivery truck driver and has a 4-year-old son. This is what she says about her life: "I work all day long as a clerk in a drugstore. When I get off work, I'm dead tired, but I still have to go pick up my son from his day care, go home, cook, and clean up. Non-stop fun! And what makes things worse is that my husband doesn't feel like doing housework after lifting things on and off the truck all day. Life has turned out to be a lot harder than I thought. Sometimes I dream about leaving everything behind and doing something totally different."

*Figure 9-2  Stowell's Group VI in New York*

**Images that attract**
- Reasonably priced middle-class comforts
- Saving time, things that are convenient
- Affordable family vacations
- Dreams coming true, becoming wealthy
- Leaving one's troubles behind
- Husbands/wives equally sharing housework
- Heartwarming scenes of people with children

**Images that Alienate**
- Implicit criticisms of working mothers
- Traditional sex roles
- Conservative people
- Spoiled people who appear to have it all without trying
- Prices they cannot afford

**KEYWORDS**

| | |
|---|---|
| looks like more... | family |
| smart | children |
| economical | caring |
| quick | warm |
| convenient | happy |
| easy | comfortable |

*Source: Leigh Stowell & Co.*

Contrast Diane in New York with Fort Wayne's Group III archetype, who is a homemaker married to a machinist. They have two children, a 10-year-old boy and an 8-year-old girl. Although this woman (let's call her Elaine) used to work, she says now that she doesn't think a woman can take care of a home and children the way it should be done while holding down a full-time job. "The most important thing is to learn to live within your means," Elaine says. "I think many working mothers end up spending a lot of their money foolishly because they don't have enough time to organize themselves....I sew a lot, I knit a lot, and I'm always doing things for our home. It's all the special things that women do that make the home feel so warm and nice." If Elaine really exists, she may be proof that little isolated pockets of the old mass market still exist. The more things change, the more some things remain the same.

If a marketer were to look at Diane and Elaine purely from a demographic standpoint, there would be little apparent difference. The essential differences—Diane's feeling of being trapped, Elaine's pride in making her money go farther—only emerge at the psychographic level. These profiles illustrate the kind of information that psychographics can provide.

*Figure 9-3  Stowell's Group III in Fort Wayne*

**Images that Attract**
- Traditional family scenes and contemporary settings
- Women nurturing husbands and children
- Women being good homemakers and creating a pleasant home atmosphere
- "Cute" things for the home
- Men fixing things around the house
- People being friendly, neighborly
- Budget-stretching ideas
- Smart shopping

**Images that Alienate**
- People disregarding family
- Avant-garde lifestyles
- Technical jargon
- Gloomy scenes, negative feelings
- High prices

**KEYWORDS**

| | |
|---|---|
| family | trusted |
| home | popular |
| homemade | affordable |
| friendly | smart, best value |
| reliable | budget |
| tough, strong | sale, clearance |

*Source:  Leigh Stowell & Co.*

## Psycho-Selling:  The Pros and Cons

The glimpses that psychographics can give into consumers' psyches are appealing to people in the selling game, and nowhere more so than in broadcasting. For both Marshall and Stowell, psychographics is an added carrot to use when pitching to clients. And it's an appeal that's working in today's cut-throat media environment.

Television has typically come up short where local advertising revenues are concerned. In 1989, $54.9 billion was spent on local advertising. Television captured only 6 percent of that, compared with 23 percent for newspapers, according to the Television Bureau of Advertising.

Marshall and Stowell are giving TV stations the ammunition they need to go after other media vehicles with a vengeance. As Craig Marshall puts it, "When I was back at the station level, I was trying to beat the other stations' heads in. But it's frightening when the stations are trying to clobber the other stations, and print and direct mail are attacking television. Everybody's attacking television, and television is attacking itself. Isn't that kind of crazy?"

As broadcasters fight shoulder-to-shoulder, psychographics is being billed as the secret weapon in their arsenal. For years, newspapers have given advertisers custom reader surveys that show where the money gets spent, although few have typically offered psychographics as part of the deal. But in turning psychographics into a selling tool, for themselves and for their clients, broadcast research firms run the risk that, in the end, psychographics will be dismissed as all talk and no action. The research itself may become lost in the maze of hype and smoke. And perhaps most significant of all, the danger that psychographic information will be misused becomes magnified at the local level.

## Now that You've Got It, What Are You Going to Do with It?

Take away the fancy names and the complicated methodologies, and what are you left with? Ideally, psychographics is a tool that helps business better communicate with and meet the needs of customers. But without the required training and the time and personnel resources necessary to put psychographics research into action, it's about as useful as a Mazarati with no ignition key or a computer with a manual written in a foreign language; the power is there, but there's no way to access it.

Furthermore, it is important to emphasize that as psycho-graphics filters down to the local level, the probability increases that it is being used incorrectly by people who are not properly trained, and that its sellers are promising more than the data can deliver. Both Stowell and Marshall say they emphasize the need for training staff when they deal with client stations. However, it is ultimately up to the stations to determine how well psychographic data are implemented and whether they are used at all.

Both of the firms' psychographics systems require preliminary training sessions, so that users can understand the information and become comfortable with the software. Both databases are delivered on disk and can be manipulated with proprietary software. Some original Marshall clients have needed additional support to adapt to VALS2 after using the original VALS, which was replaced in 1989. "You can't just hand this to a research person and say, 'Here you are, have fun,'" says Marshall's Marikos. "Someone needs to direct its use and establish priorities. It takes a real commitment from management." Stowell's Schlee also emphasizes that stations with the most success using the information are those with management that understands research is a long-term commitment.

In many cases, this commitment extends to dedicated personnel. KPNX-TV in Phoenix became Stowell's second client in 1981. The station hired a research director in the second year of the survey. "It became clear to us that if we really wanted to make it work for us, we needed to add a full-time specialist," says Jeff Morris, general sales manager.

Morris says that the psychographic edge doesn't always produce a sale for the station. Sometimes station reps determine that TV isn't the most cost-effective way to reach the client's target groups and that another media mix, perhaps outdoor and print, will work better. "I admit that doesn't happen very often," Morris says. "But it does happen, and it shows that we're in the business of serving our advertisers' best interests. It may not result in an immediate sale. It's more of a long-term approach."

## CASE STUDIES
Many Marshall and Stowell client TV stations say that the major challenge to implementing psychographics has been teaching sales staff how to convey the value of the information. The more familiar the sales staff is with psychographics and other data, the better they can explain to advertisers what the information can do for their business.

• **Sporting Goods:** "The most obvious obstacle we faced was the advertisers who don't believe in this new-fangled research," says Scott Blumenthal, general sales manager of Indianapolis' WISH-TV, a Marshall client. Blumenthal says the most resistant are the retailers who have been in business 20 or 30 years and who have seen steady, if unspectacular, profits by spending frugally on print advertising. "You study these businesses and you find out that although they're making money, they aren't maximizing their potential in the marketplace. They aren't doing as well as they thought they were doing." VALS2 has allowed Blumenthal to show these most resistant advertisers who they are missing.

One Indianapolis sporting-goods store, considered the home-town store with several major locations in the city, was suddenly faced with potential competition for the first time. Several national chains were considering entering the market. WISH-TV presented research findings to the owner showing that future growth would depend on three things: developing a client base of women, emphasizing low price in the image, and showing customers that they were conveniently located. Marshall data had shown that women were avoiding the store because of its macho image—dark paneled walls hung with stuffed moose heads and merchandise displayed on tables. The data showed that the store was especially unpopular with Believer and Maker women, who preferred to buy sporting merchandise from large discount stores. WISH reps suggested that the chain emphasize low prices and convenient location, because these are attributes that especially appeal to Believers and Makers. "VALS allowed us to talk to those people," says Blumenthal. "We knew what to say because we psychographically knew the people who weren't coming in."

WISH-TV ran an ad campaign emphasizing the images and keywords that appealed to the target groups. The owner of the chain also agreed to remodel his stores. "He had some beautiful women's clothes, but they were not displayed in a setting that was conducive to female shopping," Blumenthal says. Out went the stuffed moose heads and the shotguns decorating the walls. The paneling was lightened to brighten the atmosphere, and merchandise was put onto display racks. "Psychographics tells us that guys will go through merchandise on tables, but women won't," Blumenthal says. "The audience that he wasn't getting wants service. They want nicely displayed features and easy-to-find items. Good selection, convenience." The remodeling was also promoted in the ads.

Within the first six months of the ad campaign, the chain's sales increased 37 percent, Blumenthal says. Interestingly, one of the national chains that had entered the market closed its stores a few months later. The local chain owner attributes this competitive victory to the increased traffic at his stores.

• **Auto Dealership:** By using Stowell data, McDougall Honda of Charlotte, North Carolina, increased its customer traffic and sales by 40 percent without increasing ad spending. McDougall competes head-to-head with five other Honda franchises in the market, so the competitive environment necessitates regular ad spending. McDougall's regular ad was a generic spot showing factory footage of Hondas and the exterior of the dealership. Using the Stowell psychographic data supplied by WBT-TV, McDougall learned that there were two likely targets in the Charlotte market—Group I, the "Yuppie" segment, and Group IV, the more traditional segment. Group I consumers were ambitious, demanding, selective, and time-conscious. They wanted service and didn't like to be talked down to. Group IV, on the other hand, was older, more conservative, and patriotic. They were not particularly brand- or style-conscious, and they liked their information straightforward and presented in easy-to-understand language.

The key to the sales increase was changing from a standard product appeal to a testimonial format. To get the attention of the two key segments, McDougall opted for two separate commercials. Although this meant added production costs, the dealership didn't increase its overall ad budget. The first spot showed an employee of WBT-TV, who represented Group I. She was pictured with her Honda Prelude just about to dash off to the tennis courts. She described her "relationship" with McDougall and said that the dealership "answers my questions without talking down to me." The second commercial featured another station employee who had actually purchased a Honda from the dealership. He was pictured washing his Honda in the driveway of a neat home. He emphasized the honesty and fairness of McDougall's salespeople and said that the service department kept his Honda "running like a dream."

Dr. Schlee, developer of the Stowell segmentation, says that McDougall's new strategy worked because it shifted the message focus from the dealership to the customer. The standard approach is, "We've got too many cars, we need to move them out, so now we're dealing." That doesn't work as well as an appeal that portrays a spokesperson who shares the age, gender, and vocabulary of the target customers. Psychographics was the inside information the dealership needed to find out who the spokesperson should be and what message would work best to get the attention of the target audience.

# 10 Getting Specific: Attitudes and Behavior of Users and Doers

*"Along with the growth of data, data providers, and information products comes a danger. It's like trying to get a drink of water from a gushing fire hydrant. Without the right tools, there is a danger of drowning. To be useful, information has to be general enough to be understandable and specific enough to be actionable."*

—Peter Francese and Rebecca Piirto
Capturing Customers

A NYTHING YOU WANT to know about the attitudes of Americans probably has been put to the public in the form of a survey or a poll by somebody somewhere. Life in these United States has never been more thoroughly documented, as thousands of universities, research firms, media companies, government, and nonprofit organizations get into the act of opinion polling. Every year, Americans are asked about everything from their views on AIDS and their feelings about acid rain to their impressions on teenage violence and how often they attend zoos.

A vast sea of information about attitudes, opinions, and behaviors now exists, and its sheer volume is increasing exponentially every year. To prove that point, Walker Research of Indianapolis conducts its own annual poll of the polling industry. The Walker poll revealed that 72 million Americans spent approximately 42 million hours answering survey questions in 1990—13 million more people than participated in 1988 and a 33 million increase from 1980. Clearly, there's a growing thirst for knowledge about what Americans think and how they live.

With all the data out there on the general public's attitudes on many issues, companies are narrowing their own research to concentrate on the people they really want to attract. The triple threat of increasing population diversity, media saturation, and product proliferation necessitates a more targeted approach to marketing. Target marketing, by definition, requires a narrowing of research focus. As Americans become harder to figure out, psychographic research has had to become more user specific.

## Anatomy of a Survey

A survey is by nature trilateral. On one side are the people being surveyed, on another is the group sponsoring the survey, and on the third is the type of information. These three pieces provide infinite variety. The following diagram represents part of the range of survey possibilities:

| SPONSOR | GROUP | INFORMATION |
|---|---|---|
| Manufacturer/service co. | Users of product/category | Attitudes on brand/category |
| Nonprofit organization | Demographic segment | Opinions on social issue/problem |
| Government agency | General population | Attitudes on candidate/policy |
| Media company | Readers, subscribers | Opinions on current events |
| Professional organization | People who do something | Attitudes pertaining to behavior |
| Advertising agency | (grocery shop, golf, sky-dive) | Full-range psychographics |
| Research firm | Nonusers of product/category | (demographics, media, |
| | | purchasing, lifestyle, |
| | | psychological traits) |

Any combination of the above elements is possible. But what good are all these data if nobody knows what anybody else is doing?

For the last decade, the *American Public Opinion Index* has been collecting, cataloging, and disseminating information on pollers—who is asking what and of whom. Dennis Gilbert, president of Opinion Research Service of Boston, came up with the idea for the index in 1981 after a frustrating experience with his own survey. Gilbert checked the Library of Congress prior to conducting a survey on the political implications of tax-exempt status and felt confident enough to claim his research was unique. Two months later, he found that another organization had conducted an identical survey. "There was a definite need for something like this," Gilbert says. "People who had data to share had no way of knowing who would be interested, and people who needed information had no idea what was being done." The first index included only opinion polls, but by 1984, it was expanded to include behavioral data, such as who buys cosmetics, eats vegetables, or commutes to work. The 1990 version is the biggest ever, spanning more than 1,500 pages and including results from more than 200 polling sources.

The existence of an index like Gilbert's is significant, because it represents the democratization that has occurred in the availability of attitude information. From the 1950s through the 1970s, most, if not all, attitudinal information was the property of a specific company or agency. To be sure, much attitudinal data are still kept under proprietary lock and key, but more are out there in the public realm—just waiting for someone to find them useful or interesting. "Most of our contributors are genuinely pleased if somebody is able to use and appreciate their work," says Gilbert.

The microfiche version of the *American Public Opinion Index* with the actual survey results numbered more than 15,000 pages in 1990. Using the microfiche index (available at nearly any major library), a researcher can find out, for instance, that 55 percent of Americans said they would save more in 1989 than they had in 1988, 25 percent washed their cars at least once a week, and 51 percent of householders said that providing for their families was their greatest worry. Not only are the numbers readily available, but the meat of the surveys, the questionnaires, are often included on the microfiche index. This makes it relatively easy for those who want to survey attitudes on similar subjects to adapt the questionnaires or to use the results as baseline data with which to compare their own findings.

This chapter will examine several types of attitudinal inquiries currently being done. They range from a Roper psychographic segmentation of environmental consumers to a Quest/Harris poll that segments women according to their attitudes about perfumes. Though these examples are not psychographic studies in the traditional sense (including psychological, demographic, media, and purchase behavior data, which is then cluster analyzed), they illustrate the wide range of attitude studies done today under the umbrella term "psychographics."

## Attitudes at Issue: Roper and Environmentalism

When Roper, Gallup, and Crossley started their competing polling firms in the 1930s (see Chapter 1), they did full-service research work for their major clients, usually businesses. This included everything from survey design and the actual door-to-door legwork to the interpretation of results. Sometime in the 1950s, Elmo Roper and his son, Bud, noticed that more companies were starting to do their own design and interpretation and just wanted Elmo Roper & Associates to do the legwork. "We resisted this as much as possible," says Bud Roper, now president of The Roper Organization. Roper toughed it out, and in the 1980s started to see a renewed demand for full-service research as companies downsized and decimated their research departments, partially in response to increasing competition from abroad. "It's come full-circle again," Roper says. "One of our clients used to have 45 employees in the department we work with. Now it has 5. So they have to turn to the outside. They don't have the staff to do the research they used to do."

Increasingly, major corporations are going to outside firms to conduct all types of research. These information suppliers range from the established polling organizations, such as Roper and Gallup, to smaller shops and consultants. Roper, for example, is regularly hired to do custom surveys; periodically, this includes major psychographic studies. Roper's recent psychographic research includes a study of smokers and nonsmokers for the tobacco industry and one on attitudes about alcohol for a liquor producer. These are proprietary studies, but Roper has publicly released the results of a 1990 study on environmental attitudes and behavior.

"We felt the conventional wisdom that was emerging was that everyone was now concerned about the environment, but from our own data, we believed it was a much more complicated picture than that," says Ed Keller, Roper executive vice president. "Concern about the environment was rising, but various behavioral measures, such as the number of people involved in recycling, weren't showing any change." Roper put together a proposal for a segmentation study of the issue and took it around to companies. S.C. Johnson and Son ended up sponsoring the study. Roper polled a representative sample of 1,500 Americans the old-fashioned way—door-to-door. The results of these hour-long interviews confirmed that saving the environment is a high priority for most citizens, but not everyone acts on their beliefs.

The study, "The Environment: Public Attitudes and Individual Behavior," was designed to identify Americans' degree of concern about environmental issues and the extent to which they were accordingly altering their behavior. Were they willing to pay more for environmentally safe products? Did they pay attention to "green" ads and base product decisions on them? Why weren't they doing more to back up their concerns? What issues were the most serious on both a national and local level? What kinds of policies did they support to address the problems? Other questions dealt with broader issues such as the depletion of the ozone layer, which was of particular interest for S.C. Johnson because of the nature of its products (cleaning wax, etc.).

Most Americans (78 percent) say that our nation should "make a major effort to improve the quality of our environment." That's up a significant 22 percent from a similar study in 1987. But a majority also thinks that individuals can do very little to solve most serious environmental problems. Americans tend to blame businesses and government for the state of the environment. Eighty-one percent said that factories and plants cause pollution, and 71 percent said the government does not enforce anti-pollution laws strongly enough. People also place the responsibility on these authorities for making things better. When asked why they didn't personally do more about the environment, 61 percent said that "companies, not people like me, should solve the problem." Other major reasons were time-related: fully 56 percent said "alternatives are too hard to find" and they had "no time to shop around," and 54 percent said they were "too busy to get around to making changes." The next most common reason was chosen by 52 percent, who said, "alternatives are too expensive." Credibility or environmental product claims were issues for the 58 percent who said they "don't believe the labels."

Consumers can impact the environment in two ways—at point of purchase and afterwards. They can use their purchasing ability as a vote, to support green products and reject others, or they can alter what they do with the packaging or other waste once the product has been consumed. What, if anything, are consumers doing about their environmental concerns?

Recycling appears to be the fastest-growing pro-environmental action. Between 1988 and 1989, the proportion of Americans who said they recycled bottles and cans rose from 41 to 46 percent. The share of those who recycled newspapers rose from 20 to 26 percent, and those who sorted their trash rose from 14 to 24 percent. Point-of-purchase behaviors have been slower to catch on. Only 14 percent said they regularly buy products made from, or packaged in, recycled materials, or buy products in packages that can be refilled. Just 16 percent said they avoid buying products from companies they don't see as environmentally responsible. Less than one-fourth said they avoid buying aerosol products or that they prefer to use biodegradable or low-phosphate soaps and detergents. But 62 percent said they regularly or sometimes read labels to check for environmental safety.

An interesting insight emerges from comparing attitudes and behaviors. Americans express a preference that government enact legislation to solve environmental problems. This preference is reflected in their behavior. Recyling, which is often mandated by law, is the fastest-growing behavior. Legislation, then, has stimulated the widest-reaching behavioral change.

In order to get a better picture of the gradations in environmental concern and action, Roper segmented Americans into five behavioral groups, based primarily on whether or not they engaged in a list of environmentally friendly practices. Roper determined that three factors influenced a person's predisposition to be committed to the environment: income, education, and gender. More affluent people, better-educated people, and women are most likely to be green consumers. The five groups are the True-Blue Greens, Greenback Greens, Sprouts, Grousers, and Basic Browns:

**TRUE-BLUE GREENS** (11 percent of adults) These people are the leaders of the green movement. They are the ones who really act on their concerns: 54 percent won't buy from environmentally insensitive companies, 59 percent regularly recycle newspapers, and 55 percent avoid buying aerosols. They support carpooling laws, use biodegradable soaps and detergents, and depend on environmental groups as their major source of related information. They are politically active, with 26 percent considered "Influential Americans," based on a Roper index of political-social activism that identifies leaders and trendsetters. Their political views are more likely than other groups to be liberal, but they are also more likely to be conservative. True Blues are least likely to label themselves "middle of the road" on political or social issues. This supports the idea that the environment is one issue not divided along partisan lines, but bridging the ideological gap.

Demographically, True Blues tend to be more female (66 percent), more affluent (median income $32,100), and more educated (half have at least some college) than the general population. Twenty-five percent are professionals, 51 percent live in large metropolitan cities, and 55 percent live in the Northeast or West.

**GREENBACK GREENS** (11 percent of adults) This group is most willing to pay more for environmentally safe products. Greenbacks say they would be willing to pay 20 percent more, compared with the 7 percent that the general public is willing to pay. However, they are less willing than True Blues to practice any pro-environmental activity that requires individual effort. For example, they will pay more for safer gasoline, but they won't give up convenience or use their cars less often. Most of them (59 percent) say they are too busy to change, which might be because more of them have children under age 13, compared with the general public (43 percent vs. 34 percent).

Demographically, Greenbacks are 58 percent female and have a median income of $31,600. Fifty-two percent have at least some college, and 45 percent are executive/ professional or white-collar workers. While 37 percent of Greenbacks call themselves conservative, this group has a higher proportion of people who say they are middle-of-the-road (33 percent) and liberal (29 percent) than the general population.

**SPROUTS** (26 percent of adults) They aren't sure which side to take when confronted with the tradeoff between environmental protection and economic development. They come down on the side of the environment, but with little conviction. Their views concerning environmental regulations are also ambivalent. Despite these vacillations, this group is almost as likely as True Blues to alter their lifestyles for environmental reasons. A solid majority (75 percent) supports regulations requiring that household products be sold in refillable containers, 42 percent regularly recycle newspapers, and 40 percent believe that individuals can do a lot about pollution from automobile exhaust. Their political views (41 percent conservative, 35 percent moderate, 21 percent liberal) closely resemble those of the general population. This and their larger numbers makes them highly desirable as a swing group—if something passes their muster, it is likely to be accepted by the other two pro-environmental groups and may have a chance with the Grousers.

Demographically, they, like the other two pro-environmental groups, are more affluent (median income $32,000), better educated, and more likely to hold executive or professional jobs than the general population. They are also the group most likely to be married (71 percent).

**GROUSERS** (24 percent of adults) are indifferent about the environment, but they rationalize their indifference by seeing it as the mainstream attitude. They seem to be looking for excuses. Eighty percent or more say that six of the eight reasons for not participating applied to them. A substantial majority (88 percent) says it's up to companies, not individuals, to solve the problem. They also say they're too busy to change (84 percent); they don't believe the environmental claims on product labels (81 percent); and 77 percent say that others aren't making sacrifices, so why should they.

They are less likely to recycle—7 percent do compared with 26 percent of the general public—and they're only willing to pay 4 percent more for environmentally safe products, compared with the general public's 7 percent.

Demographically, Grousers are less affluent (median income $24,900), less educated (69 percent have a high school education or less), and more likely to work in blue-collar jobs (31 percent).

**BASIC BROWNS** (28 percent of adults) could be classified as environmental couch potatoes or the Archie Bunkers of the environmental scene. They realize the environment is in trouble, but they participate in none of the pro-environmental activities. Nor do they attempt to rationalize their behavior as the Grousers do. They simply chalk it up to impotence; they feel the individual has little power to affect change in any environmental problem except litter. A majority (55 percent) also says that they don't have the knowledge to understand environmental problems. Basic Browns are the least likely to buy products made from recycled goods (1 percent), to support stricter governmental regulations (43 percent), and they're only willing to pay 3 percent more for environmentally safe goods.

Demographically, this is the most socially and economically disadvantaged group. Their median income is the lowest ($21,200), and three out of ten have not finished high school. This group has the highest percentage of men (55 percent), and blue-collar workers make up a larger proportion of this group than any of the others. Politically, they tend to be apathetic: they have the lowest percentage of Influential Americans, and four out of ten Browns describe themselves as middle-of-the-road.

### WHAT DOES IT ALL MEAN?
Because Roper has historic data from surveys going back 10 or 20 years, it can offer a perspective that others cannot. For instance, one of the major findings shows that environmental concern is increasing faster than any other issue Roper monitors. In 1989—for the first time in 16 years—a majority said protecting the environment should take precedence over acquiring adequate supplies of energy.

Marketers, however, should consider carefully before jumping on the environmental band wagon. A majority of consumers already believes that businesses are more motivated by profit than by the public good, and are appropriately skeptical of environmental claims in advertising and on product labels. Since the most environmentally active consumers are well-educated, affluent, and among the most Influential Americans, any environmental claim has to be valid, well conceived, and intelligently communicated.

Another important finding of the Roper report is that pro-environmental behavior is still growing, and concern levels have not yet peaked. While environmental action is not universal now, it is almost certain to become more widespread for the following reasons:

- The groups that act most on their environmental concerns—True Blues and Greenback Greens—are the two groups that contain the highest proportion of Influential Americans, the leaders and trendsetters.

- Support for mandated changes in products and packaging to help the environment is broad-based, even if it involves added costs to consumers.

- Recycling is rising, which increases awareness of and involvement in the solid-waste problem.

- More companies are developing and offering green products as consumer demand for them increases. As the selection of environmental products increases, the laggard groups may also start opting for green alternatives over their old standbys.

One scenario might threaten the universal adoption of pro-environmental activities, and that is a prolonged economic downturn. The propensity to act on environmental concerns seems to be related to the degree of affluence of the individual or household. What's more, the rapid growth in environmental concern occurred during the 1980s—a period characterized by unprecedented economic growth. As of this writing, the economy is in a recession, and it is possible that concern about the environment will diminish among less-advantaged groups as concern about unemployment and economic well-being increases.

It seems quite likely, however, given the depth of their commitment to the environment, that the issue will remain a priority with the True Blues and Greenback Greens, and perhaps even the Sprouts. These groups disagree with the statement, "First comes economic security and well-being; then we can worry about environmental problems."

Taking the long-term perspective, it seems clear that environmentalism is here to stay. The solid-waste problem is worsening, and more people are personally experiencing the consequences of past disregard for the environment. In this scenario, one thing is certain: both government and business would be wise to organize their policy-making and research and development efforts with environmental concerns in mind during the 1990s and beyond.

## Consuming Attitudes: Women and Fragrance

No attitudes are so important to marketers as those that pertain directly to product consumption. This is especially true of products that involve consumers' egos, such as cars, clothes, and perfume. Louis Harris & Associates conducted the "Quest for the American Woman" study for Quest International, a fragrance and flavor supplier. The survey found that women with higher levels of self-confidence prefer more subtle fragrances.

The survey, which updated a similar one done in 1976, was based on personal interviews with 866 white, black, and Hispanic women aged 16 or older. It included questions on lifestyle trends, psychographics, attitudes toward social issues, brand preferences, and shopping habits relating to several toiletry product groups (toilet soaps; colognes, toilet waters, and perfumes; deodorants and antiperspirants; hair-styling aids; shampoos, hair conditioners, and cream rinses; bath and shower additives; hand and body creams and lotions; and facial creams and treatments).

One of the most significant findings was that women today are more independent, confident, self-reliant, and assertive than they were in 1976. More than half of those who work view their work as a career, not simply a job, and they feel strongly that they would have risen further and faster if they were men. Working women also feel that they've had to work twice as hard as men to get ahead. Only 37 percent say it is more important to have a husband to take care of them than to make it on their own, down from the 57 percent who said that was important in 1976. But 77 percent of women agree that "my children are the most important thing in my life." That's up remarkably from the 10 percent who agreed with that statement in 1976.

Using multivariate analysis, Quest/Harris identified several segments of women based partly on their fragrance preferences. The groups include:

**Fledgling Career Woman**—She has a positive and optimistic attitude about her future. Fragrance is important to her and is a major influence in her product choices. She tends to prefer highly perfumed products.

**Working-Class Woman**—She is dissatisfied with her life and buys highly perfumed products to add a little color to her ordinary existence. How a product smells is a big influence in her product preferences.

**Frustrated Professional**—This woman has little interest in fragrance. She feels impeded from achieving her ambitions because of her sex.

**Traditional Housewife**—This woman is somewhat dissatisfied with her life, and she likes highly perfumed products. But she doesn't necessarily base her toiletry choices on fragrance.

**Successful Professional**—She is self-assured, confident, mature, and prefers subtle fragrances that please her. Fragrance is not a basis for her toiletry preferences.

**Senior-Set Woman**—Traditional values are at the core of her very satisfied attitude. She doesn't like fragrance that makes an overt statement.

Quest has used this information to provide an edge in the highly competitive fragrance business. Executives say it helps Quest monitor and evaluate consumer preferences and feelings about specific brands, enhancing the company's ability to create products consumers will desire and buy. The company finds the historic data particularly useful because they offer a perspective on changing fragrance preferences. Harris/Quest plans to do a similar survey in 2000 to find out how preferences in this category have further evolved in relation to the changing roles and attitudes of women.

## A Matter of Behavior: American Express and Travel

An increasingly popular type of survey studies people who participate in an activity, whether it be rock climbing, working out, or buying a particular product. One example is The American Express Global Travel Survey, which was conducted in the U.S., West Germany, the United Kingdom, and Japan. American Express researchers screened participants according to their travel habits, defining travelers as those who had spent at least one night away from home in the past year. They found that roughly six in ten adults meet this criterion.

A goal of the survey was to identify shared attitudes and behaviors of certain groups that crossed national lines. It found five types of travelers defined by their shared likes, dislikes, and desires: Adventurers, Worriers, Dreamers, Economizers, and Indulgers. The most affluent groups were the Adventurers and the Indulgers, and the two of interest to American Express.

Adventurers' major motivation is seeing and experiencing new things. They value diversity, are independent and confident, and maintain control in a variety of travel situations. The actual act of travel plays a major role in their lives and helps shape their sense of self. They are well-educated and affluent, more so than other groups. Fully 57 percent are male, and 44 percent are young (between 18 and 34). They also are the most frequent travelers, taking an average of 3.8 trips a year.

The Indulgers' style is somewhat different than the Adventurers'. Their major motivation, as the name suggests, is indulgence. Travel in itself is not as important to them as the opportunity it affords to pamper themselves and treat themselves to the best. They are willing to pay for the best service. They are not intimidated by travel, nor do they find it stressful. Equally divided between male and female, they are more affluent than other groups, and they are the second most frequent travelers, taking an average of 3.4 trips a year.

As a group, Indulgers tend to spend more per trip than other travelers, except in the U.S., where Adventurers spend $700 per trip, compared with $600 for Indulgers. This may be due to the current popularity of high-cost adventures like white-water rafting and guided tours of New Age energy zones. West Germans are the biggest spenders across the board—both Indulgers and Adventurers spend an average of $807 per trip.

The United Kingdom has the highest share of Adventurers (43 percent), followed by the U.S. (27 percent). Germany led in the Indulger group, with 48 percent of Germans fitting this style of travel. The U.S. was also second in the proportion of Indulgers, with 23 percent of Americans falling into this category.

American Express, long considered a research leader in financial services, does a variety of specific psychographic research. As far back as the 1970s, American Express researchers were segmenting cardmembers and prospects to identify their shared attitudes and behaviors. The possibilities of this type of research when done well are great, say American Express researchers. A study like this provides a basis for developing marketing strategies in each of the countries studied.

## Psychographics of Demographic Groups

Perhaps the most prevalent psychographic research today is the kind that focuses on specific demographic groups. Media companies and packaged-goods companies frequently screen their survey participants by sex and age. In addition, numerous market research firms now specialize in specific racial or ethnic groups, such as blacks, Hispanics, or Asians.

Sex, age, race, and ethnicity are not the only demographic criteria for psychographic study; there is an increasing interest today in the psychographics of affluence. Who's got the money, and what do they want? Mendelsohn Media Research Inc. of New York does an annual survey focusing on the purchase behavior of affluent adults ($60,000-plus household income). Publications such as *Affluent Markets Alert* (Alert Publishing Inc., Long Island City, New York) chronicle everything from the magazines preferred by affluent Americans to their attitudes on political issues and motivations related to home remodeling. Recent issues, for example, featured surveys showing that 85 percent of Affluents own VCRs. Affluents are 39 percent more likely than average to watch CNN and 155 percent more likely to read the *Wall Street Journal*. As for their brand preferences, Affluents prefer Coor's over Strohs, Coke over Pepsi, Mercedes Benz over BMW, United over American Airlines, and HBO over Showtime. Exactly who are these Affluent Americans? The newsletter has the answer to that, too. They are most likely to be married males between the ages of 45 and 55. Above all, they hate waiting in lines.

Increasing attention is being focused on the psychographics of minority groups, because the most vigorous population growth in the coming decades is expected to come from the nonwhite population. Yankelovich Clancy Shulman currently has a Hispanic Monitor and is developing an Asian Monitor.

The Hispanic Monitor is a syndicated psychographic study done jointly by YCS and Market Development Inc., of San Diego. "That the U.S. Hispanic market is showing occupational and income growth five times that of the general market is an important socioeconomic trend," says Dr. Henry E. Adams, senior vice president of Market Development Inc. That income growth, combined with a very positive attitude toward saving money, suggests a future rise in demand for high-ticket items such as homes, mortgages, and automobiles in the U.S. Hispanic market.

The Hispanic Monitor was designed to help businesses gain better insights into the Hispanic market, and the findings are poking holes in some long-accepted theories about U.S. Hispanics. According to the study, Hispanics voice a stronger commitment to both earning and saving than their general market counterparts. They tend to hold more traditional, middle-class values, and are not as fatalistic as stereotypes portray. Hispanics have an optimistic belief in the Horatio Alger, pull-yourself-up-by-your-bootstraps philosophy. If one works hard enough in America, they believe, one can succeed. In addition, they don't like to live on borrowed money; three out of four Hispanics agree that cash, not credit, is the best way to make purchases.

The Hispanic Monitor has identified four Hispanic consumer clusters in the population: Hopeful Loyalists, Recent Seekers, Young Strivers, and Established Adapters.

*Figure 10-1*

## Psychographic Profile

|  | % Share of Hispanic Market | Age 16-34 (Index) | Mid/Upper Income (Index) | High School or More (Index) |
|---|---|---|---|---|
| Hopeful Loyalists | 43 | 94 | 112 | 82 |
| Recent Seekers | 24 | 96 | 70 | 95 |
| Young Strivers | 15 | 123 | 106 | 111 |
| Established Adapters | 18 | 106 | 112 | 129 |

*Source: YCS/MDI Hispanic Monitor, 1988*

The first two segments are primarily foreign-born Hispanics, and the latter two are mostly native-born Hispanics. The groups were derived from the extent to which Hispanics agreed or disagreed with statements that measured nine attitudinal and motivational dimensions. Due to the proprietary nature of the study, information on the nature of the segments is limited.

The study found that assimilation is influenced more by the place of birth than by the length of time Hispanics have been in the U.S. Foreign-born Hispanics have more in common with each other, despite their length of residency, than they do with U.S-born Hispanics. For instance, native-born Hispanics are far more likely to speak English than the foreign-born, even those who have lived in the country for years. In addition, there

*Figure 10-2*                    **Segmenting Hispanics**

| Most Savings Oriented | Most Conservative | Most Self-Indulgent | Most Fatalistic | Most Self-Driven |
|---|---|---|---|---|
| ➤ Recent Seekers | ➤ Recent Seekers | Hopeful Loyalists | Hopeful Loyalists | Young Strivers |
| Young Strivers | Hopeful Loyalists | Established Adapters | Young Strivers | ➤ Recent Seekers |
| Established Adapters | Established Adapters | ➤ Recent Seekers | Established Adapters | Established Adapters |
| Hopeful Loyalists | Young Strivers | Young Strivers | ➤ Recent Seekers | Hopeful Loyalists |

*Source: YCS/MDI Hispanic Monitor, 1988*

are fewer attitude similarities among Hispanics with similar national backgrounds (Mexico, Guatemala, Puerto Rico, etc.) than previously thought.

One of the most significant findings is that a "melting pot" type of Americanization does not seem to be happening in Hispanic communities. In these communities, Spanish is the language of trade as well as socializing, so there is less need to use English to get by. Combined with increasing immigration, this is creating a new cultural force that is neither American nor Hispanic, but a synthesis of the two—a hybrid market that encompasses the best of both cultures.

"Marketers now have a way of reaching Hispanics psychographically, giving the Spanish-language advertiser one more important tool in developing effective advertising," Adams says. Because the Hispanic segments are similar to other segments identified by national psychographic studies, Adams says, the study shows that marketers can reach the Hispanic market successfully if they use a national approach that emphasizes these attitudinal insights.

## One Step Beyond: Linking Demographics and Behavior

One research firm took the American Express idea a step further and queried a specific demographic group on a specific topic. This study, done by Strategic Directions Group of Minneapolis, Minnesota, looked at the travel preferences of the over-50 population. These consumers are significant because one out of four Americans is now over the age of 50. The group also accounts for about 80 percent of all leisure travel in the U.S. The study identified four segments among over-50 travelers defined by their income and attitudes:

**Insecures** (32 percent of over 50 population) Aging is not fun for this pessimistic group. More than one-fourth make no trips at all. Those who do are six times more likely than average to travel by bus. Their annual household income is $12,700.

**Threatened Actives** (26 percent) Crime is their major concern. One-fourth have taken a trip two days long in the past year. The automobile is the preferred mode of transportation; 81 percent drive their cars on vacation. Their annual household income is $11,400.

**Upbeat Enjoyers** (20 percent) take the attitude that their best years are still to come. They are financially secure, and nearly one-third have taken more than two trips of two or more days in the past year. They are more likely than any other group to take escorted tours, with 38 percent having taken one in the last year. One in five plans a European trip in the next year. Their annual household income is $26,400.

**Financial Positives** (23 percent) are the most affluent group, with a median income of $30,100. They're also the most frequent travelers—they've taken an average of two trips of two or more days in the past year, compared with 0.5 for all people over age 50. They are positive and financially secure, and they prefer to travel by air. About 20 percent plan a trip to Europe in the next year.

## The Lesson of Specificity

Researching psychographics is like looking at a fractal equation. The deeper and more specific you get, the more you notice a recurring pattern. If you look closely, you see a degree of similarity in each of these segmentations that stems from the scaler rating systems on which they are based. The groups generally go from highly enthusiastic/ liberal to very resistant/conservative.

But the closer you get to real consumers, the people who use your product or service, the closer you get to the truth of what makes people buy the product or service you offer. As far as research is concerned, the more specific the better. If you're in the aluminum-siding business, the best psychographic research you could get are the attitudes of your most likely customers toward siding. Only then can you gain clues about the unique attitudes and concerns that motivate people to buy one type of siding over another.

The other question that arises from the proliferation of survey data is that of validity. To the information customer, the operative caveat should always be "buyer beware." Good psychographic research is done by reputable social scientists who have proven track records. Surveys done for show are easy to spot by the simplicity of their results and the inapplicability of their findings.

# 11 Retailing in an Era of Diversity

*"Three basics are key in knowing the consumer: age and income, life experience, and basic values. To be a winner in this industry, we are going to have to put the best system in place to meet the diversity of the target consumer's physiological and psychological needs in a cost-effective and timely manner."*

— Corrin Corbin
Director of Apparel Marketing, DuPont

NOWHERE DO the fickle winds of consumer change wreak more havoc than in the retail industry. In fashions for clothing, home furnishings, and accessories, this season's rage is next season's bargain basement markdown. Trend spotters were paid huge sums to predict that a fondness for Third World primitivism and the Santa Fe look would replace the glossy black-and-silver minimalism of the late 1980s. Add to the already capricious nature of fashion demand the increasing diversity of consumer lifestyles, and it's no wonder small and large retail firms alike are floundering as they search for a stable foothold in an ever-changing market.

Today, the winds of demographic change are so obvious that some fashion lords have taken notice. No longer can designers dictate what Americans wear, as evidenced by the miniskirts that remained unsold on racks in the late 1980s. Older, more demanding consumers refused to buy clothes that made them look ridiculous. Today's popular fashions are an eclectic mix that places equal emphasis on comfort and style while offering quality and simplicity—all in direct response to consumer demands.

Today's shoppers are not only older, they're more savvy. There is an increasing demand for quality. But perhaps the most important current lifestyle trend is time pressure.

More women are working, and most new families have two earners, so shopping time must be deferred to nights, weekends, or mail order. The phenomenal success of the mail-order apparel and home accessory businesses during the past decade shows that customers appreciate a new way to shop that offers quality merchandise with a minimum of hassle. This trend toward mail order, combined with an economic downturn, has made 1991 one of the most dismal years in recent memory for the retail industry. Stores around the country are looking for new ways to induce consumers to come in and shop. Instinctively picking up on consumers' growing dislike for being kept waiting, many retailers are emphasizing better customer service. The Washington, D.C.-based Woodward & Lothrop/Wanamaker's chain, like many around the country, has increased weekday and Sunday hours and is trying to increase the efficiency of register transaction time to reduce customer waiting time.

Others create a total shopping experience that is part theme park and part savvy merchandising. Victoria's Secret and The Gap cater to shopping-weary consumers with mood-altering ambiences that enhance the total shopping experience. Some shopping malls go so far as to recreate a summer day in the middle of winter—complete with real birds flying overhead and summer-scented potpourr—to lull customers into lingering and spending more money.

Still others are turning to psychographics, often using research for the first time, to find out what customers want from the shopping experience. K mart, the nation's third largest retailer, launched a new ad campaign showing that the discount store stocks much of the same merchandise found in fancier stores. "Our pricing is still important, but we wanted to emphasize our new quality and customer service," CEO and chairman Joseph E. Antonine told the *Wall Street Journal*. The new strategy is based on extensive in-depth customer interviewing conducted by psychologists. The technique, called "value structuring," reveals that the most important thing customers want from their shopping experience is to be treated with respect. They also say they prefer stores that are clean and comfortable. As a result of the research done by the New York agency Hirsch & Spector, K mart is remodeling its 2,200 stores and has started workshops to help employees better understand what customers need.

## Turning to Consumer Research

Tough financial times often cause businesses to turn to research, and the current crisis in retailing is no exception. The Retail Merchants Association reports an increased interest from many members in studies about customers' shopping styles and preferences. It seems that after years of resistance, many retailers are now looking at customers' psychographics for answers to the disturbing question, "Why aren't they buying?"

This renewed interest in shopping habits has resulted in a flurry of surveys. One of the most publicized was a 1989 Roper and Hart poll commissioned by the *Wall Street Journal*. From two separate surveys of 4,000 shoppers emerged a profile of seven shopper types:

- **Agreeable Shoppers** (22 percent) are the consumers who go along with the consensus, are especially susceptible to advertising, and shop at discount stores.

- **Practical Shoppers** (21 percent) are the ones who research their purchases to find the best deal and shop at stores that sell off-price, brand-name clothing.

- **Trendy Shoppers** (16 percent) are shopping fanatics who buy on impulse and stock up on the latest fashion fads at trendy boutiques.

- **Value Shoppers** (13 percent) are traditional, price-sensitive shoppers who believe that the best products have been around for a while. They don't often buy top of the line, and they prefer mid-priced department stores.

- **Top-of-the-Line Shoppers** (10 percent) believe their hard work has earned them the right to buy the best—products that have an established reputation for quality. They tend to shop in upscale department stores.

- **Safe Shoppers** (9 percent) are the ones who look for familiar brands that make them feel comfortable, such as the brands their parents used. They prefer to do their shopping at established mass merchandisers.

- **Status Shoppers** (5 percent) may sometimes be impractical and buy things they can't really afford, but they love to own designer labels, and many believe that buying a new gadget a day keeps the doldrums away.

Some smaller retailers like Hess's of Allentown, Pennsylvania, seem to be just getting into the research habit. Hess's recently did an analysis of under-45 customers and over-45 customers to discover their shopping differences. They found older customers more responsive to attentive service, while younger customers like being self-sufficient and even resent over-anxious salespeople breathing down their necks. Armed with this information, the company changed the setup of its women's sportswear departments. Skirts, blouses, and slacks for over-45s were grouped separately, and salespeople were trained to take customers through to help them choose outfits. Junior sportswear, however, was set out in matching outfits to make it easier for customers to choose coordinated outfits themselves.

Mervyns, a Hayward, California-based chain with 225 stores in 17 states, began doing attitude research in 1989 to better discern how the company fits in with competitors like J.C. Penney and Sears. The company began by trying to assess the shopping experience from the consumer's perspective. The marketing manager conducted a series of roundtable discussions including eight to ten customers and several company people. Company executives, store managers, and district managers have all gained valuable insights from the focus group sessions, according to Judy Jones, manager of market research. "It's really powerful," Jones says. "It gets our executives in touch with our customers. It's had a big impact on the way we talk about our business, the way we plan our business, and it's permeating the ranks of the organization."

One strategy that has worked well for Mervyns is to send a customer out onto the floor for 15 or 20 minutes to buy a selected item. The customer, fresh from the shopping experience, can tell company representatives how well the store performed in customer service, ease of locating merchandise, presentation, and sizing. One customer returned saying she couldn't find any large sizes, and when she looked at the stacks she couldn't tell which sizes were which. That information inspired the company to test alternate size labeling on shelves and ultimately produced sales improvements in the test areas.

Jones says that including managers in the process has paid off because the managers now have a better understanding when she presents results of quantitative studies. "Managers now understand what I mean by 'an easy to shop environment.' By sitting in those groups, they see how the customer is experiencing it."

## Fashion Shoppers: Management Horizons Shopper Typologies

Clothes have been said to make the man, and the woman..For clothing, home accessories, and fashion items, psychology plays an especially important role in determining why people buy what they buy. Matching stores and product mix with the right type of consumer is a complicated task that has been made simpler for some companies by a shopper segmentation scheme developed by Management Horizons, a market research and consulting subsidiary of Price Waterhouse.

Management Horizons, based in Dublin, Ohio, has about 140 clients in the apparel, catalog, and home furnishing businesses. The firm began to develop the shopper typology in 1987, after an informal survey of clients revealed that many were having difficulties applying existing psychographics systems such as VALS to their everyday businesses. "Retailers were most interested in finding out how to alter merchandise presentations and selling techniques to different shoppers," says Mandy Putnam, research manager and developer of the typology. "Our typology is more specific to the fashion industry than VALS, which makes it easier for marketers to use."

This specificity, she says, also provides better insight into how customers buy clothes and fashion items. "We wanted to isolate people who behaved differently in the marketplace, then link their behavior back to their attitudes," says company chairman Dan Sweeney.

The typology began with a pilot study of 400 people and an initial questionnaire with about 200 statements that respondents rated on a six-point scale from 'strongly agree' to 'strongly disagree.' Researchers weeded out the questions that had little relationship to fashion-buying behavior and ended up with a battery of 54 questions that seemed most predictive of behavior. The questionnaire was sent out to 5,000 consumers through National Family Opinion's (NFO) consumer panel database. The responses were factor analyzed, and an algorithm was set up to place individual consumers into groups. The process took just under two years, and by late 1988 the firm had begun marketing Management Horizons' Six Shopper Typologies.

The typologies measure consumers according to three pairs of polarized attributes found most predictive of fashion-shopping behavior: autonomy or affiliation, resistance or embracing of change, and impulsiveness or self-sacrifice. The final questionnaire consists of 15 shopping and behavioral attitude statements:

_It is important to me to wear fashionable clothing._
_I feel I am more self-confident in my decisions than most other people._
_I will often postpone a purchase rather than buy on credit._
_I feel it's important to make present sacrifices for the future._
_I like to experiment with different looks._
_I like styles that help me create new images for myself or my home._
_I shop only when I need to replace items._
_At times, I enjoy being outrageous._
_Having artistic things in my environment is important to me._
_An important part of my life and activities is being stylish._
_Things are changing too fast these days._
_I am a spender, not a saver._
_I am open-minded regarding different alternative lifestyles and values._
_I like to wear clothes that represent my individuality._
_I am more of a practical person than an imaginative person._

The groups are also profiled by demographics, media usage, and purchase behavior, including general consumption, store patronage, and price sensitivity. "The result is a very rich lens for looking at the customer," says Sweeney. The segmentation can help predict consumers' likely fashion shopping behavior. Are they browsers? Heavy credit users? Do they buy on impulse or comparison shop? Do they like fashion innovations? Do they like special attention from sales personnel? How much exposure do they have to competitors?

Management Horizons attaches the psychographic questionnaire to a demographic segmentation system, the Consumer Market Matrix. The Consumer Market Matrix segments consumers by income and household composition, and was developed by examining the income and life stages of about 50,000 households in the NFO panel. The six Life Stage segments are:

- Younger Singles (under 45, no children)

- Younger Couples (married couple, household head under 45, no children)

- Younger Parents (head under 45, children present)

- Mid-Life Families (head between 45 and 64, children present or supported)

- Mid-Life Households (head between 45 and 64, no children present or supported financially)

- Older Households (head 65 or older, retired, no children)

These are further segmented into three income categories within each life stage:

- Down Market—lower quintile of income for lifestage

- Middle Market—three middle income quintiles for lifestage

- Up Market—upper quintile of income for lifestage

The Down Market Younger Single, for example, makes under $12,500, while the Up Market Younger Singles' income reaches $32,500 and over. Older Households in the Down Market may have incomes of less than $7,500, while the Up Market income in that lifestage reaches $22,000 and over.

Demographics is the first step in understanding the market; psychographics provides an extra layer of understanding. Putnam advises that the shopper typology be used as an extension of a demographic analysis. "I believe demographics are the essential first layer to the puzzle," she says. "You might be a self-actualized person, but you're not going to spend that way if you don't have the income to support that spending."

## THE SIX SHOPPING TYPOLOGIES
### *YESTER YEARS—17 percent of primary shoppers*
**Who They Are:** Yester Years are concentrated in the Down Markets of the older lifestages, especially in the Older Households lifestage. Their average age is 50, and they are more likely to be female, married, with or without children. They have completed high school but probably not college, and their average household size is 2.7 with 0.9 children. Many of the female heads are either retired or housewives. They tend to live in lower-to-middle income sections of rural areas and towns.

**Median income:** $19,600

**What They Think:** This group seeks conformance to traditional, established patterns. They are resistant to change and reluctant to take risks. They tend to be insecure, conservative, and somewhat antisocial (i.e., low participation in activities).

## How They Shop:
- Clothing: They look for everyday low prices and like stores that make it easy to find merchandise. They respond well to good guarantees and convenient store location.
- Electronic equipment: Everyday low prices, ease of finding merchandise, and speedy service.
- Furniture: Everyday low prices and knowledgeable sales personnel.

**What They Buy:** They are homeowners and more likely to own a domestic than a foreign car. Except in buying women's casual clothing and women's and children's shoes, they are low-velocity spenders and show below-average spending rates (percent of group buying in the past year). Their consumption rates of consumer electronics (except for color TVs) is also below average.

**Where They Shop:** They are most likely to shop in mass market, discount stores.
- **Apparel Spending:** Light spenders for below-average price points. They spend less than other groups on clothing and fragrances. Except for women's shoes, they buy mostly on discount.
- **Fashion preferences:** Yester Years are casual dressers and like to wear simple, practical styles. They tend to purchase private-label brands in women's tops, jeans, and fragrances.

**Credit Usage:** They use credit cards less regularly than other groups.

## What Media They Use:
- Television: Above-average viewers (4.3 hours during last weekday). Lower-than-average tendency to subscribe to cable television.
- Radio: Below-average, but with an above-average tendency to listen to country/western, all news, religious, and agricultural/farm formats.
- Newspapers: Below-average readers.
- Magazines: Below-average subscribers, but with an above-average tendency to subscribe to media guides.

### *POWER PURCHASERS—15 percent of primary shoppers*
**Who They Are:** Power Purchasers are found in the Middle and Up Markets of the younger lifestages. Equally male and female, and married with children, their average age is 42.6 years. They are college graduates and hold professional or technical/sales positions. Their average household size is 2.7, with an average of 0.9 children. They tend to live in wealthy, urban affluent, and urban middle-income areas.

**Median income:** $31,650.

**What They Think:** They like to indulge themselves and their families liberally, and they have the income to support it. They look for variety and enjoy taking risks. They are more likely than average to exercise or go to jazzercise, participate in team and spectator sports, socialize with friends, and go to movies. They also frequently travel by air and use ATMs more often than other groups.

**How They Shop:**
- Clothing: Power Purchasers like merchandise to be easy to find and friendly sales personnel. They look for stores with a wide selection of high-quality clothing and speedy service.
- Electronic equipment: High quality, good sales or promotions, availability of specific, preferred brands.
- Furniture: High quality, pleasant atmosphere.

**What They Buy:** Purchasing rates are well above average for most categories, including clothing, shoes, furniture, appliances, home furnishings, jewelry, sporting goods, toys, and cosmetics. They are also more likely to own consumer electronics, and their use of lawn-care and maid services is high.

**Where They Shop:** They frequent department stores, national chain stores, and specialty stores. Above-average patronage of catalog showrooms and home improvement centers.

**Apparel Spending:** Heavy buyers at above-average price points. They buy more than average of women's shoes, dresses, casual tops, jeans, men's slacks, dress shirts, sports shirts, and fragrances.

**Fashion Preferences:** Business or dressy clothing of contemporary styling. They look for designer brands in women's tops, jeans, and fragrances.

**Credit Usage:** They frequently use credit cards at above-average rates to pay for purchases.

**What Media They Use:**
- Television: Watch slightly less than average (3.9 hours during last weekday), but their tendency to subscribe to cable is above average.
- Radio: Below-average with a tendency toward top 40, progressive, and golden oldies formats.
- Newspapers: Above-average readership of local Sunday newspapers.
- Magazines: Above-average number of subscriptions (4.5), especially travel/leisure, business, news, media guides, home, fashion, entertainment, and metro magazines.

### *FASHION FOREGOERS—16 percent of primary shoppers*
**Who They Are:** This group is more scattered among the sex/age and income matrix

than other groups. They can be lower-income singles, middle-income couples, or upper-income oldsters. Their average age, however, is 47.5, and they are most often single men living alone. Men tend to be well-educated college graduates and employed in professional occupations, while women tend to be employed in blue-collar jobs. Their average household size is 2.4 with 0.7 children, smaller than other groups. They tend to live in a mix of geographic areas, but are more heavily concentrated in metro areas of 50,000 to 499,999 population.

**Median income:** $25,350.

**What They Think:** Fashion Foregoers are fashion laggards who are totally unconcerned with their image. Their income may be higher, but they are more likely to spend it on hardware than clothes. This makes them what Mandy Putnam calls, "the bane of the fashion industry." They are mundane and somewhat antisocial. The only activity they participate in with any regularity is do-it-yourself projects.

**How They Shop:**
- Clothing: Everyday low prices, ease of finding merchandise, and convenient store location are big selling points with this group.
- Electronic equipment: Everyday low price, wide selection of merchandise.
- Furniture: Everyday low price.

**What They Buy:** Except for electronics, home entertainment, tools/hardware, and building materials, Fashion Foregoers exhibit below-average buying rates in most categories.

**Where They Shop:** They are infrequent shoppers in all types of stores except for home-improvement centers. In categories where women make most purchasing decisions, this group shops in discount stores.

**Apparel Spending:** Lower-than-average spending at lower-than-average price points.

**Fashion Preferences:** Function and durability are key drawing points for these shoppers. They tend to dress in ordinary, basic clothes, and they are not brand conscious.

**Credit Usage:** They are average credit-card users for Visa and MasterCard, but exhibit lower-than-average use of retail store cards and American Express.

**What Media They Use:**
- Television: Lower-than-average use (3.7 hours/weekday).
- Radio: Below-average (3.1 hours/weekday), with preference for classical, sports, and progressive formats.
- Newspaper: Lower-than-average readership of local weekday newspapers, but average readership on Sunday.

- Magazines: Above-average subscribers (4.5), especially to sports, literary, science, and news magazines.

### *SOCIAL STRIVERS — 20 percent of primary shoppers*
**Who They Are:** Social Strivers can be Younger Couples in the Down and Up Markets, Younger Parents in the Down Market, and Mid-Life Families in the Down Market. Their average age is 44.3, and they tend to be female, single or married with children. They are more likely to be high school graduates, and they are employed in pink- or blue-collar positions. Their average household size is 2.7, with 0.9 children. They tend to live in lower-income areas of rural towns and suburbs.

**Median income:** $21,550.

**What They Think:** They spend a lot of money they don't necessarily have, to maintain a fashionable image. They are extremely style-conscious and experimental in their fashion choices and look for status-enhancing brands. They are avid shoppers but try whenever possible to buy on sale. Very socially oriented, they are more likely than average to listen to tapes or records, play or watch team sports, join clubs, go to movies, and socialize with friends.

**How They Shop:**
- Clothing: They respond to guarantees; friendly, courteous sales personnel; and wide selections.
- Furniture: Wide selection.

**What They Buy:** Above-average buyers of many categories, including women's dress and casual clothing; infants', boys', and girls' clothing; children's shoes; furniture; appliances; home furnishings; tableware; housewares; domestics; jewelry; sporting goods; toys; and cosmetics. They also show above-average purchase rates for consumer electronics.

**Where They Shop:** Nearly every retail outlet attracts above-average numbers of Social Strivers, except home-improvement centers, where their patronage is only average.

**Apparel Spending:** Frequent shoppers with above-average spending at low to moderate price points.

**Fashion Preferences:** They prefer somewhat dressy clothes and contemporary styling, often buying the newest trendsetting fashions. Extremely brand conscious, they look for national or designer brands for women's tops, jeans, and fragrances.

**Credit Usage:** They use retail store credit cards more frequently than MasterCard, Visa, and American Express, which they use at below-average rates.

**What Media They Use:**

- Television: Heavy viewers (4.5 hours/weekday) and above-average subscribers to cable.
- Radio: Heavy listeners (3.6 hours/weekday), with preference for top 40 and black formats.
- Newspapers: Above-average subscribers (3.4), with preference for fashion magazines.

### DUTIFULS—16 percent of primary shoppers

**Who They Are:** They are concentrated in older, Down Market households, and their average age is 50.6, the oldest of any group. Mostly married, they tend not to have children at home. They are more likely to be high school graduates, and many are retired or working in blue- or pink-collar jobs. Their average household size is 2.6, with 0.8 children. They live in lower-income, non-metro areas, towns, and cities, and in middle-income areas of towns.

**Median income** is lowest of all groups: $17,800.

**What They Think:** As the name implies, Dutifuls are sacrificial by nature and comparison shoppers by necessity. They are highly practical. You won't find them buying expensive designer clothes for themselves. They like routine and go out of their way to avoid taking risks. Very conservative, they are careful, thrifty shoppers.

**How They Shop:**

- Clothing: They like everyday low prices, guarantees, easy-to-find merchandise, convenient store locations.
- Electronic equipment: Friendly sales personnel, ease of finding merchandise, speedy service.
- Furniture: Everyday low price and ease of finding merchandise.

**What They Buy:** They are homeowners, but they seem to have passed the acquisitive stage in life. They are below-average buyers for all categories.

**Where They Shop:** Infrequent shoppers, Dutifuls show above-average patronage only at warehouse grocery stores.

**Apparel Spending:** Light spenders for average or less-than-average price points.

**Fashion Preferences:** Tastes run toward simple, practical looks or ordinary, basic, durable clothes. Brand preferences are either generic or private label for women's jeans and cologne.

**Credit Usage:** Less regular usage of credit cards than any other group.

**What Media They Use:**
- Television: More than average (4.2 hours/weekday).
- Radio: Average listening (3.3 hours/weekday) with preference for instrumental, all news, sports, and agricultural/farm formats.
- Newspapers: Above-average readers of weekday papers.
- Magazines: Below-average magazine subscribers, but average subscribers for health/ lifestyle magazines.

### *PROGRESSIVE PATRONS—16 percent of primary shoppers*

**Who They Are:** Progressive Patrons are concentrated among Younger Singles in the Middle and Up Markets. To a lesser degree they are Younger Singles in the Down Market, Younger Couples in the Middle and Up Markets, and Mid-Life Families in the Up Market. Their average age is 42.1, and they are often male and single. They tend to be college graduates, and men tend to be employed in professional occupations, while women hold either professional or technical/sales positions. Their average household size is 2.4 with 0.8 children, and they tend to live in large urban areas and suburbs.

**Median income: $28,650.**

**What They Think:** They have discerning tastes and the income to buy the best. Highly self-confident, Progressive Patrons have an artistic streak in their clothes consumption. They seek variety and are open-minded and risk-taking. They like to be innovative and imaginative in their shopping as well as in their lives, which makes them among the first to buy adult high-tech toys and gadgets.

**How They Shop:**
- Clothing: Stores that make it easy to find merchandise and have good availability of high quality clothing will win Progressive Patrons.
- Electronic equipment: Availability of high-quality, wide selection, and availability of specific preferred brands are factors rated highly by this group.
- Furniture: Availability of high quality.

**What They Buy:** The group shows above-average purchasing rates for many categories, such as men's dress and casual clothing and shoes, furniture, home entertainment, appliances, home furnishings, tableware, domestics, jewelry, sporting goods, tools/ hardware, and cosmetics. This group also has higher-than-average ownership of consumer electronics, and their ownership of innovative electronic products, such as personal computers and answering machines, is relatively high.

**Where They Shop:** They shop frequently in specialty stores, home improvement centers, catalog showrooms, and convenience stores.

**Apparel Spending:** Heavy spenders for relatively high price points. They buy more than average of women's shoes, dresses, casual tops, jeans, and men's slacks, dress shirts, and sport shirts.

**Fashion Preferences:** Progressive Patrons tend to wear business attire and prefer traditional or contemporary styles. They buy designer brands for women's tops and jeans.

**Credit Usage:** Their use of Visa, MasterCard, and American Express is above average, but their use of retail credit cards is average.

**What Media They Use:**
- Television: Less than average (3.6 hours/weekday), but greater likelihood to subscribe to cable.
- Radio: Above-average listening (3.6 hours/weekday) and preference for classical, progressive, and jazz formats.
- Newspapers: Above-average readers of local Sunday papers.
- Magazines: Above-average subscription rate (4.7), especially sports, travel/leisure, literary/science, business, news, fashion, entertainment, and metro/city magazines.

## How the Typology Is Used

The retailers' prize targets are Progressive Patrons, Power Purchasers, and the Social Strivers, who spend most heavily on apparel, home furnishings, and other categories. In order to find out which typologies their customers fall into, retailers have two options. They can administer Management Horizons' questionnaire to a sample of their customers, or they can have it administered through a diary panel such as MRCA's.

MRCA Information Services of Stamford, Connecticut, has a diary panel of 11,500 households that report monthly on their purchases of apparel, jewelry, and household textiles; 5,000 of the panel households have been typed by the Management Horizons questionnaire.

Linked with MRCA's diary panel, the typologies show which shopper types buy certain items and which are responsive to which retailers. This linkage also allows larger retailers to use the typologies without having to do primary research. MRCA data show, for example, that Power Purchasers are two times more likely than average to buy women's dresses at Macy's, while Progressive Patrons are three times more likely to shop for their dresses at The Limited. Strivers buy dresses at T.J. Maxx.

Once retailers understand their customer mix, they can create more effective appeals. For Social Striver customers, retailers can tailor their selling approach to the group's high affiliation needs. "They need a lot of hand-holding and respond well to friendly and attentive salespeople," Putnam says, whereas Progressive Patrons prefer nonpersonal selling techniques such as interactive computer systems.

*Figure 11-1  Men's Dress Shirt Buying by Brand*
*(percent above or below average in consumer behavior by shopper type)*

## Discount Private Store Brands

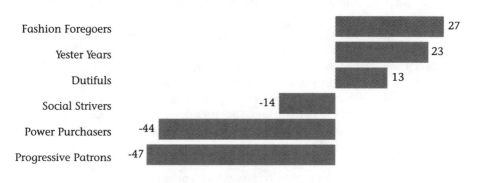

| | |
|---|---|
| Fashion Foregoers | 27 |
| Yester Years | 23 |
| Dutifuls | 13 |
| Social Strivers | -14 |
| Power Purchasers | -44 |
| Progressive Patrons | -47 |

## Designer Brands

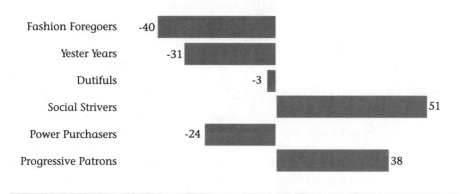

| | |
|---|---|
| Fashion Foregoers | -40 |
| Yester Years | -31 |
| Dutifuls | -3 |
| Social Strivers | 51 |
| Power Purchasers | -24 |
| Progressive Patrons | 38 |

## National Manufacturers Brands

| | |
|---|---|
| Fashion Foregoers | -4 |
| Yester Years | 12 |
| Dutifuls | 10 |
| Social Strivers | -4 |
| Power Purchasers | 9 |
| Progressive Patrons | -6 |

*Source:  MRCA Information Services*

MRCA data like those above show which shopper types are attracted to various types of stores. The more fashion-oriented shoppers, Social Strivers and Progressive Patrons, are usually considered the most valuable targets. As the data above show, however, that isn't always so. While these two types prefer to buy designer-brand men's dress shirts, they are least likely to buy national manufacturer brands or brands from discount stores.

Fashion Foregoers may not be the most attractive target for designer brands or high-fashion merchandise, but even these fashion illiterates can be worthwhile targets for clothiers. They are the biggest consumers of men's dress shirts at Sears, J.C. Penney, and Mervyns. They also are the ones most likely to shop at discount stores. And there are some items of clothing they are willing to pay more for. "These guys will pay for something like Gore-tex®," Putnam says. "But they don't care if it comes in red, green, or blue, as long as it covers them." It shows that no customer type is beyond reach, providing the approach and the product is right.

Psychographic measures are especially important for fine apparel, Putnam says, because clothing is such a vehicle of personal expression. "Clothing creates an impression, so there's the element of psychological risk in buying it," she says. For some customers with high-affiliation needs, wearing the wrong item of clothing can cause a series of complex psychological and emotional responses in certain social situations. Someone who is sensitive to the status connotations of clothing brands can feel out of place, inferior, or at the very least uncomfortable when surrounded by designer labels.

## Shared Experiences:  DuPont's Cohort Study

Perhaps the most important factor influencing retail buying, and consumer spending in general, is the aging of the population. The scales are tipping as more American consumers enter the older age brackets. In matters of fashion, age can be a significant determinant of style preferences. Impact becomes less important than functionality and comfort as one becomes older. This is not to imply that all consumers over 45 want similar conservative styles. Nothing is as individual as fashion. But it is safe to say that, in general, the older the people, the less likely they are to go for fashion extremes.

Realizing the importance of this particular demographic variable, DuPont's Textile Division, Fibers Department commissioned Management Horizons to help on a major study to identify what factors most greatly influenced consumption patterns. The survey results were presented at DuPont's annual business forum in 1989. "These three basics are key in knowing the consumer: age and income, life experiences, and basic values," said Corrin Corbin, director of apparel marketing.

The DuPont/Management Horizon study was based on the established lifecycle concept—that one is shaped by the events one experiences during youth and that people of the same age tend to behave in similar ways because they went through the same formative life experiences. During the formative years—between the ages of 7 and 21—core values and attitudes are shaped that will affect an individual for life. The main influence in one's life changes as one matures from childhood to young adulthood. During the pre-adolescent phase, parents are the major influence. In early adolescence, peers become the primary influences, and by late adolescence and early adulthood, the individual learns primarily from personal life experiences.

As people mature, other influences take over, such as college, marriage, pursuing a career, and/or raising a family. Overriding all of these personal influences are the broader events that shape all of our lives. These are political, social, international, technological, and economic events. "These events of the future are not predictable at this point," says Corbin, "but they will definitely influence the consumer in the years to come."

To gain a better understanding of these wider-ranging influences, DuPont and Management Horizons analyzed how life experiences will affect Americans of different ages, now and in the future. This unique segmentation finds ten different groups, or cohorts, with shared core values in the population today:

- **World War I Babies,** born 1910-1919 (5.3 percent of 1990 population, 2.6 percent in 2000). These people came of age during the Stock Market Crash and the Great Depression, when frugality was not only a virtue but a means of survival. These memories of scarcity make them overcautious about spending on anything other than the necessities of life. Even where food is concerned, these people will shop for the best bargains, clip coupons, and avoid items they see as too extravagant.

- **Roaring '20s Babies,** born 1920-1929 (8.2 percent of 1990 population, 5.7 percent in 2000). Possessions are less important than experiences for these people born during the boom times of the 1920s. They will continue to spend on travel, entertainment, friends, and family, but they are less likely to spend on personal apparel as they age.

- **Depression Babies,** born 1930-1939 (8.8 percent of 1990 population, 7.3 percent in 2000). Their major expenditures today are for their children's college educations, home furnishings and improvements, big domestic cars, travel, entertainment, and other luxuries. During the next decade, however, their spending is expected to shift from status spending on the man's career to status spending on retirement.

- **World War II Babies,** born 1940-1945 (6.5 percent of 1990 population, 5.9 percent in 2000). They are divided between the achievement oriented, the traditional, and those whose dreams have evaporated (often due to divorce). Major spending is now centered on the kids, home improvements and furnishings, travel, entertainment, and automobiles. As these people age, expect them to shift back to focus on personal pleasure: as they retire, many will continue to pursue the leisure activities they enjoy now.

- **Mature Boomers,** born 1946-1950 (7.1 percent of 1990 population, 6.5 percent in 2000). Due to their experiences as young adults in the 1960s, they feel guilty when they spend money needlessly or max out their credit cards, and have a love-hate relationship with materialism. The problem is that they like to have nice things, and now that they are parents, they indulge their own children as their own parents once indulged them. Fantasies are a priority with this group, so expect that they will spend to maintain them as they age.

- **Mid-Boomers,** born 1951-1957 (11.6 percent of 1990 population, 10.7 percent in 2000). They have less ambivalence toward material things than do the older boomers. The women in this cohort are the top spenders on personal apparel because they feel they deserve nice possessions, especially when they work so hard for them. Many of the men in this cohort, however, feel that fashion is flaky and prefer functional clothing. The focus of their spending will continue to shift in the next decade away from satisfying personal whims and toward fulfilling family responsibilities, as many in this cohort are starting families for the first time. While they are expected to become more price conscious, they will continue to demand quality from the products and services they buy.

- **Young Boomers,** born 1958-1964 (12.4 percent of 1990 population, 11.6 percent in 2000). This is the cohort to which the ill-fated "Yuppies" belonged. The youngest boomers think little about spending lavishly on themselves, and their high levels of expenditure on home entertainment products, furniture, vacations, and various other luxury items reflect this. However, many in this group are now beginning families, and their spending is expected to shift to family-oriented products and services. But a significant portion of this group will continue to pursue careers while living a self-absorbed lifestyle, and their spending on personal apparel, homes, and furnishings is expected to accelerate as their incomes rise.

- **Mature Busters,** born 1965-1970 (9.1 percent of 1990 population, 8.8 percent in 2000). Peers and media are major influences in their lives right now. As they enter the job market and begin their adult lives, their spending will increase for items like home furnishings, career wardrobes, transportation, and personal computers. As some begin families, they will start spending on items like children's clothing, toys, and sporting equipment.

- **Young Busters,** born 1971-1976 (8.3 percent of 1990 population, 7.9 percent in 2000). Many members of this cohort are still in their key developmental years. Some are still living with their parents, so they control not only their own incomes (often from part-time work), but also influence what the family buys. They'll be spending their money in the next decade on first cars, entry-level career wardrobes, apartment furnishings, and electronic gadgets.

- **Mature Boomlets**, born 1977-1982 (8.5 percent of 1990 population, 8.2 percent in 2000). These are the highly indulged children of the baby boomers, many of whom have working mothers. Many have been cared for by a series of day-care providers and have become accustomed to caring for themselves and holding more responsibility at a younger age than previous cohorts. They also have disposable income and more influence on family spending than older generations. In general, they are savvy consumers due to their extensive exposure to media. They will be spending on leisure wear, tuition, books, consumer electronics, food, and personal items in the next decade, as well as continuing to influence the way their parents spend money.

The Cohort Study shows that age matters, says Corbin. Examining the life experiences of the cohorts in the market helps determine who the future customers are likely to be and how they will shop. For example, Young Busters and Mature Boomlets have grown up playing video games, and their ease with computers will make them willing and able users of the electronic shopping technology of the future. Looking at the market in terms of age cohorts, as with traditional psychographic inquiries, can help marketers make some sense of a population that is getting impossibly diverse.

"To be a winner in this industry, we are going to have to put the best system in place that will meet the diversity of target cohorts' physiological and psychological needs in a cost-effective and timely manner," DuPont's Corbin says. For retailers, facing the future with any degree of success will certainly require psychographic tools that can provide new insights into why consumers buy, how they shop, and what businesses can do to keep them coming back for more.

# 12 Packaged Goods: Attitudes of the Core Consumer

*We find the pot of gold at the end of the rainbow lies in usage and increasing usage and increasing usage as opposed to lifestyle segmentation, which is still somewhat abstract. A lifestyle segmentation may be a useful way of looking at an overall consumer market or consumer trends, but in terms of trying to explain other behaviors, the first priority is usage. Then you can look at lifestyles and emotions to better explain usage. For us, that's proven to be a much more useful approach than just trying to segment people into lifestyle groups.*

*— Anthony Adams*
*Vice President of Marketing Research*
*Campbell Soup Co.*

**P**SYCHOGRAPHIC RESEARCH has been in use longest and is the most evolved in the packaged-goods industry. The competitive environment for packaged-goods started heating up just as lifestyle research was emerging, as packaged-goods manufacturers and their agencies were forced to begin looking for better ways to understand markets. They quickly embraced the new technique, and use spread as more marketers caught on to the notion that this new way of looking at customers could provide the inside information they needed to successfully sell more of their products in a tougher market. Looking back at the early lifestyle research done in the late 1960s, we see that companies such as the Nestlé Company, Procter & Gamble, Kellogg, and Schlitz were among the first to target customers through psychographic research.

In those early days of lifestyle research, the makers of Schlitz used the new technique to get an idea of who their best customers were. They found out that the major beer drinkers were blue-collar risk-takers who fantasized about living solely for pleasure. These beer drinkers considered themselves "real men." They subscribed to *Playboy* and preferred physical, male-oriented activities. They agreed with the statements, "I would do better than average in a fistfight," "Men are smarter than women," "Beer is a real man's drink," and "A party wouldn't be a party without liquor." Out of this came the Schlitz "reach for all the gusto you can" campaign that was especially created to trigger the hedonistic, live-for-today fantasy of these men. Some of the early ads portrayed macho sea captains and built on the idea that the ocean was the last frontier for rugged he-men types.

Another early example of lifestyle research in the packaged-goods category involved Lava heavy-duty hand soap. Data from Leo Burnett's 1968 study were used to widen the market for the product, which had traditionally been aimed at the wives of blue-collar men. The advertising imagery showed men working hard at grimy jobs on oil rigs and construction sites. Demographically, this image was accurate; the heaviest users of Lava were blue-collar workers. But this group was getting older and was not a growth market, so the company ad agency decided to go after new users. Using the lifestyle data, they found that one segment of the market was made up of traditional-valued women who were entirely focused on their homes and families. They considered themselves the "gatekeepers" of their homes. This was reflected in their agreement with statements such as "I try to arrange my home for my children's convenience," "I always make my cakes from scratch," "Clothes should be dried in the fresh air and sunshine," and "People come to me more often than I go to them for information on brands." They disagreed with the statements, "I must admit I really don't like household chores" and "I like modern furniture." From the lifestyle data, the agency decided to play up the idea of the woman as the gatekeeper for the home. They decided to use all the family members in the advertisements and built the campaign around the idea that children, who hate washing up, would get all the dirt the first time with a heavy-duty soap.

## The More Things Change...

From the early 1970s, when the above ads ran, to the early 1990s, much has changed, yet much has remained the same in how packaged-goods companies explore the minds of consumers. Psychographic segmentations are still used to get the big picture of customers' lifestyles; what's changed is the content and scope of psychographic research. Today, the research has to be more specific so it can be directly applicable.

There is also a greater emphasis on understanding the specific emotions elicited by brands (see Chapter 7). This is largely due to the intensifying competitive situation in the industry as a whole. There are many more products out there vying for the consumer's dollar. More than 13,200 products are introduced every year, and the number of new-product launches nearly doubled in the last five years. But analysts say that up to 80 percent of all new products will fail. And most often, failure happens because the market for the product is misunderstood in some key respect.

Today, the industry uses a whole range of research techniques, from small-scale, one-on-one interviews to the broadest-based surveys. As shown in Chapter 7, packaged-goods companies are using qualitative psychological research in a more and more specialized way. By the same token, psychographic segmentations are becoming more specific. Packaged-goods companies are paying more attention to segmentations that emphasize product-related attitudes and specific product-usage situations. The following section looks at several ways of psychographically understanding packaged-goods markets.

## The Importance of Process

It's crucial to look at product-related attitudes or benefits, but sometimes it's useful to first look at the processes and behaviors that influence product selection. Looking at how people shop for groceries, bake, cook, or dine out will tell you something about why they make the choices they make in the marketplace.

In the past decade, myriad packaged-goods firms, either on their own or in concert with magazines or market research firms, have released psychographic studies that explore the behavior surrounding the product usage or purchase situation. For example, in 1988, Pillsbury, along with Creative Research Associates Inc. and SRI International, surveyed Americans about their eating behavior and attitudes toward food. The "What's Cookin'" study included data from food diaries kept by more than 3,000 respondents over 15 years by the Market Research Corporation of America (MRCA). The study identified five segments of the population defined by their shared eating behavior:

- **The Chase & Grabbits,** at 26 percent of the population, buy fast-food hamburgers and sandwiches, frozen dinners and carry-out frozen pizzas. They are young urbanites, mostly single, and not very involved with food. They are the people who would just as soon take a pill for their sustenance or for whom microwave popcorn can be a meal. They are adventurous in their food choices if the meal can be the means of creating an interesting social occasion. As long as it keeps hunger at bay and is convenient, Chase & Grabbits are happy.

- **The Functional Feeders,** at 18 percent of population, are time-pressured working people over the age of 45 who could use "shortcut" as their watchword. They typically eat canned soups, frozen macaroni and cheese, frozen pancakes and waffles, store-bought cookies, and instant potatoes. They aren't too adventurous about food. They use modern convenience foods, but mostly as ingredients in other dishes. They are constantly searching for quicker ways to prepare the traditional foods they grew up with.

- **The Down Home Stokers,** at 21 percent of the population, are largely southern and blue-collar, and have modest incomes and educations. They are tightly bound to their regional foods, such as farm-style meat and potatoes in the Midwest and New

England's clambakers. Their typical preferences are homemade fried chicken; fresh-baked breads such as cornbread, rolls, or biscuits; vegetables cooked with bacon; and fried eggs. By stoking up on the foods of their heritage, they are reaffirming the values represented by their traditional cuisine. They are closed to foreign foods unless they come in forms corresponding to their established tastes.

- **The Careful Cooks**, at 20 percent of the population, are distinguishable by both their lifestage and geographic region. They are concentrated on the West Coast are often retired, and many have advanced educations. They've left the red meat feasts of their past behind because of a desire to live a longer, healthier life than their parents. They sometimes miss their old eating habits, but are now comfortable with healthier ways of cooking and eating. They have acquired an extensive store of nutritional knowledge, and they regularly sample other cuisines that meet their healthy standards. They prefer wheat bread, skim milk, yogurt, fresh fruits and vegetables, fish, chicken without skin, and salads.

- **The Happy Cookers**, at 15 percent of the population, are a declining group rooted firmly in the traditional kitchen of grandma. They view cooking and baking as a way to show their love for their families and take great pride from it. Two categories make up this group—the younger mothers and older nurturers. The younger faction is more aware of the dangers of fat and sugar, but sometimes bends the rules to treat their children to a cozy kitchen full of the warm aromas of baking. Typical Happy Cooker foods are homemade pies, cakes, cookies and fruit crisps; homemade meat dishes; homemade casseroles; fresh fish; and fresh vegetables, both raw and cooked.

With 15 years of MRCA panel diaries, the researchers were able to chart the rise and decline of the various groups over time. They found that the Chase & Grabbit segment had grown the most (by 136 percent) over 15 years and was likely to become the largest segment by 2000. The Careful Cook segment also showed substantial growth between 1971 and 1986 and was likely to reach one-fourth of the population by 2000. In contrast, the more traditional types, the Down Home Stokers and Happy Cookers had declined by almost 35 percent since 1971 and were likely to either stabilize or further decline by the year 2000.

Such an inquiry is valuable, say Pillsbury officials, because trends are a continuum. Knowing how people ate in the past provides a solid bedrock from which to predict how they will eat in the future.

## Category-Specific Attitudes

Research that goes even further into attitudes and behaviors surrounding specific product decisions helps to put more pieces of the consumer puzzle into place. The Quaker Oats Company, for example, manufactures dozens of brands in several product categories including hot and cold cereals, grains, mixes, frozen foods, syrups, snacks, and pet foods. Each brand competes for market share in categories that are becoming more crowded every year. Psychographic segmentations have been done in practically every division to give researchers a better understanding of the complicated markets for each category.

Quaker's pet-foods division, for example, competes for customers in a category that grew by 165 new products in 1990 alone. Understanding the pet-food market is like trying to understand what makes some people cat people and others dog people. This is no petty distinction. Fully 43 percent of U.S. households have a pet, while only 38 percent have children. Thirty percent have at least one dog, 22 percent a cat, and 8 percent have some other type of pet, according to Mediamark data. To complicate matters, half of the people who have cats also have dogs, but only one-third of dog owners also own cats.

There are an estimated 170 million pets in the U.S. consuming more than $7 billion worth of pet food annually. To better understand this large and complex market, Quaker's pet-foods division psychographically segmented the market to find out what roles pets play in people's lives. "If your dog is your baby, you treat it differently than if it's a working dog," says Eileen Thompson, Quaker's director of market research, new ventures. This attitudinal distinction translates into different buying patterns for pet food. The consumer who considers a dog a member of the family will buy more expensive brands of pet foods in a greater variety of flavors. Someone buying food for a hunting dog or a watch dog will buy top-of-the-line scientifically formulated food, but care little what flavor it is as long as the dog eats it. Quaker wouldn't discuss the specific results of the pet food segmentation, but other companies have released product-attitude segmentations that illustrate how this type of inquiry can be used.

## Food for Life: HealthFocus™

Over the last decade, there has been an explosion in the number and variety of foods billed as low in fat, low in cholesterol, and low in salt. No longer are people with hypertension or heart disease the only markets for such products. These days, the market for healthy food crosses age, sex, and income boundaries and extends to the consumer mainstream.

Ninety percent of all food shoppers in 1990 said they base their food choices on health factors. Not only are consumers more aware of potential health problems; they're willing to change their eating habits to help prevent problems later in life. They are also quick to change brands, and many say they're willing to sacrifice product benefits like convenience and lower prices to eat healthier. Such a large group of consumers can no longer be adequately defined as a single market. Packaged-goods companies are looking for better ways to understand and capture niches of this quickly expanding market, and they're using psychographics to do it.

A market consulting firm called HealthFocus, in Emmaus, Pennsylvania, has developed an impressive clientele by filling the demand for insights about consumers' attitudes on health and nutrition. The company was started in 1988 by the people who ran the test kitchen at Rodale Press, publisher of *Prevention* magazine. Since then, they have produced a psychographic segmentation of health consumers that has been used by most major packaged-goods companies. Quaker Oats has used the segmentation to help position its Pritikin line. More than a dozen other companies, such as Carnation, Kraft, General Foods, General Mills, Campbell Soup, Purina Mills, and Procter & Gamble have also used the study, "HealthFocus on U.S. Consumers: The First Comprehensive Study of Public Attitudes and Actions Toward Healthy Food Choices."

In 1990, HealthFocus selected a representative sample of Americans and then prescreened them by telephone for health awareness. The resulting sample of 1,100 Health Active consumers was sent a 300-question survey to complete and send back. The response rate was 56 percent. Questions covered food-related actions, attitudes, and concerns, social and health attitudes, shopping and eating patterns, company/brand perceptions, perceptions of organic foods, product usage, personal medical history, and demographics. The attitudinal questions were measured on a five-point scale, from strongly agree to strongly disagree, and included statements such as:

*I enjoy eating healthy foods.*
*Eating healthier foods has required me to change brands.*
*I feel better physically when I eat healthy foods.*
*My physical appearance is more attractive through general health and nutrition habits.*
*It's very important to me that I feel attractive to the opposite sex.*
*Environmental issues have impacted my selection of food products.*
*The health hazards of daily living (pollution, stress, etc.) are greater than in the past.*

HealthFocus found that consumers had five major reasons for buying healthy food. The number-one reason, chosen by the majority of the survey sample, was preventive. Fully 68 percent said they ate healthy to ensure future good health. The second most common motivation was medical—13 percent said they ate healthy to treat or control an existing health problem. Another 11 percent said they ate healthy because it provided extra day-to-day energy and stamina, 7 percent said they did it to lose weight, and 1 percent said they did it for spiritual or philosophical reasons.

These motivations provided the basis for the segmentation. Based on motivations, food attitudes and actions, personal health attitudes, and social attitudes, HealthFocus™ identified five groups in the health consumer market:

**INVESTORS** (45 percent of adults) make health-conscious eating choices for preventive reasons, to ensure that their health will remain good in later years. They don't need to change their diets, but they believe that doing so now is an investment in future good health.

Demographically, Investors are more likely than average to be men and to have four or more years of college education. They are more likely than the other groups to be employed, especially in professional/technical positions, and they work more hours per week than any other group. Their age distribution is similar to that of the overall survey. They are the second most affluent group, with a median household income of $33,600.

MANAGERS (36 percent of adults) choose healthy foods for short-term performance reasons. Managers are seeking glowing health now, not just the future absence of disease. Like Investors, they don't have to make changes, but they find that eating better makes them feel and think better.

Demographically, Managers are better-educated than average; more have college degrees or graduate training. Proportionately more are employed as managers or administrators, and Manager households with children typically have two preschoolers. They are concentrated in the Midwest region of the country and one-third live in suburbs, compared with 28 percent of the overall survey. Fewer live in small towns or rural areas. Median household income is $33,400.

HEALERS (9 percent of adults) are most often older people who have discovered healthy eating later in life due to health reasons. They are compelled by their doctors and by their pressing health problems to make immediate, and often drastic, dietary changes. Because they feel it's eat healthy or die, they will often sacrifice taste and convenience for nutritional benefits.

Demographically, the Healer group shows more distinct differences than the rest. They are proportionately more female (84 percent, compared with 79 percent of the overall survey). Proportionately more are in the 50-to-64 (34 percent, compared with 20 percent overall) and over-65 age groups (29 percent versus 13 percent overall). Healers are least likely to be college graduates, employed, or employed in professional/technical positions. They are more likely to be retired or clerical workers, and higher proportions are married or widowed. They have the smallest households, and they are more concentrated in urban than suburban areas. Income-wise, they are concentrated at both ends of the scale. A higher-than-average share have incomes both below $15,000 and over $65,000. Median household income, however, is below average, at $27,500.

STRUGGLERS (7 percent of adults) are always torn between their love of junk food and their awareness that certain foods are better for their health. They are always yo-yoing between healthy and unhealthy eating, and they're the least likely to stick to a healthy diet. Many feel impeded by life's obstacles (time and work pressures) from consistently eating healthy foods.

Strugglers are more likely to work in service occupations and less likely to have managerial/administrative or professional/technical positions. Strugglers are most likely to have children (59 percent, compared with 50 percent overall). They are also more likely to have two or more children (37 percent versus 32 percent). Struggler households are also most likely to have teenagers or adult children. Stragglers are the least affluent group (median income $26,200, compared with $32,600 for all respondents).

**DISCIPLES** (3 percent of adults) follow a restricted diet because they feel it is philosophically or spiritually the right thing to do. These are the animal-rights activists, the Buddhists, or Seventh-Day Adventists who maintain strict vegetarian diets. It also includes those on macrobiotic diets for health reasons. For this group, their dietary regimen is a way of life as deeply rooted and immutable as are their convictions.

Demographically, Disciple households are the least likely to have children. They are slightly more rural than average, and fewer live in small towns. They are found in higher proportions in the New England and Pacific states and are least likely to live in the Central region of the country. Disciples, the most affluent group, have a median household income of $33,800.

Like the original VALS, the HealthFocus segmentation is theory-based, rather than data-based. HealthFocus developed the theory that the healthy foods market was composed of five groups in 1988, but didn't field the first study until 1990. Also similar to the original VALS theory (see Chapter 3) is the overlap between groups depending on product and circumstance. All Health Active consumers demonstrate the tendencies of one particular group, but they can sometimes exhibit characteristics of other groups, depending on the product they're buying or the usage situation. For example, a person diagnosed with high cholesterol who is under stress and has a parent who died of cancer will probably buy low-fat dairy foods like a Healer to deal with his high cholesterol. But he'll buy calming herbal teas like a Manager to manage his stress, and choose high-fiber cereals like an Investor to guard against developing cancer later on.

Likewise, a consumer will vary his or her dietary food choices to correspond to changes in health status. A sudden illness could cause a member of any of the other groups to start behaving like a Healer, while an improvement in health can cause a Healer to start acting more like an Investor or a Manager.

A number of products now use advertising messages targeted to appeal to one segment or another, says Sara Starr, vice president and cofounder of HealthFocus. New lines of light junk food—lower-fat Twinkies and potato chips—are nearly irresistible to Strugglers, who are torn between healthy and unhealthy eating. These products allow them to ease their consciences without sacrificing too much. The current ad campaign for V-8 vegetable juice shows people walking at 45-degree angles, signifying they haven't kept their diet straight because they haven't eaten their daily requirement of vegetables. With one drink of V-8, their diet is straight again, and they're walking straight up. This campaign is perfectly targeted to Managers, says Starr. Managers are interested in the day-to-day management of their health, but they want quick and painless ways of doing it.

## HOW CLIENTS USE IT

One of the most valuable ways to use a motivational segmentation like HealthFocus is as an entry point to an unfamiliar market. Quaker Oats used the HealthFocus segmentation to upgrade its Pritikin line of products to appeal to a younger, broader market. The Pritikin line is the original Healer family of products, created by a doctor for patients who had to follow stringent diet guidelines to manage serious health problems.

With help from HealthFocus, Quaker developed cleaner, more stylish packaging and got Pritikin products moved from the special dietary foods section of supermarkets to the general sections next to competing products. In addition, Pritikin adopted the line, "Live your Life in Your Prime." "That's a much more Manager kind of message," says Starr. "That's a market they were kind of ignoring, and one we said they should look at because they would be receptive to the products."

Quaker now has a better chance to capture the younger, information-oriented Managers. According to Starr, "Managers like to read information, but they like it presented in a pretty clean, graphic way. They're not willing to sacrifice taste for health, and they don't like to be associated with anything that suggests that they're going to sacrifice taste. So having a cleaner, more updated look would appeal to them more than something that speaks of old-style health food."

Purina Mills used the HealthFocus segmentation to better understand the potential market for a new product, Lean Cuts by Mariah. The fresh pork product, in test market as this book went to press, is to be positioned as a low-fat alternative to chicken, says Paul Poe, director of marketing.

Poe says the segmentation has helped the company decide which product benefits would be most important to the target markets. "It's very helpful in terms of prioritizing our approach," says Poe. Purina Mills expects Lean Cuts to appeal primarily to Investors and Managers, who eat healthy foods but aren't willing to sacrifice taste. Poe says Purina Mills could use the HealthFocus information to target recipes, nutritional information, package copy, and advertising at Investors or Managers. An advertising approach that might work with these groups would first emphasize the great taste and then the low-fat aspect of the product. Other important appeals to these targets would be the variety of product use and fast cooking time.

The down side for Purina Mills, however, is that the HealthFocus segmentation has not proven useful as a way to identify those groups in the marketplace. "I'm not sure that any of those psychographic groups are definable," says Poe. "I think they're strategically and attitudinally correct, but I don't think they're necessarily targetable because I'm not sure we can find those people utilizing mass media." HealthFocus included some media-use information in its survey, but a product like Lean Cuts that's just getting started needs more detailed media information. "Given the scope of our product and the fact that we're only in a couple of test markets," Poe says, "the use of that information would be difficult. Something like *Walker's Weekly* probably has a circulation of 25,000 nationwide, and we need it much more confined than that."

Although there are limitations to the segmentation technique, Poe says, it serves a distinct and valuable purpose in the process of marketing research. "It gives you a good starting place to focus in on," Poe says. "Once you get through that and begin to do your own market research, you begin to see some twists and turns from what you thought it would be."

Eileen Thompson, market research director of Quaker's new ventures division, says that a segmentation such as HealthFocus is just one step in a laborious process of understanding a market. "We do a lot of qualitative work in all of our businesses—focus groups," Thompson says. "But we try to make sure we have fairly high-level people going to them and really understanding what people are saying. Then we try to turn that into a number of statements or questions that will help pull apart those different kinds of attitudes. Then that becomes the basis for a quantitative segmentation study."

The key goal is to really get at what makes people attitudinally and behaviorally different. That involves probing every conceivable aspect of consumers' thought processes. It can also involve doing more than one segmentation per category. For example, Quaker did its own health and nutrition segmentation study last year to try to better understand the key issues involved in healthy eating. The results were fairly similar to what HealthFocus found, but Thompson says it provided even more detailed information. "We were focusing on general health and nutrition behaviors, which brought in things like attitudes toward medicine and attitudes toward exercise."

Thompson does not agree that psychographics is most useful for new-product research. "Even the most standardized businesses can use psychographic segmentation to look at their business in a different way and to help in positioning," she says. "While it's certainly critical to new-product development, we also use it fairly extensively to figure out where we're going on the main businesses as well."

## Campbell: Who Is the Core User?

Rated as one of the most recognizable American brands next to Coca-Cola, Campbell Soup Company is one company that's taking psychographic research to new levels. Campbell's investment in understanding consumers' mindsets predates the motivational research that equated soup with nurturing substances such as mother's milk and amniotic fluid. Over this long history of research, Campbell has learned to have a healthy respect for its customers. The company considers brand equity with its best customers as something with bottom-line value.

"We've found that 5 percent of Campbell consumers are worth $8.34 each in earnings before interest and taxes to our company," says Anthony Adams, vice president of marketing research. "Our brand equity is our most important asset. If it appeared on our balance sheet, it would have more value than all our plants combined." Campbell has discovered that a core of enthusiastic customers buys about 102 cans of soup per household every year. And there is an even more loyal extra-enthusiastic consumer who buys up to 320 cans a year. "We should start paying them rather than vice-versa," Adams jokes.

Once they began to understand where business was coming from, Campbell researchers made a serious commitment to finding out everything they could about these most loyal customers. "The most productive group is what we're calling the core enthusiast," Adams says. As a group, they may be fairly small, much smaller in some cases than heavy users, but their attitudes, emotions, and behaviors provide key insights into why Campbell Soup sells.

Adams has developed a unique way to correlate the usage data from Mediamark with scanner sales data from IRI. Campbell segments households based on their degree of profitability and enthusiasm for the brand. Enthusiasm is measured by tenacity and frequency of use. Once they rate panel participants on enthusiasm, they replicate the sample and get attitudinal and emotional data from them.

This method of segmenting takes psychographics one step beyond and shifts the focus from potential market segments to actual product users. "Users are a much more useful topic for research than a lifestyle segment per se," Adams says. "We find the pot of gold at the end of the rainbow lies in usage and increasing usage and increasing usage as opposed to what to me is still somewhat abstract, lifestyle segmentation. A lifestyle segmentation may be a useful way of looking at an overall consumer market or consumer trends, but in terms of trying to explain some other behaviors, the first priority is usage." Once the core users are identified, Adams adds, lifestyle and psychographic research becomes valuable as a way of better explaining usage.

After attitude and lifestyle comes emotions, says Adams. To gain insight into core consumers' emotional bonds with the brand, Campbell uses a computer program called Emotional Sonar™, developed by Emotion Mining Company of Wellesley, Massachusetts (see Chapter 7). This interactive computerized interview helps people articulate the exact emotions they felt at a certain point in time, such as the first time they ate Campbell's soup or saw a piece of advertising. This gives Campbell direct access to consumers' hearts and minds, helps position its products against competitors, and creates ideas for advertising.

Above all, Campbell wants to find out what keeps these core customers coming back. "We want to understand the brand's essence," Adams says. "These are the people who would put an 'I Love Campbell's' bumper sticker on their car. What makes them want to do that?"

Some of what keeps them coming back undoubtedly has to do with the brand's imagery. Campbell developed its latest generation of ads after analyzing the Emotional Sonar tests. In one, mom feeds her chilly little boy a bowl of soup and wraps him in a scarf, to the tagline, "Once a Campbell kid, always a Campbell kid." A nurturing mother, a child, and warmth are all part of Campbell's imagery summed up nicely in the symbol of the scarf, Adams says. "Soup is like a nutritional scarf. It warms you, whether you're physically or psychologically cold." The company has been "close to ecstatic" with the early tracking results of these new ads, Adams says.

Adams admits that this imagery, which relies heavily on the warmth of a nurturing mom, is uncannily similar to the images suggested by those early motivational researchers. "Soup is a liquid food, and there have been analogies to mother's milk," he says. "It's not that we're returning to motivational research, but we are realizing more than ever that emotion is an extremely important part of the communication package for any brand that has a heritage like Campbell's Soup. Customers don't respond well at all to a 100 percent rational sell."

What makes Campbell's unique among packaged-goods giants is its new emphasis on the core customer. Adams says that the Value of the Customer Process, which has been in use for about five years, is now the basis for Campbell's entire research process. It's valuable, because it underscores the importance of core customers to the success of the business and recognizes the importance of finding out what makes them buy. "'Value of the Customer' is going to be written on Times Square by 1995, because it has applications to all products and services," Adams says. "You save immense amounts of time and money, and there are going to be more case studies that show it. It's going to become the way to do research."

# **13** *Geodemographics: You Are Where You Live*

"As American society has become increasingly fragmented due to shifts in family composition, labor distribution, and the economy, marketing companies have pioneered many ingenious methods to quantify the changes and incorporate them into their product strategies. In 1974, a computer scientist turned entrepreneur named Jonathan Robbin devised a wildly popular target marketing system by matching zip codes with census data and consumer surveys. Christening his creation PRIZM (Potential Rating Index for ZIP Markets), he programmed computers to sort the nation's 36,000 zips into 40 'lifestyle clusters...'

Here was a new way of looking at the nation—not as 50 states but rather 40 neighborhood types, each with distinct boundaries, values, consuming habits, and political beliefs."

— Michael Weiss
The Clustering of America

THE 1988 PUBLICATION of *The Clustering of America* by Michael Weiss was such a sensation that *USA Today* devoted nearly a column to it, as did most other major dailies. A surprising response, considering the book is about Claritas Corporation's PRIZM geodemographic clustering system. What captured the imagination of the people who bought the book was the notion that address matters. PRIZM, which identifies the average demographic characteristics of people living in certain units of geography, operates on the theory that you can tell a lot about a person by where that person lives.

In the strictest sense, a geodemographic system like PRIZM is not psychographic research, although many people think it is a more applicable alternative. Geodemographic systems are demographically driven, while psychographics is based on attitudinal differences. Psychographic insights come from representative surveys that include questions about demographics, attitudes, leisure activities, opinions, purchase behavior, and media use. Geodemographic clustering systems like PRIZM are based on demographic information derived from the U.S. census. The demographic characteristics of people living in a particular geographic area are averaged, and the area is defined by those shared characteristics. Though it isn't directly psychographic at all, geodemographic clustering looks a little like a psychographic segmentation of neighborhoods.

Consider PRIZM's most affluent cluster. PRIZM classifies the zip codes of Beverly Hills, California; Palm Beach, Florida; Scarsdale, New York; and McLean, Virginia, into a cluster called "Blue Blood Estates." Behind the privacy hedges and security gates that shield homes in these neighborhoods, you'll find the stately colonial and English Tudor mansions of old monied families as well as the baroque neo-Spanish excesses of California's new celebrity royalty. One in ten American millionaires can be found residing in these areas. Political power brokers, corporate kingpins, and high-priced professionals, like brain surgeons and entertainment lawyers, also live in areas at the top of America's socioeconomic hierarchy. What do these disparate neighborhoods have in common? According to PRIZM, they are the few, the proud, and the rich. They make up only 1.1 percent of the population, but they hold one-third of the private wealth, 60 percent of corporate stocks, and almost 10 percent of the nation's real estate.

## You Are What You Buy

The real reason people think that geodemographic systems like PRIZM are comparable to lifestyle research is because they have links to purchase and attitude information. Though cluster systems are demographically based, they can be tied to psychographic systems, such as VALS, and consumer panel data, such as those from Mediamark or Simmons. This allows researchers to understand a cluster of people not only by where they live and their shared average demographics, but also by the types of products they buy.

Though these linkages make geodemographics similar to lifestyle or psychographic research, it doesn't mean they can be used interchangeably. Lifestyle research finds out what people buy by asking a representative sample and extrapolating to the general population. Geodemographic systems categorize panelists into geodemographic clusters. What the representative panel members say they buy is then considered true for the other people in their respective clusters.

Four other companies besides Claritas now offer cluster systems for the U.S.:

- **ACORN**, by CACI

- **ClusterPLUS,** by Donnelley Marketing Information Services

- **OASYS**, by National Demographics & Lifestyles

- **MicroVision** by National Decision Systems

To get an idea of how geodemographics and psychographics differ, here's a simple comparison. PRIZM data from Simmons and Mediamark show that Blue Blood Estates residents are big consumers of bottled water, imported cheese, Irish whiskey, and air-travel credit cards. They are also more likely than average to attend live theater and belong to country clubs.

*Figure 13-1  Blue Blood Product Use*

|  | National Average | Blue Blood Estates | Cluster Index |
|---|---|---|---|
| Air-travel credit cards | 1.5% | 7.9% | 530° |
| U.S. Treasury notes | 0.7 | 3.6 | 521 |
| Irish whiskey | 1.5 | 6.0 | 401 |
| Rental cars | 4.9 | 19.5 | 398 |
| Imported cheese | 6.9 | 26.1 | 379 |
| Downhill skiing | 4.2 | 13.6 | 322 |
| Personal computers | 7.0 | 20.2 | 288 |
| Valid passports | 10.2 | 29.3 | 287 |
| Men's business suits | 8.0 | 20.9 | 261 |
| Bottled water | 9.3 | 23.6 | 253 |
| Book clubs | 8.9 | 19.9 | 224 |
| Croissants | 12.3 | 26.4 | 215 |
| Country clubs | 1.2 | 2.5 | 207 |
| Attend live theater | 15.4 | 29.9 | 194 |

*Source: SMRB & MRI, Claritas Corporation, 1987*

Index indicates the percentage of people in each category indexed against the national average. An index of 100 represents the U. S. average, and an index of 200 signifies usage that's twice the national average. Many researchers believe that a product-use profile, like the one above, is an alternative to psychographics. It's true that it tells you what Blue Blood Estates buy, but it doesn't tell you why.

If you profile the Blue Blood Estates cluster by VALS 2 types, you can learn more about this group's motivations. The VALS 2 linkage shows the proportions of Blue Blooders in each of eight pre-established segments (Achievers, Believers, Actualizers, etc.). But even that picture is somewhat broad. You can find out the specific attitudinal motivators only by doing a special psychographic segmentation.

If you did a psychographic study of a representative sample of people who live in Blue Blood Estates geodemographic cluster areas, you might find several prevailing attitudes—the traditional old money segment, the guilt-ridden heir segment, the middle-of-the road professional segment,  and the liberal but self-indulgent celebrity segment. You might also find a segment of Hangers On. This combination of demographic, locational, attitudinal, and consumer information provides a more complete picture of what and why people buy.

To put it another way, the most direct way to identify the psychological traits and attitudes of a given group of consumers is to pull a representative sample and do a psychographic study. Geodemographics can provide some of the same information, but it does so through a filter of demographic averages. If you are comfortable that consumer panel data and VALS 2 psychographic categories are relevant for your particular market, then geodemographics probably will be a convenient alternative to conducting a full-blown psychographic survey.

## The Value of Clustering

Coincidentally, or maybe not so coincidentally, geodemographics and psychographics are linked historically as well as functionally. The wizard who invented PRIZM, Jonathan Robbin, got his start in the early 1970s as a graduate student doing experimental work in factor analysis for Russell Haley at Grey Advertising. Haley was one of the first to coin the term "psychographics," and he invented benefit segmentation—the practice of segmenting markets by the benefits people want from products (see Chapter 2).

"I brought Jon in to handle our statistical work, and we got interested in television markets," Haley says. "We used census data to profile television markets, and Jon got interested in the zip code phenomenon." Though the rest as they say, is history, Haley admits with some chagrin that the future of zips wasn't immediately apparent to him. "I didn't see a lot of potential in being able to get the profiles of individual zip codes because direct mail was really the only way to reach them," Haley says.

By the early 1980s, however, major companies like Time, General Motors, and American Express were using Robbin's new tool to tailor their products and advertising to various PRIZM lifestyle clusters. Geodemographics was considered a marketing breakthrough, because it told marketers not only how target consumers lived and what media they used, but more importantly, it told them where to find those consumers.

Today, increasing numbers of companies selling everything from toothpaste to financial services have used geodemographics to successfully identify and reach potential consumers. Phillip Morris, J.C. Penney, 3M, Toyota, and Gannett are just a few of the major corporations that have used a geodemographic system with good results for everything from locating new-car dealerships to deciding in which media to advertise.

In *The Clustering of America,* Weiss tells how geodemographics was used by Virginia Intermont College (VIC) in Bristol, Virginia, to recruit new students. Analyzing current enrollment, college officials found that a majority of students came from Blue Blood Estates areas. Recruiters subsequently mailed brochures emphasizing things like equestrian studies, new horse stables, and VIC's strong business program—features they expected would be especially attractive to Blue Blood Estates households—directly to selected Blue Blood Estates zip codes.

The direct-mail use of geodemographics is perhaps the most obvious, but many companies find that geodemographic companies provide convenient one-stop shopping for other types of consumer information, most important, media use. The advertising agency Chiat/Day/Mojo recently used Donnelley's ClusterPLUS to help a rapidly expanding retailer develop a targeted advertising strategy. Agency researchers had to start from scratch, because the retailer had no client data whatsoever. This is perhaps one of the areas that geodemographics can be most useful—as a place to start understanding customers where little prior knowledge exists.

Chiat media researchers looked at the retailer's major New York City store and one of its suburban mall stores. About the only information they had to start with was that the New York City store generated more traffic but fewer sales than the suburban location. To find out why, they did a customer profile for both stores. Researchers staked out the two stores and wrote down the license numbers of all the cars that came to the customer pick-up area that day. The license numbers were matched to the car owner's zip code and census tracts by the Detroit-based demographic research firm, R.L. Polk, and the geographic information was imported to Donnelley's Conquest Advertising system. The system produced maps that showed where customers were coming from.

With this, it was relatively easy to cluster code customers to find out what types of people lived in those neighborhoods and to match these clusters with media and purchase data. Chiat researchers found that most customers were concentrated in a few clusters. Using Conquest's television module, with links to Nielsen audience data, they found out which television stations and programming the people in those clusters preferred.

Geodemographics gave Chiat an effective new business tool. Using the Conquest system, Chiat's media research director was able to walk into a meeting with the retailer armed with impressive knowledge about its customers. He also had specific suggestions to target advertising at neighborhoods with similar geodemographics that weren't producing any customers.

## To Cluster Or Not to Cluster

The 1990 census data are expected to make cluster products like PRIZM and ClusterPLUS more accurate. Between 1980 and 1990, geodemographic companies had to base their data on updated estimates from the 1980 figures; such estimates were often of dubious reliability.

For many companies, geodemographic systems may be the easiest and fastest way to get a picture of the entire marketplace. But keep in mind that cluster products were designed for one purpose—to boost local response rates of national marketing campaigns. They are by no means the ultimate level of detail where small local or regional markets are concerned.

## How Good Is Average?

One of the reasons that *The Clustering of America* generated such interest was because it raised some interesting questions. The idea that marketers were using such devices to target products at certain types of people based on their zip codes was unsettling to many people. What's more, the concept behind geodemographic clustering—that people of like lifestyles, attitudes, and demographics tend to live in proximity to each other—goes against the individualism that is the core of many Americans' national identity.

Some have correctly argued that while it's true that one neighborhood, zip code, or census group might house a group of people who live, think, and behave in more or less similar ways, it may well also house many people who don't. Geodemographics relies on averages, and averages, while easy to understand, are ultimately generalizations. Geodemographic systems, then, possess the same Achilles heel as broad-based national psychographic segmentation systems like VALS—their generality tends to blur the richness that comes from differences within the target market. Geodemographics has its uses, but some marketing veterans follow it up by examining actual census numbers or conducting their own specific psychographic research.

Fairfield, Connecticut, and Beverly Hills, California, may both qualify as Blue Blood Estates communities, but they are very different places. The people who live in each area want different things in products and services. Local styles and traditions and differences in household types, ethnicity, and locally produced products do not show up in the clusters. When competition gets tough, it's those subtle nuances that provide a competitive edge in a new market.

# 14 *Advice from the Experts: Avoiding the Pitfalls of Psychographic Research*

S INCE PSYCHOLOGY WAS FIRST APPLIED to consumer behavior in the early part of this century, commercial researchers have steadily learned more about how psychological factors affect the decision to buy. The first studies officially termed "psychographic" attempted to tie consumers' personality traits to purchase behavior, with limited success. Later, psychographics became lifestyle research and attempted to profile the total consumer by gathering diverse bits of information on anything that influenced the way he or she lived. Still later, researchers in various industries shifted their focus to specific attitudes and behaviors directly relevant to the product or category. At each stage, the process of psychographic consumer analysis was refined.

Why, then, are some in the marketing profession still doggedly pursuing avenues that others abandoned long ago as fruitless? In the course of researching this book, I posed that question to many marketing experts and got a variety of responses. Some, like Joseph Plummer, said that in searching for the logical evolution of psychographic research, I was looking for something that didn't exist. The field of marketing, it seems, is not like others where practitioners embrace and reject new theories and techniques more or less simultaneously. Marketing is not like science. When a theory is discredited in the sciences, proponents either recant, convert, or retire. In marketing, researchers often learn their craft by trial and error. Whatever works for them is what they use, regardless of what leaders in the field have proved or disproved. Corporate marketers work in relative isolation and rarely share what works for fear of relinquishing ground to the competition.

And too, academe has produced some useful research that corporate marketers have all but ignored. Whether the problem is miscommunication or an academic versus real-world focus is difficult to say. One truth has emerged, however. The researchers with the most success under their belts are those who have monitored advances in both the academic and corporate spheres and manage to adapt aspects of each to their own research.

It is no doubt true, as many veteran marketing researchers say, that there is no one right way to do market research. On the other hand, most are willing to admit that there are wrong ways to do it, and the consequences of making mistakes are getting greater every year.

Each of the previous chapters contains suggestions about how and how not to do psychographic research, derived from extensive interviews with noted market researchers, some of whom are members of the American Marketing Association's Attitude Research Hall of Fame. These suggestions can be synthesized into 11 basic lessons for avoiding psychographic pitfalls.

**Lesson #1: Know where you've been.**
Chapter 1 outlines the twists and turns in the market research field as the psychological aspects of consumers began to play a greater role in how businesses looked at markets. In most disciplines, it is a prerequisite that novices first understand the origins of the flow of knowledge before embarking on uncharted tributaries of their own. This is true in the more established disciplines of sociology, psychology, and anthropology, but unfortunately, it is not so true in marketing, which draws on all of these other disciplines for its theoretical basis.

As Daniel Yankelovich says, it is probably due to this collective disregard for the past that market research seems to flounder without a theoretical basis of its own. "If you don't read and approach this field from a scholarly perspective, you reinvent the wheel every year," Yankelovich says. This shortness of collective recall among many practitioners is one reason why psychographic research is so poorly understood. Because it is poorly understood, it is sometimes not done well, which may be one underlying reason that many researchers have become disillusioned with it.

**Lesson #2: Extract the best from both quantitative and qualitative research.**
As Chapter 2 suggests, the ultimate lesson we should learn from the qualitative versus quantitative debate that divided the marketing research community in the 1950s and 1960s is that both techniques are useful. Most market researchers today use both quantitative and qualitative research and value both techniques for their respective strengths. Psychographics, which combines survey sampling with qualitative information about attitudes, merged the best of both types of research. So why is it still true today that it is the qualitative aspects of psychographic segmentations—the catchy names like "Achievers" or "Healers"—that corporate executives will remember when it's time to make decisions? Venerated market researcher William Wells says that it's because, in several key respects, qualitative research is intrinsically superior to quantitative.

First, Wells says, there's the time factor. In a pinch, a set of qualitative interviews can be done in a week, while a typical survey takes much longer. Second, there's the cost factor. Qualitative research tends to be less expensive than a large-scale survey. Third, qualitative research comes in a form that's easy to understand and full of human insights, while a typical survey is "homogenized and dehydrated, packed into sanitary little tables." Executives remember the insights they heard or read about from focus groups, because they have actively processed those words spoken by real people. The words and the images evoked have more cognitive staying power than do mere numbers. Finally, qualitative research (and this is the ultimate purpose of psychographics) bridges the distance between the person who needs the information and the person who supplies it.

When it's not possible to do the quantitative part of psychographic research, qualitative is better than no research at all. To illustrate that point, Wells tells a story he heard from Bud Roper. A Rhode Island politician coming up on a difficult re-election bid once asked Roper for help. The problem was that both time and money were short, so Roper had two choices—refuse the job or do something quick and cheap. He chose the latter and sent two interviewers to ask people at Rhode Island shopping centers why they supported or opposed the incumbent. The incumbent ended up winning a close election, thanks in part to what he learned from Roper's study. Roper was the first to admit that this particular study could not be considered "scientific" by any stretch of the imagination. He says: "Few studies have been so unscientific (yet few) have better served the purposes for which they were intended." How could the head of a leading polling organization and such a noted advocate of survey research take this position? Wells explains the seeming contradiction by looking further into the meaning of "scientific." "Science has to do with the pursuit of knowledge. Of insight," he states, "one can be scientific or unscientific with or without quantitative survey methods."

While ideal market research includes both quantitative surveys and qualitative insights, fast and cheap can be better than nothing. The crucial variable is this: Does the research seek to discover the truth? Good market research, like all scientific inquiry, attempts to find out the whole truth about the consumers, the products, the markets, or the issues in question. "Let's be more interested in truth and less interested in data," Wells told an audience of quantitative researchers. "We are justly proud of our devotion to precision. But we should be ashamed that we produce so many significant answers to insignificant questions."

**Lesson #3: Understand the underlying consumer trends.**
As Chapter 4 illustrates, the best insurance policy to guard against being caught unawares by changing consumer tastes is constant monitoring of consumer trends. This does not mean that the advice of every self-proclaimed consumer soothsayer should be heeded uncritically. Being able to distinguish bona fide trends from fads is just as important as knowing about potential trends, and doing so involves periodic measurement of consumer attitudes over a period of time. William Wells has this advice for distinguishing fads from trends. "I believe it's a mistake to drop a 'trend' just because it seems to show no change," he says of a practice by Monitor researchers. "One of the most important values of periodic measurements is that it helps provide defense against

seers who, from casual observation, suddenly discover a 'trend' that has been present all along, or that is not in fact occurring, or that is occurring only among a very small segment of the population. In our experience, only about one-half of the trends we read about in the trade press are real. It is important to know which half."

**Lesson #4: Weigh the relative value of using a syndicated broad-based segmentation.** As we learned in Chapters 3 and 5, some researchers steadfastly maintain that syndicated psychographic segmentations like the Values and Lifestyles Program of SRI International are convenient and less-expensive alternatives to original psychographic studies of individual markets. Others feel that such broad-based national segmentations are too general to offer real insights into consumers of specific products. Only a small portion of any market falls into any one psychographic segment, and most marketers find it defeats the purpose to focus on one small segment while ignoring or alienating the majority of real customers. On the other hand, proponents assert that such segmentations are a valuable starting point for getting to know an unfamiliar market. Both sides would probably agree, however, that broad segmentations are more useful for some categories than for others.

Before signing up, make sure you understand what these products can and cannot do relative to your product category. As the marketing director of one packaged-goods giant says, "The psychology of selling cars is very different from the psychology of selling coffee." Whether or not you start with a broad-based segmentation, eventually you have to understand the precise discriminators that drive product choice at the category and brand level.

**Lesson #5: Use whatever technique you're most comfortable with to get a psychographic profile of all potential customers.**
Advertising agencies, as illustrated in Chapter 6, use a wide range of tools and techniques to gain insight into their clients' customers. No agency uses only one technique, and all emphasize the importance of using a multilayered approach to get the most comprehensive portrait possible of current customers, as well as noncustomers. Analyze them by lifecycle, segment them by demographic aspects, or do a lifestyle study to learn their attitudes about cleanliness versus their product preferences. Understand what discriminates customers from noncustomers, and you're halfway to solving the behavioral mystery that's at the core of all market research—why some people buy and some don't.

**Lesson #6: Identify the underlying motivators.**
Behind this simple statement, as we saw in Chapter 7, lies a complicated maze of hidden drives and desires. One current motivational expert advises clients to think of the human mind as a lake bed. The conscious is everything above the water and the subconscious is everything below the surface. Only a small fraction of that subconscious material—the layer immediately below the surface—has any relevance to the superficial act of choosing what things or services to buy. Don't repeat the mistake of the early

motivational researchers and look too deeply for product choice motivators. "You can array an automobile market or some other product according to the particular values and attitudes people have toward that product category," says Daniel Yankelovich. "But the level of personality that gets into the really deep stuff—whether it's Freudian or Jungian—is simply too deep to have much bearing on product and brand choices, which are relatively superficial choices. It doesn't make that much difference to your life, and it doesn't reveal fundamental aspects of your personality."

**Lesson #7: When entering large foreign markets, market to the similarities, but make sure you understand and never underestimate the differences.**
In Chapter 8, advertising researchers working on large multinational accounts empha- sized the importance of recognizing both the differences and similarities when marketing in numerous cultures. The similarities are important because they allow companies to establish uniform brand images and standardize some aspects of advertising and marketing. Knowing how Germany is different psychographically from France, however, is also crucial. Such local differences can mean the difference between ads that work and those that don't.

Large cross-national psychographic segmentations are useful because they provide a common general framework against which to assess large populations and to gain an initial understanding of complex new populations. A cross-cultural psychographic study, however, is only the first step, and it should be followed up by more focused original research in each culturally distinct new market.

**Lesson #8: Understand the uniqueness of each local or regional market.**
Another way of using psychographics effectively is at the local or regional level. Chapters 9 and 13 explore two ways in which large national markets can be broken down into small geographic regions. In Chapter 9, we examined two ways to psychographically survey local broadcast markets. Chapter 13 discusses the common misconception that geodemographic systems such as Claritas's PRIZM can be substi- tuted for psychographic research.

The increasing popularity of both approaches, however, underscores the fact that marketers today, more than in the past, need to understand how local and regional markets differ from the national norm. Finding customers in today's tough competitive environment is like trying to find perfect specimens in a picked-over vegetable bin. Psychographic differences are often behind those regional differences, and the more marketers can find out about local psychographics, the more accurately they can identify potential market niches hidden in distant corners of the vast American landscape.

**Lesson #9: Carefully consider the sample size.**
This might seem like basic advice to most researchers, but as the opinion pollers in Chapter 10 point out, it is the size and quality of the sample that largely determine the

reliability of any survey. To illustrate the importance of the sample, one researcher points to the 1936 presidential election, the one that first proved the value of survey sampling. Sample bias was the reason the *Literary Digest* (with a 2 million-ballot survey) predicted Landon would beat Roosevelt, while Gallup and Roper (with 5,000 people each) correctly predicted a Roosevelt victory. The *Literary Digest* surveyed subscribers, who, back in the 1930s, were much better educated and more affluent than the general electorate, says Dennis Gilbert, president of Opinion Research Service. Gallup and Roper, on the other hand, surveyed fewer people, but those people were representative of the American public.

"The randomness of the sample is a key to the quality of any survey," says Gilbert. Guaranteeing the randomness of the sample might take more doing in the future, Gibson warns. More people are refusing to take part in surveys—some have been burned by telemarketers disguising sales pitches as surveys, and others are just too busy. The result could be increasing survey bias if researchers don't take special pains to ensure that samples are representative of their true markets. "Who are all those people saying no?" asks Gibson. "You want to find out if the ones who say no are just like everyone else or different. If they're different, you have to make an extra effort to get more of them to protect the quality of the sample."

### Lesson #10: Make the ultimate goal of your psychographic research to identify product-specific attitudes and behaviors.

As we saw in Chapters 11 and 12, psychographic research is alive and well in industries as different as retailing and packaged goods. But market researchers today are focusing on the attitudes, emotions, and behaviors that have direct relevance to each category, product, or brand. Sometimes corporate market researchers use both existing psychographic segmentations and their own proprietary psychographic research to gain better understanding of a market.

The more quickly a market is changing, the more frequently it needs to be surveyed. In the last decade, Nestlé has done six separate psychographic studies of the pet-food category alone. "It's really a type of study that we use the first time to understand how people are differentiating between brands, what are the key dimensions that differentiate products, and then, of those dimensions, which ones are most important in determining their brand preferences," says Mary Beth Rymers, director of consumer research for the Nestlé Food Company.

### Lesson #11: Know everything you can about your core customers.

The ultimate lesson of this book has to be the one offered by Tony Adams of the Campbell Soup Company—recognize that each loyal customer has bottom-line value to your company, and focus your research on finding out what keeps them coming back for more. Corporations like Campbell are using state-of-the-art techniques to identify the precise emotions elicited by their brand names. Emotions are but one aspect, however, in the total research mission. Of primary importance is finding the individuals who account for the core of your business. As Adams predicts, you'll be hearing more about this "Value of the Customer" approach to market research in the future. It melds a new recognition of the old axiom "happy customers are the key to success" with the whole philosophy behind psychographic research.

The fundamental purpose of psychographic research (and market research in general) has always been to get to know your customers on a more personal basis so as to provide them with products and services that better meet their needs. American companies, especially, should understand the risks of taking customers' needs for granted. The Big Three U.S. automakers may never regain the customers they lost through past disregard for changing consumer needs.

## A Multifaceted Reflection

Understanding what makes people buy is a never-ending and exceptionally difficult endeavor, complicated by the inherent complexity of the individual human beings who make up markets. Psychographics was developed as a way to understand increasingly diverse markets. It provides a way to separate groups by shared characteristics beyond mere age, sex, income, and education characteristics. It tries to create order out of the chaos of wants, needs, motivations, activities, interests, opinions, and personality variables comprising that complex creature, the American consumer.

Psychographic research may not always provide a perfect reflection of the market, but it has its uses. It helps in strategic planning and product innovation by bringing the seller of goods and the advertiser of products one step closer to real people. It helps in the creation of effective advertising because it provides clues about how to communicate with those who are predisposed to buy the product. It paints a human face on the amorphous mass that is the target market.

Psychologist Dr. Joseph Smith, president of Oxtoby-Smith, has been a leader in psychological research for more than 30 years. It was at his suggestion that NBC adopted the peacock logo, and airlines decided to give customers room for carry-on luggage. Smith welcomes a resurgence of psychological research if it helps companies better meet customers' needs, but he warns that the best research is multilayered and that companies looking for quick and easy answers will get what they deserve. "There are no easily accessible answers," Smith says. "To suppose that there's a magic tool for discovering what motivates consumer behavior is naive. It disparages the complexity of the human experience and of marketplace behavior."

Like the engineer who solves a difficult problem by looking at it from a fresh perspective, the marketer gains insight by looking at the individuals in a market and focusing on a number of variables that all play a role in consumer choice. As each layer is peeled away and understood, another piece of the puzzle that is the consumer is put into place.

When these separate facets are assembled, they form a portrait of customers that marketers with insight recognize as the key to future business success, both on a macro and micro level. Corporate leaders with vision are using these tools today to create the goods, services, and company policies that will meet the demands and address the concerns of consumers, now and in the future.

# *Appendix*

## *A Listing of Advertising Agencies and Market Research Firms*

# Advertising Agencies

Ally & Gargano
805 Third Avenue
New York, NY 10022
212/688-5300

Backer Spielvogel Bates, Inc.
405 Lexington Avenue
Chrysler Building
New York, NY 10174
212/297-7000

Batten, Barton, Durstine, & Osborn,
Inc.
1285 Avenue of the Americas
New York, NY 10019-6095
212/459-5000

Chiat/Day/Mojo
79 Fifth Avenue
New York, NY 10003
212/807-4000

Della Femina
350 Hudson Street
New York, NY 10014
212/886-4100

DDB Needham Worldwide
437 Madison Avenue
New York, NY 10022
212/415-3180

D'Arcy Masius Benton & Bowles
1675 Broadway
New York, NY 10019-5809
212/468-3419

Grey Advertising, Inc.
777 Third Avenue
New York, NY 10017
212/546-1597

J. Walter Thompson USA Inc.
466 Lexington Avenue
New York, NY 10017
212/210-7293

Leo Burnett Company, Inc.
35 West Wacker Drive
Chicago, IL 60601
312/220-5959

McCann-Erickson USA
750 Third Avenue
New York, NY 10017
212/697-6000

N.W. Ayer
825 Eighth Avenue
New York, NY 10019
212/474-5000

Ogilvy & Mather, Inc.
Worldwide Plaza
309 West 49th Street
New York, NY 10019-7399
212/237-5460

Young & Rubicam
285 Madison Avenue
New York, NY 10017-6486
212/210-3000

# Marketing Research Companies & Consultants

Ernest Dichter
24 Furnace Brook Road
Peekskill, NY 10566
914/739-7405

DYG, Inc.
555 Taxter Road
Elmsford, NY 10523
914/347-7200

Emotion Mining Company, Inc.
44 Washington Street
Wellesley, MA 02181
617/235-4520

Russell Haley & Associates, Inc.
8 Orchard Drive
Durham, NH 03824
603/868-2313

HealthFocus
216 North Fourth Street
Emmaus, PA 18049
215/967-2233

Impact Resources, Inc.
125 Dillmont Drive
Columbus, OH 43235
614/888-5900

Information Resources, Inc.
150 North Clinton Street
Chicago, IL 60606
312/726-1221

Langer Associates, Inc.
19 West 44th Street, Suite 1601
New York, NY 10036
212/391-0350

Louis Harris & Associates, Inc.
630 Fifth Avenue
New York, NY 10111
212/698-9600

Management Horizons
570 Metro Place North
Dublin, OH 43017-1398
614/764-9555

Market Development, Inc.
1643 Sixth Avenue
San Diego, CA 92101
619/232-5628

Market Facts, Inc.
676 North St. Clair Street
Chicago, IL 60611
312/280-9100

Marshall Marketing &
Communications, Inc.
1699 Washington Road
Pittsburgh, PA 15228
412/854-4500

Mediamark Research Inc.
708 Third Avenue
New York, NY 10017
212/599-0444

MRCA Information Services
4 Landmark Square
Stamford, CT 06901
203/324-9600

NFO Research, Inc.
2 Pickwick Plaza
Greenwich, CT 06830
203/629-8880

Opinion Research Service
P.O. Box 9076
Boston, MA 02114
617/482-1534

Oxtoby-Smith, Inc.
215 Park Avenue South
New York, NY 10003
212/614-0040

R.L. Polk & Co.
1155 Brewery Park Boulevard
Detroit, MI 48207-2697
313/393-0880

The Roper Organization Inc.
205 East 42nd Street
New York, NY 10017
212/599-0700

Simmons Market Research Bureau
380 Madison Avenue
New York, NY 10017
212/916-8900

Solutions Marketing Research
(division of Executive Solutions, Inc.)
152 Forest Avenue
Locust Valley, NY 11560
516/674-3070

SRI International
333 Ravenswood Avenue
Menlo Park, CA 94025-3493
415/859-4324

Leigh Stowell & Company
2025 First Avenue
Seattle, WA 98121
206/726-5550

Strategic Directions Group
119 North Fourth Street
Minneapolis, MN 55401
612/341-4244

Walker Research, Inc.
3939 Priority Way South Drive
P.O. Box 80432
Indianapolis, IN 46280-0432
317/843-3939

Yankelovich Clancy Shulman, Inc.
8 Wright Street
Westport, CT 06880
203/227-2700

# Geodemographic Companies

CACI Marketing Systems
9302 Lee Highway
Fairfax, VA 22031
703/218-4400

Claritas Corporation
201 North Union Street
Alexandria, VA 22314
703/683-8300

Donnelley Marketing Information
Services (DMIS)
70 Seaview Avenue
P.O. Box 10250
Stamford, CT 06904
203/353-7000

Equifax National Decision Systems
539 Encinitas Boulevard
Encinitas, CA 92024-9007
619/942-7000

National Demographics & Lifestyles, Inc.
1621 Eighteenth Street
Denver, CO 80202-1211
303/292-5000

# Bibliography

Appel, Valentine. "Motivation Research." In *International Encyclopedia of Communications*, edited by Erik Barnouw. New York: Oxford University Press, 1989.

Boote, Alfred S. "Psychographic Segmentation in Europe." *Journal of Advertising Research* 22 (December 1982–January 1983): 19–23.

Cheskin, Louis. *Color for Profit*. New York: Liveright Publishing Co., 1951.

Cheskin, Louis, and L. B. Ward. "Indirect Approach to Market Reactions." *Harvard Business Review* 26 (Winter 1948): 572-80.

Demby, Emanual H. "Psychographics Revisited: The Birth of a Technique." *Marketing News* 23 (January 1989): 21.

———. "Psychographics and From Whence It Came." In *Lifestyles and Psychographics*, edited by William D. Wells. Chicago: American Marketing Association, 1974.

Dichter, Ernest. "Whose Lifestyle Is It Anyway?" *Psychology & Marketing 3* (Fall 1986): 151–63.

———. Typology. Peekskill, N.Y.: Institute for Motivational Research, 1958.

———. "Psychology in Market Research." *Harvard Business Review* 25 (Summer 1947): 432–43.

Dickson, Peter R. "Person-Situation: Segmentation's Missing Link." *Journal of Marketing* 46 (Fall 1982): 56–63.

Evans, Franklin B. "Psychological and Objective Factors in the Prediction of Brand Choice: Ford Versus Chevrolet." *Journal of Business* 32 (October 1959): 340–69.

Francese, Peter, and Rebecca Piirto. *Capturing Customers*. Ithaca, N.Y.: American Demographics Press, 1990.

Gallup, George H. *A Guide to Public Opinion Polls.* Princeton: Princeton University Press, 1944.

Gottlieb, Morris J. "Segmentation by Personality Types." In *Advancing Marketing Efficiency,* edited by Lynne H. Stockman, 148–158. Chicago: American Marketing Association, 1959.

Greenberg, Marshall G., and Paul E. Green. "Multidimensional Scaling." In *Handbook of Marketing Research,* edited by Robert Ferber. New York: McGraw-Hill, 1974.

Haley, Russell I., ed. *Attitude Research in Transition.* Chicago: Attitude Research Committee of the American Marketing Association, 1972.

———. "Beyond Benefit Segmentation." *Journal of Advertising Research* 11 (August 1971): 3–8.

———. "Benefit Segmentation: A Decision-Oriented Research Tool." *Journal of Marketing* 32 (July 1968): 30–35.

Hughes, David G. "The Measurement of Beliefs and Attitudes." In *Handbook of Marketing Research,* edited by Robert Ferber. New York: McGraw-Hill, 1974.

Kassarjian, Harold H. "Projective Methods." In *Handbook of Marketing Research,* edited by Robert Ferber. New York: McGraw-Hill, 1974.

Kahle, Lynn R. "Social Values in the Eighties: A Special Issue." *Psychology and Marketing* 2 (Winter 1985): 231–37.

Kahle, Lynn R., Sharon E. Beatty, and Pamela Homer. "Alternative Measurement Approaches to Consumer Values: The List of Values (LOV) and Values and Lifestyles (VALS)." *Journal of Consumer Research* 13 (December 1986): 403–9.

Koponen, Arthur. "Personality Characteristics of Purchasers." *Journal of Advertising Research* 1 (September 1960): 6–12.

Lazarsfeld, Paul F. "The Art of Asking Why: Three Principles Underlying the Formulation of Questionnaires." *National Marketing Review* 1 (Summer 1935): 24–31.

Lockley, Lawrence C. "History and Development of Marketing Research." In *Handbook of Marketing Research,* edited by Robert Ferber. New York: McGraw-Hill, 1974.

McGregor, Douglas. "Motives as a Tool of Market Research." *Harvard Business Review* 19 (Autumn 1940): 42–51.

Maslow, Abraham H. *The Farther Reaches of Human Nature.* New York: Viking Press, 1971.

———. *Motivation and Personality.* New York: Harper & Row, 1970.

Merton, Robert K., and Paul F. Lazarsfeld, eds. *Continuities in Social Research: Studies in the Scope and Method of "The American Soldier,"* Glencoe, Ill.: The Free Press, 1950.

Mitchell, Arnold. *The Nine American Lifestyles: Who We Are And Where We Are Going.* New York: Macmillan, 1983.

———. "Values Scenarios for the 1980s." Values and Lifestyles Program. Menlo Park, Calif.: SRI International, 1981.

———. *Consumer Values: A Typology.* Values and Lifestyles Program Analytical Report, No. 1. Menlo Park, Calif.: SRI International, 1978.

Nelson, Alan R. "Psyching Psychographics: A Look at Why People Buy." In *Attitude Research Reaches New Heights,* edited by Charles W. King and Douglas J. Tigert. Chicago: American Marketing Association, 1970.

Pitts, Robert E., and Arch G. Woodside, eds. *Personal Values and Consumer Psychology,* Lexington, Mass.: Lexington Books, 1984.

Plummer, Joseph T. "Applications of Life Style Research to the Creation of Advertising Campaigns." In *Lifestyle and Psychographics,* edited by William D. Wells. Chicago: American Marketing Association, 1974.

———. "The Concept and Application of Life Style Segmentation." *Journal of Marketing* 38 (January 1974): 33–37.

Riesman, David, with Reuel Denney, and Nathan Glazer. *The Lonely Crowd: A Study of the Changing American Character.* New Haven: Yale University Press, 1950.

Rogers, E. M. *Diffusion of Innovations.* New York: Free Press, 1962.

Rokeach, Milton. *Beliefs, Attitudes, and Values.* San Francisco, Calif.: Jossey-Bass, 1968.

Roper Organization. *The Environment: Public Attitudes and Individual Behavior.* New York: Roper Organization, 1990.

Settle, Robert B., and Pamela L. Alreck. *Why They Buy.* New York: John Wiley & Sons, 1989.

Skelly, Florence R. "Using Social Trend Data to Shape Marketing Policy: Some Do's and A Don't." *Journal of Consumer Marketing* 1 (Summer 1983): 14–17

———. *"Development of Social Trends Measurements."* Paper presented at the Spring Conference on Research Methodology of the American Marketing Association, New York, May 1970.

Thomsen, F. L. "How Good Is Marketing Research?" *Harvard Business Review* 24 (Summer 1946): 453–65.

Wallendorf, Melanie, and Gerald Zaltman. *Readings in Consumer Behavior, Individuals, Groups, and Organizations.* New York: John Wiley & Sons, 1984.

Weiss, Michael. *The Clustering of America.* New York: Harper & Row, 1988.

Wells, William D. "Psychographics: A Critical Review." *Journal of Marketing Research* 12 (May 1975): 196–213.

Wells, William D., John Burnett, and Sandra Moriarty. *Advertising Principals and Practice.* Englewood Cliffs, N.J.: Prentice-Hall, 1989.

Wells, William D., and Douglas J. Tigert. "Activities, Interests and Opinions." *Journal of Advertising Research* 2 (August 1971): 27–35.

Yankelovich, Daniel. *New Rules: Searching for Self Fulfillment in a World Turned Upside Down.* New York: Random House, 1981.

———. *"Research for Social Change."* Presented to the American Association for Public Opinion Research, May 1967.

———. *"Planning Advertising Strategy: A Theory of Consumer Research."* Paper presented as the American Contribution to the Esomar Conference in Deauville, France, June 1966.

———. "New Criteria for Market Segmentation." *Harvard Business Review* 42 (March–April 1964): 83–90.

———. "A Marketing Concept Should Be the Sum of Psychoanalysis and Nose-Counting." *Printers' Ink* 263 (April 1958): 75–76.

Ziff, Ruth. "The Role of Psychographics in the Development of Advertising Strategy and Copy." In *Lifestyles and Psychographics,* edited by William D. Wells. Chicago: American Marketing Association, 1974.

# Index

## A

Attitudes, Interests, and Opinions
  (AIO) 21, 24, 27, 30, 34, 111
adjective check lists 21
Adler, Alfred 12, 24
advertising expenditures and cuts 98
Advertising Research Foundation's
  Qualitative Research Council 134
affluent 234
Affluent Markets Alert 198
alcohol consumption 62
Ally & Gargano 135
ambiguous stimuli 127
America's New Grownups 100
American mainstream 100
American Airlines 14
American Association for Public
  Opinion Research 8
American Express Global Travel Survey
  197
American Marketing Association 239
American Public Opinion Index 189
American Soldier, The 12
analgesic market 87
anthropomorphization 130
AT&T 139
Attitude Research Hall of Fame 239
automobile industry 51

Case study 187 (See also specific
  automotive companies)

## B

baby boomers 62, 99, 218
baby boomlet 219
baby bust 218
Backer Spielvogel & Bates Worldwide
  147
Global Scan 147
Baird, Mary 35
Battan, Barston, Durstine, and Osborn
  114, 138
  deck photos 138
beer, wine, and spirits industry 62
Benefit Chain 132
Benefit Segmentation 23
Betty Crocker 6
bi-polar rating scale 21
Blood Donors LifeStyle, profile of 119
Boote, Alfred S., study 145
Boston vs. Fort Wayne typology 180
brands 91
  acting workshops 131
  changing image of 94
  consumers' perceptions of 128
  emotional bonds 126
  equity 230

image in relation to self image 90
personification of 130
Bud Light and Spuds McKenzie 115

# C

cable television users, LifeStyle profile of 116
CACI's ACORN segmentation system 233
California Psychological Inventory 12
Campbell Soup Co. 71, 139, 229
  with Swift-Armour in Brazil 142
Canadian Global Scan 151
Carnation 225
Category Sculpting 130
CBS television 52
change-leader groups 157
Chavez, Cesar 47
Cheer detergent 26
Cherington, Paul 10
Cheskin, Louis 15
Chevrolet experience with Nova in Spanish 143
Chiat/Day/Mojo 236
chocoholics 135
Christen, Francois 75
Chrysler 13, 52
Clairol 46
Claritas, PRIZM segmentation system 45, 232, 242
Clustering of America, The 232
ClusterPLUS segmentation system 235
Coca-Cola 139
collage techniques 130
Color Research Institute of Chicago 135
Columbia University's Bureau of

Applied Social Research 11
Combat vs. Raid 129
Committee on Motivation Research 9
Consumer Market Matrix 206
Consumer Market Profile 176
consumer snapshots 83
convenience foods 136
Creative Research Associates Inc. 222
Crisco 137
Cronbach, Lee 75
Crosley, Archibald 10, 190
Cross Cultural Consumer Characterizations™ (4 Cs) 161
cross-cultural psychographic segmentation, dangers of 146
Curtis Publishing Co. 9
customer service 203, 205

# D

D'arcy Massius Benton & Bowles 129, 159
DDB Needham 110
  Life Style Study 31, 71, 99, 110
  Planning for ROI strategy, heavy, medium, and light users 115
decline in consumption-oriented trends 63
defense mechanisms 126
Demby, Emanual 22, 26, 29
depth interviews (see in-depth interviews) 53
Dichter, Ernest 6, 12, 19, 71, 126
direct marketing 63
Donnelley's ClusterPLUS segmentation system 236
Doyle Dane Bernbach (see also DDB Needham) 114

Dr. Pepper 46
dual-income households 102
DuPont's Cohort Study 216
DYG, Inc., Scan Survey 67

# E

E.I. DuPont and De Mours Co. 9
eating behavior 222
EC 1992 142
economic pressures 125
effect of scanner technology
   economic pressures of ad industry
   125
Elgin, Duane 36
Emotion Mining Co. 139, 230
Emotional Bonding 138
Emotional Lexicon 126, 138, 139
Emotional Sonar 127, 138, 139, 140,
   230
environmental product claims 194
environmentalism attitudes vs.
   behavior 191
ethnography 135
Euroconsumer 159
Evans, Franklin B. 15
Exxon 14

# F

Fashion Shopper Typologies 207
Fast Food Users
   LifeStyle profile of 115
Feminine hygiene 136
focus groups 47, 133, 240
   importance of the moderator 134
Folonari wine 47
Ford 27, 52
Fort Wayne market vs. New York City
   173

Fortune 52
Freud 13, 24, 127
Freudian 242

# G

Gale, Harlow 11
Gallup Organization 190
Gallup, George 10
Gardner, Burleigh 15
General Electric 129
General Foods 71
General Lifestyle Segmentation 28
General Mills 6, 71
General Motors 51
Geodemographic clustering systems,
   based on demographic information
   45, 232
Getchell, J. Sterling 14
Gilbert, Dennis 189
global attitudes 148
Global Scan 147
global segmentation strategy 142
Golfers
   Life Style profile of 117
Gottlieb, Morris 20
Gough, Harrison G. 12, 75
Grape Nuts 47
Grey Advertising 21, 100, 128, 137, 235
grocery shopping styles 136
guided imagery 131

# H

Haire, Mason 15, 127
Haley, Russell 21, 34, 235
HealthFocus study 224
Hegel's dialectic process 66
Heinz 14
Herzog, Herta 15

Hess's 204
Hidden Persuaders, The 16
Hispanic Monitor 200
Holman, Rebecca 42
Houghton, Dale 11

# I

images that alienate 182
images that attract 182
in-depth interviews 6, 8, 16, 17, 53, 97
indirect questioning 127
Information Resources, Inc. (IRI) 230
inner directed 23, 37, 40, 73
Institute for Motivational Research 14
interactive computer programs 138
interconnection of segments 91
International Organization for Displaced Scientists 13
Iron City beer 92
Ivory soap 13

# J-K

Japan 151
Jell-O 47
Jung, Carl 12

Kahle's List of Values 69
Kahle, Lynn 69
Kellogg Co. 9
Kellogg's 1911 9
key words and key images 90, 181, 182
Kmart 203
Koponen, Arthur 20

# L

ladies' foundation garments 51
Langer Associates 134

Lava heavy-duty hand soap 221
Lazarsfeld, Paul 11, 13, 14, 126
Lazer, William 24
Lean Cuts by Mariah 228
Leigh Stowell & Co. 169
Leo Burnett 24, 25, 126, 135, 139, 144
    1968, study 223
levels of human consciousness 126
Lever Bros. 139
Life Magazine 30
Life Style Study 34, 71, 99, 110
lifecycle
    concept 104, 216
    effect on apparel buying 217
LifeStages 104
    size projections 108
lifestyle studies 24
Literary Digest 10
local psychographics 185
Lonely Crowd, The 37
Looking Glass 131
Louis Harris & Associates 195

# M

mail-carrier study, ethnographic 137
Management Horizons 205, 216
Market Development Inc. 198
Market Facts Inc. 24
    nationally representative consumer
    panel 111
Marshall Marketing & Communications Inc. 169
Maslow's needs hierarchy 74
Maslow, Abraham H. 35
MasterCard 47
Mather, John 93, 96
McCann-Erickson 129, 138
McDonald's 139

McNamee WCRS Inc 92
Mediamark Research, Inc. 42, 87, 233
Merrill Lynch 44
Mervyns 204
Michelin ads 115
Microwave product users
  Life Style profile of 116
Minute Rice 133
Mitchell, Arnold 34, 35
Monitor's theory of social change (See
  also Yankelovich Monitor) 66
motivation research 7, 13, 15, 16
MRCA Information Services 214, 222

# N

1936 presidential election 10
N.W. Ayer 9, 99, 131, 138
  Adversary Groups 131
  Balloons 132
National Decison Systems,
  MicroVISION segmentation systems
  233
National Demographics and Lifestyles
  OASYS segmentation system 233
National Geographic 45
NBC 244
  peacock logo 244
Needham Harper Worldwide (See also
  DDB Needham) 114
needs hierarchy 35
neo-traditionalism 57
Nestlé Food Company 243
New Rules, 33
New Wave program 109
New York City market versus Fort
  Wayne 173
NFO Research 205
Nine American Lifestyles, The 35

Nissan Motor Corporation, suit against
  137
nondemographic segmentation 3, 20
nonprofit organization 120

# O

Ogilvy & Mather 44
  New Wave Program 109
olfactory sensations 131
  to trigger memory 131
one-on-one depth interviews 133
opinion polling (See also specific public
  opinion organizations) 9
Opinion Research Service 191
other-directed 37
outer-directed 37
Oxtoby-Smith 15, 133, 246

# P

Packard, Vance 16
paper-and-pencil inventories for
  personality assessment 12
PepsiCo 144
PepsiCo standardized global strategy
  144
Pernica, Joseph 28
person-situation segmentation 70
personality assessment 12
personality constructs 23
personality inventories 20
personality traits 27
pet food 224
picture sorting techniques 93, 128
Photosort 129
Pictured Aspiration Technique 128
Pillsbury 222
Pinto 27
Pitts, Robert Jr. 38

Pittsburgh Brewing Company 92
Planning for ROI 115
Playtex 51, 128
Plummer, Dr. Joseph 25, 44, 135, 141, 144, 240
Politz, Alfred 7
popular culture 52
post-boomers (See also baby bust and baby boomlet) 66
Power Group 99
Pritikin health-food products 225, 228
PRIZM segmentation system 232
Procter & Gamble 13, 26
product
    benefits 132
    low-involvement 70
    problems of product differentiation 125
    product-related attitudes 222
    product-related benefits 222
    product-specific psychographic profile 28
    usage situation 70
Projective techniques 126, 138
    depth interviews 12
    problems with projective techniques 138
    Rorschach Ink Blot Tests 12, 16, 127
    Thematic Apperception Test 12, 16, 127, 128, 129
Protestant Work Ethic 52
Psycho-Economics Institute (Wirtschafts Psychologices Institute) of the University of Vienna 13
psychographic information as a single source 170
psychographics
problem of defining 26
psychometric techniques 20

Purina Mills 228

**Q**

Quaker Oats 223, 225
qualitative research 126
quantitative vs. qualitative research 7, 17, 20
Quest for the American Woman study 195
Quest International 195
Quest/Harris 196

**R**

R.L. Polk 236
Raid vs. Combat 129
Reader's Digest 46
real estate 47
recycling 192
Riesman, Glazer and Denney 23, 37
roachkillers 129
Robbin, Jonathan 232, 235
Rogers' theory on the "diffusion of innovations" 74, 109
Rogers, Carl 133
Rokeach's Value Survey 69
Roper and Hart poll 203
Roper Organization 8, 190
Roper, Bud 8, 10, 192, 240
Roper, Elmo 8, 9, 192
Rosenzweig Picture Frustration Test 132
Ryoshiki 155

**S**

S.C. Johnson 193
Saatchi & Saatchi 55
scaler rating systems 21
scan technique 67, 109

scanner tracking data 98
scientific vs. unscientific approach 240
Schlitz 25, 220
self-image 19
  in relation to brand image 93
self-orientation 78
Sensations™ 131
shifts in social values 32
shortening uses 137
Simmons Market Research Bureau 42, 233
single-source use of psychographics 168
Skelly, Florence 50
Smith, Dr. Joseph 15, 133, 246
Smith, G.H. 15
Smith, George Lesley 133
Snyder, Dr. Tom 127
social intelligence 155
soft-drink market 46
Solutions Marketing Research 130, 133
sporting goods 186
SRI International 32, 34, 68, 224 (See also VALS)
Starch, Daniel 10
statistical researchers vs. motivationists 7
status orientation 78
stomach-remedy segmentation 28
Strategic Directions Group 200
Strategic Shopper 136
Strong, E.K. 11
subscriber studies 29
survey sampling 10

# T

Target Dollar$ program 179
The Chicago Tribune 9

theory of social character 23
Thompson, J. Walter 11, 45, 104
Thunderbird 52
Tigert, Douglas 30, 34
time 13
time pressures of consumers 101, 136
Timex 46
toothpaste market 23
traditional values 57
travel 200
  American Express Global Travel Survey 197
  train travelers 117
  preferences of the over 50 population 200
  trend monitoring 109

# U

U.S. census 233
U.S. Postal Service 137
United Farm Workers 47

# V

validity criteria 54
VALS 32, 44, 51, 68, 241
  criticisms 68
  real estate market 47
  typology 36
VALS 2 169, 234
  approach 178
  framework 80
  linkage 234
Value of the Customer Process 231
values 69
  Kahle's list of values 69
  link to product use 69
  link to products 69

measurement system 69
values structures of women in Europe
  145
Visa 129
Voluntary Simplicity Lifestyle 36

# W

Walker Research 187
Watson, John B. 11
Weiss, Michael 232
Wells, William 16, 21, 24, 27, 30, 33,
  239
Wexberg, Erwin 12
What's Cookin' study 222
White, Arthur 50
Wilson, Clark 29
Wood, Richardson 10
Woodside, Arch G. 38
working women 64

# Y-Z

Yankelovich Clancy Shulman 56, 57,
  62, 198
Yankelovich Monitor 34
  35 trends 55
  changes in trends 59
  current 45 trends 60
  development 51
  distinction from VALS 51
  original trends 55
Yankelovich, Daniel 3, 9, 20, 33, 50,
  242
Yankelovich, Skelly & White 50
yogurt category 72
Young & Rubicam 9, 42, 44, 137
  Four Cs global segmentation 161

Ziff, Ruth 97

# *Colophon*

The book text is set in 9/13 Stone Serif™. Chapter titles are set in 18 point bold Italic and the major section headings are 12 point Stone Sans™ bold.

The Stone type family was designed by Sumner Stone and is distributed by Adobe Systems, Inc. of Mountainview, California.

The book was electronically typeset with Aldus PageMaker™ software. The figures were produced with Aldus FreeHand™.

# Also From American Demographics Books

**CAPTURING CUSTOMERS: How to Target the Hottest Markets of the '90s**
*Peter Francese and Rebecca Piirto*
Explains how to integrate psychographic information with media preference data, demographic data, and geographic information. This perspective allows you to fully understand who your customers are and how to market to them most effectively. In a highly competitive, information-driven business environment, marketing efficiency is the key to success.

**DESKTOP MARKETING: Lessons from America's Best**
*Richard Thomas and Russell Kirchner*
Dozens of case studies show you how top corporations in all types of industries use today's technology to find tomorrow's customers.

**THE INSIDER'S GUIDE TO DEMOGRAPHIC KNOW-HOW:**
**How to Find, Analyze, and Use Information About Your Customers**
*Diane Crispell*
Using her behind-the-scenes knowledge of the data industry, the editor of the award-winning newsletter, *The Numbers News*, shows you how to find and analyze the data you need to make important decisions—and do it at the most economical price. Features a directory listing over 600 sources of data and related services.

**THE ALMANAC OF CONSUMER MARKETS:**
**The Official Guide to the Demographics of American Consumers**
*Margaret K. Ambry, Ph.D.*
Organized by age group, this ground-breaking reference profiles American consumers by the variables that separate buyers form nonbuyers—education, income, health, household type, and much more—and highlights the demographic changes that will be creating new markets in the 1990s.

**SELLING THE STORY: The Layman's Guide to**
**Collecting and Communicating Demographic Information**
*William Dunn*
This handbook offers a crash course in demography and solid instruction in writing about numbers. Learn how to use numbers carefully, how to avoid misusing them, and how to bring cold numbers to life by relating them to real people.

**THE SEASONS OF BUSINESS: The Marketer's Guide to Consumer Behavior**
*Judith Waldrop*
A unique guide to seasonal marketing that examines, for every month, the primary marketing events, participation in sports and leisure activities, health-care issues, and personal attitudes. Learn which demographic groups are the principle players and which consumer concerns are most pressing.

Books may be ordered by calling
800-828-1133
For more information write to

**AMERICAN**
**DEMOGRAPHICS BOOKS.**
P.O. Box 68, Ithaca, NY 14851